# HALF-TIME WHISTLE

*Other Robson titles by Frank Keating*

Gents and Players

Long Days, Late Nights

Passing Shots

# HALF-TIME WHISTLE

# FRANK KEATING

## An Autobiography

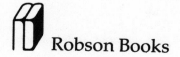

Robson Books

# To our Mum, of course

First published in Great Britain in 1992 by
Robson Books Ltd, Bolsover House, 5–6
Clipstone Street, London W1P 7EB

**British Library Cataloguing in Publication
Data**
A catalogue record for this book is available
from the British Library

Typeset in 11 on 13pt Sabon
by Columns of Reading Ltd.
Printed in Great Britain by
Butler & Tanner Ltd., Frome and London

# Acknowledgements

For all that Life is one long practice session in the nets for
the Big Match that never actually gets played, in this case
applause and gratitude is due to just about everybody with
whom I have padded up and shared a partnership or two.
Even notorious, world-class shits seem not to have gone out
of their way to run me out for some reason. You will see I
have been as lucky with schoolmasters, editors and
producers as with provincial and 'Fleet Street' pals from the
posh papers to the pop; thanks to them all, doorsteppers
and deskmen, for the laughter and company and kindness
and cribs. Successive sports editors on my beloved *Guardian*, John Samuel and Mike Averis, have been absolute
bricks in their different ways, ditto Alan Coren on *Punch*,
Dominic Lawson of the *Spectator*, and the still lamented
Grahame Turner of ITV. Gratitude down the years to a host
of heavenly girl guides in their summer dresses, and in their
flannel-nightie winter-warmers, too; to all Gloucestershire
cricketers, Fulham footballers, and Irish rugby players –
well, to all good fellows of the sportsfields really: and the
more famous, the finer fellows they always seem to be in my
experience.

Jeremy Robson proposed this venture, and amiably

nagged away – still against my better judgment; Maureen Lipman says Jeremy makes old Job seem like John McEnroe. He gave me an enthusiast of an editor in Louise Dixon who has been, as Mike Brearley remarked on another occasion, 'particularly helpful and helpfully particular'.

Who else on these occasions? Well, St Francis for the name, St Andrews for the golf, St Emilion for the slurp and, certainly, St Bruno for the baccy; I owe a large drink to Lindy Glover for an immaculate typescript, another to my agent, Lou Cooper, and to my cousin, Margaret Arnold, for scaling the family tree – which has suddenly blossomed even more thanks to darling Jane and the miraculous arrival of Patrick and Tess.

FK
Hereford
1992

# 1

Not long before he died in 1991, I enjoyed a day with the former world welterweight champion, Jack 'Kid' Berg. The old 'Whitechapel Windmill', 80 and still full of the joys, whisked me at a lick around the East London haunts of his childhood in his racy little dodgem-red motorcar. After he won his world title, at the Albert Hall in London in 1930, he took it to America and successfully defended it 12 times in 12 months. In a total of 192 contests, Jack fought everywhere and everyone – from the Hollywood Forum to the New York Polo Grounds, from Kid Chocolate to Mushy Callaghan – yet why, he kept asking with exasperation that day, did I particularly want to know every possible detail of his mundane, non-title victory on points over Glasgow's 'Bellshill Belter', Jake Kilrain, at the Empress Hall, Earl's Court, on October 4, 1937?

Because, I said, that was the night I was born.

And just as Jack 'Kid' Berg, the 'all-action crowd-pleaser' with the egg-whisk overarm style, had been weighed-in preparatory to being swabbed down a few times between rounds that evening – well, so had I. For the very first time. Apart from Jack's little matter with Jake in the Empress Hall and mine with our Mum in a redbrick Victorian nursing home a million miles away in Hereford, nothing else of much note seems to have happened on that autumn Monday.

A couple of days earlier, mind you, and I might well have popped out – applause! applause! – to the cheers of the Edgar Street throng, for the handsome rust-red house still stands just across the road from Hereford United Football Club. Not that there would have been much of a din. United were not even in the Southern League then and, except for every other Saturday afternoon, their wide and scrubbily unpretentious paddock served as a grazing patch and loading park for the city's vast and busy cattle market. But the sense of 'place' is surely one of one's most crucial possessions. And, just think – I was born only two corner-kicks away from the spot where Raddy Radford spin-nakered then mighty Newcastle United's net with his gale of a 35-yarder that glistening and watery winter tea-time in the FA Cup 40 years later. That certainly caused one heck of a noise in Edgar Street.

But my first sounds, apart from my own squeals of panic or relief, must have been the moohing and maahing of Hereford heifers under the auctioneer's hammer: the nursing-home was even nearer the cattle market than the football pitch. Funny: 17 years later, when my poor father, in despair of his layabout, games-obsessed dunce, suggested it was time I began living in the big wide world of muck and perhaps took up farming, I said 'Sorry, Pa, I've been frightened of cows since that day I was born'.

It was a good birthday to share. It was St Francis of Assisi's 711th and Buster Keaton's 42nd. Hollywood's 'Charlton Athletic', Mr Heston, was 13 on October 4, 1937; equally far away from Hereford, in a Cape Town shanty, skinny Basil D'Oliveira was six. I wonder if Baz was dreaming his dreams even then. Two score years later, his sister stood with me on the hut-speckled hill of wasteland where the family had been brought up and we looked across the blue waters of Cape Town's bay to sombre, khaki-coloured Robben Island, which had been Nelson Mandela's enforced home for 13 years already. And he had another 13 to go. D'Oliveira escaped much more quickly; he is now snug and celebrated and 60, and has been living in Worcestershire for half a lifetime. Just down the lane, and I love him.

On that very first Monday of mine, the auctioneers and steers having finished their bellowing business, Dad and Uncle John were at last summoned to the bedside from the Market Tavern to view the produce after, by all accounts, a long and premature session at wetting this muler's head. Then the dinky Austin milk-churn van zigged them up the Ross road, zagged off left at Little Birch – and, who knows, they might even have been in a fit state to hear on the wireless that The Kid had beaten the Bellshill Belter on points at the Empress Hall.

To be a farmer's son. Dad was a grand strapping fellow with curly jet hair and an enchanting grin under his big curl of a nose. He was nothing remotely to do with the Welsh borders. What Hereford made of him, the Lord only knows. He was Cockney alright, born and bred in Pimlico; but as well as a great dollop of first-generation Irish in him, a nice streak of Jewishness had run in the family for a century. It made for an irresistible mix – sentiment and solidity, daring and caution, vulnerability and self-sufficiency, sensibility and sense.

There was also a dandy deep down in his lovely nature. He went to his grave, at 81 in 1989, regretting I had never taken up his permanent offer of an account at The Famous in Cheltenham ('Outfitters to Empire and Colonial Officers & Servants'). He could never understand the 'second generation's' compunction to dress down and not up. In those fuzzy, stamp-sized sepia snapshots at the farm in Little Birch, he wore a dashing moustache and, invariably, tweedy plus-fours, as if he'd always made sure he was decked out in his 'number ones' before winding a film into the camera for Mum or Uncle John. 'Uncs' was no relation. He was an all-sides Cork man. At the Christian Brothers he had shown such a flair for mathematics that he had sailed up to University in Dublin, there to apply his special talent exclusively to devising unbeatable systems for the green-baize card tables and roulette wheels. He made as hefty a profit as he did a loss, but just as a system was on the point of becoming infallible, the college authorities slung him out as a 'dangerous influence', with never a thank-you, a degree, or a penny. He caught the boat-train to London, and met Dad in 1930 the day after he had been fired from his first job as a pioneer petrol-pump attendant for, apparently, telling the supercilious young Randolph Churchill where to get off when the swell made a pit-stop in his limousine on a forecourt near Marble Arch. Dad had said, 'No worries, come and join the Distributist League and we'll redistribute the land to the people'.

They were inseparable friends – arms akimbo, dancing down the long lane with darling, swirling-skirted Mum – to the day Uncle John was killed in a road accident near Kidderminster less than a year after he had taken me to my first Ireland v England rugby international at Twickenham in 1960. He had telephoned full of urgent excitement the week before: 'The new boy from Cork has been picked at full-back – AND I'VE GOT US TWO TICKETS. Meet me at the Challoner Club and we'll take it from there'. We did, pub-crawling our way across the river to the ground by bus and tube, toasting each time for Luck to the Corkman, Tom Kiernan, in extravagant slugs of that syrupy monkish concoction, Green Chartreuse.

In a kindly, cheerful review a few years ago of some waffle of mine, that irrepressible scribbler Roy Hattersley chaffed, 'Keating is a quiet unassuming man who portrays one of the most glaring and tell-tale signs of the chronically incurable romantic by talking about his Irish origins as if he had not been born on a farm in Hereford'. That was all to do with Uncle John: just as he had taken me to see Cork's Tom Kiernan begin his record-breaking sequence of international rugby appearances for Ireland, he had also introduced me (from a distance, of course) to the onliest Jackie Kyle (at Oxford, for Major Stanley's XV), and to Peter Doherty, playing at inside-forward for Derby County in a League soccer match against Aston Villa at Villa Park. Both Kyle and Doherty were so electrically enthralling to a small boy, it was no wonder that, at a rugby school when we were allowed just the one annual England v Ireland St Patrick's Day muckabout soccer match, I always grabbed a shirt of green.

Dad, of course, had more important things on his mind than sport – although once, a dozen or so years ago, I was covering a world heavyweight boxing match eliminator in New York in which an amiable, lumpen peacenik was being built up as yet another New White Hope in the heavyweight division. His name was Gerry Cooney. On the morning of the contest, the hotel reception paged me an urgent message – 'Ring your father at home pronto'. Oh no, what's up, I wondered, has something terrible happened?

Full of foreboding, I phoned. 'This chap Cooney', says Dad, 'ask him if his family came from Bandon and sailed from Kinsale in 1903. If they did, he's a first cousin of yours. My mother's lot were Cooneys.' I enquired of Gerry's father. His Cooneys had done just that, via Bandon and Kinsale. Hey, I'm related to a contender. Not that I boast about it. Peaceable Gerry, as he usually did, got pulped that night.

Both Dad's grandfathers, apparently, had been pressganged into the British army from Bandon, a colonial garrison town. Annie Cooney, Dad's mam, had been born in Secunderabad, India, in 1876. But at four she was enrolled in school back in Bandon. What travels those dear, desperate people had to make – especially as they weren't even fighting for their own ruddy Empire. In many ways it must have been worse for the wives and the women. If your husband was shot dead in the cause of England's prosperity, you had to fend for yourself or get married to another soldier, sharpish. (For instance, Annie Cooney's mother,

Ellie, ended up Mrs Dwyer, having been married once in Ireland and four times, after thrice being widowed, in India).

My cousin Margaret (daughter of Dad's only brother, Vincent, in Annie Cooney-Keating's brood of nine) has enjoyed burrowing into the records. By the time she was 10, my Gran Annie was living in a damp basement dump alongside the Thames in London where the National Theatre stands today. It was a pleasant Sunday stroll over one of the bridges and along the Embankment to meet the handsome Keating boyo in Pimlico. His grandfather, Bryan – with a 'y', like Dad's – had married Esther, daughter of Sarah (née Levy) and John, who was a slipper-maker in Butler Street, Christ Church, Spitalfields. Thus did a hopefully happy, and certainly hard-pressed, marital merger of Jews and Catholics a century and more ago conspire to produce a farmer's son from the Welsh Borders who is potty in the devotional support of Ireland at rugby, England at cricket, Fulham FC at soccer, and Gloucestershire at everything.

Dad's father died young: he only had one leg. I never met him. Dad used to say he had it shot off, defending the Empire in a red coat up the Khyber. The truth was that he lost it in a road accident near the squashed, one-up house, 25 Claverton Street, Pimlico, where they nested with their six girls (Marie, Eileen, Josephine, Agnes, Kathleen and Winifred, and the two boys, Bryan and Vincent). So a peg leg had many to feed as he Long-John-Silvered it around poverty-stricken Pimlico. Grandad was a sometime sacristan at Westminster Cathedral. But his main business was 'Keating's Bath Chairs' – by appointment to the gentry. I suppose it was a profit-making social service. All the wealthy grand-dames and blimpish patricians of neighbouring Belgravia would hire him to wheel them out of a morning or afternoon – perhaps just around their own posh and leafy square – for threepence an hour, or, for sixpence,

the Big Job, up to Green Park along The Mall, or down St
James's. This strikingly handsome, peg-legged wheeler
bobbing up and down (like Long John when the waves were
churning the *Hispaniola*) behind his wicker-chair by all
accounts became one of the regular summer sights of SW1.
But, as Dad told me once – bless him, he didn't relish
talking of those old days, for some 'first generation' reason
– there was not much work for Bath chair pushers in the
London winters. And even in the summers, your wickerwork-
on-wheels might be booked – but the bastards of Belgravia,
having booked you, didn't pay if you turned up and it was
raining, or if something else had cropped up in the drawing-
rooms of the upper-middle classes.

I wish I'd known Grandad. On rainy or snowbound
winter Saturdays, when no nob would brave a wicker walk,
he would hoppity-stroll up through Sloane Square and then
down the length of the Fulham Road, to Stamford Bridge to
watch Chelsea play football. Those must have been the
royal-blue days of Viv Woodward; Nils Middleboe, the
Dane; and Harry Halse, the 'Leyton Leopard', who scored
three raspers in each half against Manchester United in the
first Charity Shield match ever played (at Stamford Bridge in
front of 70,000). Heroic leader of the line in Grandad's day
was Bobby Thomson, born in Croydon, and founder of
feasts to come for the likes of Bentley and Greaves and
Osgood. Grandad must have sympathized with Thomson,
who had only one eye. Said Thomson, 'If the ball comes
over towards me from a corner, I shut my one good eye and
play from memory'.

Such innocent diversions passed my father by. He had far
bigger fish to fry. Grandad never really recovered from his
motor accident and the big brave man, apparently, just
withered away in a great deal of pain. So at 14 Dad, the
eldest boy, was now the breadwinner. He left the cathedral
elementary school and became a junior messenger with a
Fleet Street photographic agency. Much later he would tell
tales, doubtless garlanded with embellishments to make my

eyes the wider, of racing the precious negative plates back full pelt from Epsom on Derby Day or from society weddings or royal tripperies.

Fleet Street and the printed page must have been in its glorious heyday. No broadcasting then. As well as the great trumpeting host of national and evening newspapers there was a myriad of hand-to-mouth reviews and pamphlets, monthlies and weeklies, devoted to any and every matter and devoured by any and every nutter. Dad dived in head-first and with a joyous splosh. His two bags were Catholicism and Socialism, mostly at one and the same time. He became a disciple and protégé of G. K. Chesterton. He read every sentence by Hilaire Belloc, and hung on every word at his public meetings. He joined the Catholic Evidence Guild and learned to speak with trenchant certainty and (I'm told) appealing wit on the public stump at Tower Hill and Speakers' Corner, Marble Arch. He helped out on GK's *Weekly*, and wrote snippets and paragraphs of polemic for Bill Titterton's lefty *New Witness*, and was a founder member of The Keys, the association for Catholic journalists and a body still full of beans (not to mention, bores: sorry, Dad).

Nobody could have been a more fervent member of the Distributist League than young Bryan Keating. This stood for the very crux of Christian Communism. Brimming with a beautiful battiness, a sort of Tolstoyan Thomas Aquinasism, the League would meet every Friday in the Devereaux, down an alley opposite the Law Courts, sing Chesterton's drinking songs and hammer out their objectives, which were based solely on the simple arithmetic of a long-division sum: divide the population of Britain into its acreage; and if the answer was, say, three, then each person in the country was legally entitled to a plot of that measure. No end of bright-eyed, breast-beating oratory and tin-rattling was devoted to the League's aims which, in his dotage 60 years later, and still bushy-tailed about the idea, Dad defined to me as a threefold simplicity:

a) To convince a large number of people that property must be distributed in the interests of liberty;
b) To examine ways of distributing property;
c) To distribute it.

No wonder Dad was happy to let the Saturday fortunes of Chelsea FC pass him by.

If he followed Chesterbelloc to every public meeting, the young man walked in the very footsteps of his biggest hero of all, a Dominican friar from the Haverstock Hill Priory in Hampstead, a spindly, sandalled, seemingly scarecrow-scatty saint called Father Vincent McNabb. (Had I not been born on the Feast of St Francis, I would have been christened Vincent). The good friar was an Irishman, but by all accounts an irresistible Merrie Englander and medievalist. Taking all the tenets of Distributism on board, Father Vincent inspired the foundation of the breakaway Catholic Land Association. Miraculously, money was raised to buy a farm in the Home Counties – at Old Brown's, near Chesham, in Bucks – where Catholic boys could come from the cities, live in the community and, to all intents, 'own' the strip of land they tilled and the animals they tended. In the fullness of time they would acquire more and more farms, until all of England was full of happy, ungreedy family units living off the land. Cynics hooted: the *Manchester Guardian* called them 'the sheep-and-a-cow crackpots'. But the country was blighted by the inter-war depression, and at least the crackpots were having an enlightened go at a peaceful revolution. Dad was first secretary of the Catholic Land Association in 1930. When they held the meeting to finalize details about Old Brown's Farm, the first item on the agenda was, 'Who will be farm manager?' There was only one thing for it. Dad put his hand up. Done! And he took Uncle John as assistant manager. Without a jot of experience, the Pimlico urchin strode back to the land.

As far as I can make out, the experiment prospered well enough. A second farm was acquired in the north of

England, and the Bishop of Birmingham sponsored another in the midlands. Then Dad and Uncle John made plans to move to Hereford, to uphold the CLA tenets in earnest – and start a family back on the land. For by now, 1935, Dad had married Monica Marsh. It must have been as large a leap into the unknown for Mum as it had been for Dad to up sticks and leave the city. The Marshes were originally from Retford (Derek Randall country). Mum was born in Hoddesdon, Hertfordshire, where her father – who died when she was three – owned a draper's shop. (There is a marvellous photograph of the village cricket team in the early 1900s, the usual sporty rustics of the time, few of them in whites – except for Grandad Marsh, pristine everything, casual boater jauntily adjusted, just so, like Cyril Washbrook's cap was to be, and wearing a beautifully cut, Josephite striped blazer. With his languid baby-walrus perfectly scissored at his top lip, he looks for all the world like snooty, sneering Lord Hawke surrounded by his artisan professionals of Yorkshire. He could only be a true amateur, and as a kid I used to think, well, if that's my Grandpa we must come from the real top bracket. It took a long time to twig the more likely truth – that as a modest draper in a small market town, he had the pick of no end of racks of striped blazers and boaters. Select a different one each weekend, and put it back in the window on Monday. Not bad for business either. Hey, Grandad Marsh wore sport's first-ever sponsored strip).

When he died in 1910, mother and daughter went to Felixstowe, where Gran successfully ran a boarding house. Then ditto at Brockley, in south London. Her family had been strict Protestants, but Grandma converted to Catholicism when Mum was seven. This upset the rest of the family, apparently: Uncle Charlie was manager of Barclays in Markham Square, Chelsea; Uncle Richard an estate agent nearby; and Auntie Mabel had married Arthur Quant, who had cornered the market in men's outfitters in Bristol. Mum followed the path to Rome 10 years later – and few converts in history can have lived a life thereafter of such bonnily serene saintliness.

She joined the Evidence Guild and remembers first setting eyes on Dad in 1927 when 'this passionate black-haired chap' was engaged in seriously matey debate over some obscure point of doctrine with Maisie Ward (writer and wife of the publisher Frank Sheed). Mum spoke a few times at Speakers' Corner – 'but it wasn't really for me', so she would make the tea and wash-up at meetings in 'The Hut', alongside Westminster Cathedral, or have a brew-up ready when Dad and the soapbox crew came back with their banners and stepladders. She was working as a secretary when Dad finally scooped her up to the Priory at Haverstock Hill for the wedding – en route to the tiny, hillocky farm in Herefordshire. First came Clare, last came Anne – and in the middle came me: on the night Jack 'Kid' Berg beat Jack Kilrain on points at the Empress Hall.

\*　　\*　　\*

My arrival apart, as years go, 1937 on the face of it seems to have been humdrum and predictable: Don Budge and Dot Round shot everyone down at Wimbers; Henry Cotton won his Second Open, at Carnoustie; silvery-haired Raich Carter silkily won the FA Cup for Sunderland at Wembley; and teenage Tommy Lawton took over the No. 9 jersey from Dixie Dean at Goodison. Only the second jet-black nag of the century won the Grand National – Royal Mail at 100–6 – and Sydney Wooderson, a Surrey insurance clerk in wire specs, cut the world mile running record to 4 min 6.4 sec. He wouldn't have been round the last bend if he'd have been up against Sebastian Coe. It was certainly a pretty crummy cricket year to be born in. There was only a weedy Test series of three matches against the club cricketers from New Zealand, who included the pipe-smoking Walter Hadlee, father of you-know-who; Patsy Hendren retired from Middlesex, leaving the stage clear for the 19-year-old D. C. S. Compton. Denis's first taste of the representative

big-time was that July – a duck for the Players v the Gents
(st C. R. Maxwell, b F. R. Brown).

Only a fortnight earlier, also at Lord's, there was another
first-innings quacker in his debut Test against New Zealand:
L. Hutton b. Cowie 0. The pale, frail concentrating
Yorkshire boy was only 21 that month. The next day,
Sunday, he had mooched by himself around London,
dropping into the news cinema near Charing Cross when it
opened at tea-time. The newsreels kept playing his humiliat-
ing duck of the day before and, in the dark, the audience
around him kept sighing and tutting. It depressed him so
much that he made only one in the second innings – and
thought he'd blown his career.

A drip of a King also abdicated in 1937. But that
happening, when you think about it, fades to nothing in
terms of the British culture that was to come. For in 1937,
that Raich Carter Cup final at Wembley was the first ever
transmitted live by BBC television's infant service. That
obviously was the other most momentous birth of the year.
And continents began to speak unto continents, too: exactly
five weeks before I was born, they got through on the
landline laid along the bed of the Atlantic Ocean, and the
first international live commentary of a boxing match, all
seashell static and crackle, was broadcast, when Tommy
Farr, of Tonypandy, lost to Joe Louis, of the Universe. They
heard it, as it happened, in Wales – live from the New York
Polo Grounds on the night of August 31, 1937. No more
waiting for bloated, boozy Fleet Street sports writers to sail
back on the *Queen Mary* before reading all about it. Mind
you, it was to be some years before I knew anything about
bloated, boozy sports writers.

I was, of course, oblivious. In truth I cannot remember
one day of life at Well Orchard Farm – except that there
was an orchard and that Mum, hot from life as a city
secretary, had to draw the water in chained buckets from
the well outside the tiny brick cottage. War was on its way
to curdle everyone's sweet dreams, not least Dad's ideas of

communal and domestic self-sufficiency. But for three years no babe could have gurglingly played himself in surrounded by such snug solitude as he lay, observed and safe and swaddled, in the docks and grasses halfway up a Herefordshire bank where daisy-filled meadows swept softly down to Wales. Three years, twelve seasons ... and the animals, too. It was what they called a 'mixed' farm, a bit of everything: lambs lambed, sheep were sheared, fatstock fattened; there were hens and horses, apples and pears and rootling porkers ... aahs and baahs and moohs and poohs and pongs. Just like Masefield's Hereford Childhood (he was Ledbury-born and bred) in 'Wonderings':

> ... of hopyards, orchards, grass and grain,
> Of many-coloured poultry harvesting,
> And tumbler-pigeons dropping on the wing,
> Of cows returning before the dusk,
> Smelling of hay and honeycomb and musk,
> Strawberry-coloured, or the white and red
> Great-bodied cattle that my county bred.

Most of Little Birch's maze of rustic alleys and pathways and twitchels remain to this day unmetalled. 'The green lanes', they call them, and the motor-car still won't hazard any journey there. It beats me, when Jane and I explore there now with the kids, how Dad and Uncle John carted the milk churns down to meet the lorry on the main Ross road each ice-armoured winter dawn.

I'm back in Hereford for good now. In fact, those first three years were so satisfactory a taster that, as soon as the war was over, I was back, in the charge of the Benedictines at Belmont Abbey for five years until I was 12 – and so twigged early the truth of the remark made by the businessman hostage in Iran, Roger Cooper, when he was released, grinning and carefree, in 1991: 'Anyone who has been to an English boarding school is totally at home in a Third World prison'.

Then, of course, I was back again, as a cub reporter on
the *Hereford Times*. No thoughts of sports reporting then.
Much too commonplace – not to say common. I was
looking to be a Hold-the-Front-Page ace foreign correspondent at least. If not, dwarlings, a Drama Critic, a
Shaftesbury Av. luminary in fedora and cloak, and a late-
night office limousine for 'going on' to dine; a wickedly
witty maker and slayer of reputations in the name of
Thespis with the suddenly realized appetite to have
deliciously impatient ingénues competing for my favours.

So the Kemble Theatre (an exquisite little Victorian thing
since, and quite criminally, bulldozed by the council to
make room for concrete offices) in Broad Street was to
become my haunt on my third spell in Hereford – with the
luxurious old brown-leather sofa in the languidly wide and
tip-toe-hushingly carpeted lounge of the next-door Green
Dragon Hotel being (when I could afford two halves of
cider and a threepenny-bit for a tip) my first theoretical
casting-couch.

I did not, in that teenage cubhood and pubescent lounge-
lizardry, completely forsake that other Hereford theatre –
the open-air one, with goalposts. And I see their attendance
record remains 18,114 for the famous non-Leaguers' Cup
tie v Sheffield Wednesday on January 4, 1958. Well, it
would have been 18,113 but for little me. I remain a digit in
history. John Charles, alternatively 'The King' and 'The
Gentle Giant', must be United's best ever, even though he
was almost in sepia and long past the green freshness of
youth when he was player-manager at Edgar Street. Raddy
Radford scored that television Golden Goal of the Decade
(or was it Century?) for United, and last time I spoke to him
he was happy and chipper, carpentering on a building site in
Sheffield; and good ol' Joe Wade, once captain of Arsenal,
still keeps a sports shop in the city. Herefordshire, I hear
you sniff, is a pretty remote backwater for even an Aga-
leaning, lazybones sportswriter like me to operate from. Not
much back-page info in this neck of the woods, you might

think. Well, the finest ever National Hunt jockey, Peter Scudamore, was also a Belmont boy. Scu's dad, Michael, still trains horses up above Hoarwithy. Not so hot on ball games is Hereford, I agree, though the sensational Victorian swiper C. I. Thornton was born at Llanwarne; the Edwardian 'double international' at soccer and cricket, jolly John Sharp, first came to the notice of Lancashire CCC when he scored 208 not out for Hereford against Ledbury when he was just 14; and what about Sarah Potter from Ross (daughter of playwright Dennis), who was the England women's team's demon fast bowler?

At men's cricket, it is a very minor county – indeed the last Herefordian to play in a Test match was Peter Richardson in 1963; and though he was born and schooled in Hereford, he played for Worcester (OK, OK – *and* Kent). He never lost his Hereford sense of humour though. Once, at Canterbury, he refused to take strike till the umpires had investigated, and stopped, a mysterious booming noise emanating from the balcony alongside the pavilion. It was disturbing his concentration, he insisted. The game was held up for minutes; fielders fretted, but Richardson stuck to his guns. Finally, and in trepidation, stewards and umpires approached the din and demanded it desist. It turned out to be, as Peter knew, Mr E. W. Swanton telephoning his testament through to the *Telegraph*.

I suppose Hereford's most enduringly celebrated sportsman remains Tom Spring, unbeaten heavyweight champion of England (and thus the world) in 1823 and '24, mine host at the Naked Boy (now the Green Man) at Fownhope, a Wyeside pull-up a few miles south-east of the city. He was 5ft 11in and 13½ stone, and he soaked his knuckles in vinegar for two hours each day. When he beat the Irish champion, Langan, at Worcester racecourse on January 7, 1824 (the 78 rounds took 2hr 29min, and were watched by 30,000), he rode from Fownhope in Colonel Berkeley's carriage and four. As the London reporter, Pierce Egan, described it: 'The roads in every direction beggared all

description. The adventures at the Inns would furnish
subjects for twenty farces ... the company in general so
masquerade a character that it defies the pen; even the
celebrated pencil of a George Cruikshank would be at fault
to give the richness of its effect ... in a word, it was a
conglomeration of the Fancy. Where were you, Mr Hazlitt?
What food for the imagination did it exhibit? Peers, MPs,
Yokels of every cast, Cockneys and Sheenies ....'

Both Peter Richardson and Tom Spring illustrate a
certainty about Hereford. When you want to get on, you
must move east to an adjoining county. As any cricket buff
will tell you, a *minor* county is all very well, but....

Certainly, with the war, the farm was too small to be
what the authorities called 'viable'. It had to be sold to the
next-door farmer. Uncle John joined the RAF. Dad
continued 'in agriculture' at the Government's behest (he
became a salesman in cornfeed, cow-cake and, later, new-
fangled electric milking-machines). So we upped sticks in
1940 from the warm and cuddly Wye and settled across the
wide Severn, near Stroud, with its valleys of myriad greens
and Molineux-golds and its hedges humped high with
silvery elder-blossom. I was ready. The kitten had his eyes
open. Even the great, wide world out yonder acknowledged
that Glos was no Minor County.

# 2

I daresay each of us has a particular place with a 'feel' so vivid in one's recollection that it stirs the very beginnings of our consciousness. It is a remembrance that never goes away. It does not have to be a sumptuous secret garden; it could be a copse where you first heard the scrunch of boots on leaves, or a hillock out of which grew your first rainbow, or a deserted, tumbledown building which you felt, and still insist, nobody living knew but you. Whatever it is, it is the place to which, for no explicable reason, your adult mind darts back when you think of your first seasons of childhood.

Mine is a weatherbeaten, bottom-shined, thin-slatted iron bench that stands under an oak tree in which King Charles never hid. It is three-quarters of the way up a nondescript hill above Stonehouse, a few miles west of Stroud. A family walk for us (unless the cowslips were waving in the water meadows down by the old neglected, green-slimed canal, where we caught tiddlers in muslin flour bags and where sad, mad old ladies committed suicide in Sunday hats) was invariably up the sharpest side of Doverow Hill. The bench was no more than a half-way house whereon to pant for a minute or two, to exult in the steepness of the climb. There was no dedication attached to the seat from either patron or parish council. It never occurred to me to ask who put it there, but somebody must have, an unknown genius.

Well past our bedtime it was the place where lovers learned their ropes, where knees were first touched and lips first puckered ('Gerroff! Or I'll tell our Mum!'). For us it was the saloon outside which we tied our imaginary horses after playing the sheriff's posse; or the place to examine, blue-fingered, which of us that day had basketed the most blackberries to sell to the Severn Valley Jam Factory; or to hold up in triumph and with nail-bitten, filthy fingers the most delicate bird's egg. In winter you pushed off from the bench with your gumboots to get a decent toboggan start. On Sundays it was the place to watch with wonder the Home Guard run around with rifles and with hedgerows in their helmets like Macduff's Birnam braves. It was the place to sit and smoke our illicit Craven A ('For Your Throat's Sake'!) for from that vantage point we could see a grown-up coming.

The last time I was there a small, trim housing estate had encroached on the nursery slopes. But the bench was still there. Now, in middling age, eyes are wide-angled, horizons broader: the world, ah! dearie me, is confined no more inside just the rim of this small hill. Now I realize that had we children needed to look up as we gambolled we could have seen two-thirds of all Gloucestershire. And more. Dead ahead, far beyond the lovingly restored Stroudwater canal, is plump May Hill, topped with its little toothbrush moustache of trees, and beyond it lie the orange soil and steers of Hereford. Over in the west, the glinting slash of Severn winks in the sunlight in front of the Forest dark of Dean, and behind those Grimm, but much loved, woods, the blue-Black Mountains of Wales scrawl across the skyline.

On a clear day we could have seen forever – well almost; and farther south-west, through that gap between Frocester and ancient Uley Bury, squats Dursley, and beyond it, Bristol, which some men in suits and collars and ties say is not in Gloucestershire now but in something called Avon. How daft can you get! Why, it's still where 'Glorse' plays cricket, innit? An' that's good enough for I.

It was from this iron seat of learning up Doverow Hill that our next-door neighbour, Jean Pearce, swore blind and crossed her heart that she had seen Bristol burn one night in the wartime blitz when all the rest of England was wearing blackout blinds. Swing your gaze back due north today and a friendly haze of smoke umbrellas over Gloucester, and right in the middle there pokes up the Norman tower of mellow perfection made of local Painswick stone; eyes further round and you can see the even more ancient, sea-monster humps of the Malvern Hills and Worcestershire.

Now here's something uncanny: if you put a tracing of a Union Jack on a map of Gloucestershire, the very cross-roads of St George – from, say, Tewkesbury in the north to Chipping Sodbury, and from St Briavels in the west to Lechlade – meet, as near as dammit, on my old bench on Doverow. The very heart of Gloucestershire!

Behind, eastwards up the hill and on the same ancient track where homesick Roman centurions might have marched, deadpan, past cringing, sack-clothed drovers, the path rolls down a couple of miles through Randwick and into Stroud, a jaunty jumble of a hillside town, once noted as England's centre of the broadcloth industry. In the last century there were over 150 mill factories here. Now they make green baize for billiard tables and white baize for tennis balls, and purple cloth for cardinals and scarlet coats for guardsmen, while sponsoring a thousand-and-one other tiny industries from combs to knitting needles.

Stroud parish has a census population of only 20,000, but it serves as social centre to 34,000 other folk who live in warm, mostly still employed content in the villages that speckle the sides of its five glorious valleys. (Take the BR rattler from Swindon one day to get just a fifth of the picture!) I rode in my first bus to Stroud. Its Gaumont was where I saw my first film (*Henry V*). Its Cadena café was

where I first took a girl to tea (and sandwiches, 9d extra).
My first job was on the old *Stroud News*, and I left when it
was swallowed up by a Murdoch-like empire from Dursley.
Stroud was where I scored the level HS of my career — 75
not out, for the Stroud Stragglers v Painswick. Stroud, I
used to think as a boy, is where I wanted to die.

An American in Cheltenham once asked me the way to
the Cotswold Mountains! They are nothing to do with
mountains; no men with ropes or pitons; no yoghurt-fed
Heidis pick wild flowers here. 'No peaks of power' wrote
the poet Ivor Gurney when he dreamed of home from his
prisoner-of-war camp and wrote his lovely hymn:

I will go climb my little hills to see
Severn and Malverns, May Hill's tiny grove.
No Everest is here, no peaks of power
Astonish men. But on the winding ways,
White in the frost time, blinding in full June blaze,
A man may take all quiet heart's delight —
Village and quarry, taverns and many a tower
That saw Armada beacons set alight.

When I was born, 1,000 years of village life had just been
topsy-turvy changed — when the infernal combustion engine
replaced the horse. And even in my 2½ score years here this
world has further changed. No silence: Muzak and Newsak
are piped almost into the very plumbing (Severn Sound is
the county's new noisy radio station). Proud cottages are
built, still in the lovely mellow stone of centuries, but where
once a trellis-bower was made for roses, there is now just
room for a swing-lid garage door. Once it was the adventure
of a year to go to Gloucester to window-shop in awe. Now
not only the gentry have accounts at Harrods.

Yet has it all totally vanished? Don't shepherds still
whistle; don't choirs still have choir outings? Don't vicars
still bowl lobs after tea, and doesn't the squire still stand

upright at slip? And aren't there quite a few blacksmiths left? Ah, the smell of singeing hoof! I remember that from boyhood, when the village smithy did his stuff behind the old Woolpack Inn in Stonehouse. They were great, patient, plodding dobbins with hairy ankles and they used to pull the Co-op bread van.

In fact, 'Dobbin' was the first word I ever wrote unaided. You can see it still crayoned on the fly-leaf of one of Mum's battered old cookbooks. For someone who remains nervous of getting too close to large animals, it is odd that my first remembered passion was for horses. Followed at once, I'm glad to report, by a passion for women – or rather, for a certain woman. Thus the combination of my two rapturous early yearnings was overwhelming when Betty Protheroe daily delivered the milk from the Randwick Dairy with her horse and cart. Each morning I was outside the garden gate waiting for them. I suppose I was about four, or five. Betty was in her twenties, a bonny, strapping smiler, all grin and gumboots and freckles and flying hair of honey. Her family were Labour Party people which, I was learning, made her even more 'one of us'. (A lefty Roman was considered the absolute 'it': there were very few of those around in Gloucestershire). Sometimes Betty would give me a hug even; every morning, she would ruffle my hair; and she often let me ride on her cart to the end of our short and cindery, potholed road. My devotion waned not a jot when, one morning, she said to my mother, matter-of-fact and even critically, as I buried my round, pale face in her dairy-grimed apron, 'Funny, clinging, little fellow, ain't he?'

By 1941 I was at the village school. It was scary: particularly as the playground was full of older Cockney urchins who ganged up on us more gormless, dreamy-daft locals. 'Streetwise' would be the word for them today. They were not evacuees but children of workers imported from Essex and Middlesex to the two wartime factories, Sperry's and Hoffman's, which had been set up a mile or two from the village, near the LMS railway line. I think they made

aircraft parts and ball-bearings. Certainly their kids were
factory-tough. When the bell went at teatime, I'd run home
at a lick, past Mr Hobbs's nursery greenhouse and along
Laburnum Lane, neither turning nor stopping till I reached
the Post Office on the main road. The Cockneys would not
chase any further than that. Ours was GWR territory, much
more upmarket. LMS was all goods train trundlers. The
GWR line ran at the bottom of our garden; a very superior
service. We had the 'Cheltenham Flyer' whooshing up to
Paddington and back every morning and evening. She was a
grand sight – and a frightening, sudden, screaming hul-
labaloo if you weren't used to it. Grandma Annie Keating
came down from Pimlico to stay for a bit just before she
died. Dad found her under the bed one morning when he
brought her a cup of tea. She thought the Blitz had caught
up with her. It was only the Cheltenham Flyer.

'Pendennis', in St Cyril's Road, was a thin, three-storey
semi. It seemed handsomely massive at the time. I went back
last year. It looked withered, shrunken and morose. But it
was big enough for Mum to have to take in lodgers who
worked at the two factories.' Happily, Uncle John was still
with us. His worsening asthma (he told me) having
prevented him changing his name to Rockfist Rogan a
dashing flier of Spitfires, he had been posted as a clerk to
RAF Aston Down, about 10 miles away east, above
Chalford: he cycled there and back each day. Dad, selling
his cow-cake and organizing his farmers, was away often
and returned with ghostly tales of train journeys in the
black-out. But how lucky we were: all together; and no
sweating every day on a dreaded War Office telegram.

Both men had to be, of course, staunch stalwarts of the
Home Guard. When they brought home their rifles for the
first time, they realized the bullets they'd been issued with
did not fit. 'Don't worry, Bryan', said John, 'if the Germans
come, the cut of your khaki will frighten the buggers'. Dad's
uniform made him look like a well-built Private W.
Gummidge. When an invasion did look likely, the Home

Guard boss, a former WW1 general, at nearby Painswick, would have his men dig up the main Cheltenham road every time he sensed 'Jerry' was on his way: sometimes the road was closed for days on end, apparently. On one such occasion Dad and John were 'guarding' the LMS railway bridge down below Court Farm and the canal turnaround-basin. Early in the morning, Mum sent me down to them with a billy-can of tea. They were sitting on the railway bank, bleary and smoking, with Mr Hopkins, the station master. Suddenly, the ground started shuddering alarmingly. John said, 'Bloody hell, here come the buggers!' – and as Mr Hopkins slithered down the bank in a panic, over the wall and up the lane, shouting 'I've got a wife and two kids to protect!', Uncle John dived head-first into a large, tangled and thorny blackberry bush. His upturned legs were still frenziedly kicking out of it when a snakily long Bristol-Birmingham goods train rumbled massively and innocently past.

Mr Hopkins's son, Gordon, was a special early mate of mine. A galumphing, garrulous country boy with a Just William haircut and an intent, pachyderm gait, he was particularly expert at finding smoking-cane in the quarry. And, of course, he knew everything there was to know about railway trains. When, a few years later, and wretchedly, I had to go away to school, he signed my autograph book – 'Gordon Hopkins, A Pal of Scruff'. (Why the village knew me as 'Scruff' I just cannot imagine). I had two other particular pals. One was Robin Bassett, a wiry, athletic, irrepressibly refreshing boy, who lived next door with his strictly-observing Methodist parents. Robin and I shared a newspaper round from Miss Timbrell's village stores. Today, I am in touch only with dear Peter Beard, affably precise, scholarly and studious – something big in the City now, and with a family house in Wiltshire. Pete lived up the Verney – posh and detached, on the way up to Doverow and our bench where Roy Rogers would tie up his Trigger, and which would also double as a barstool for his ol' greybeard pardner, Gabby Hayes. (Peter's Uncle Horace,

one Christmas, gave him a book on cricket by someone
called Neville Cardus. Peter was full of it. The words
seemed much too long for my liking. I suppose I read about
four lines).

The Gaumont in Stroud began a sixpenny Saturday
morning film club, and we would all pile onto the bus – Red
& White, or Western National – outside the Post Office at 9
sharp. My older sister, Clare, would be in charge of the
posse; sprog Anne was now old enough to come too – every
time we got on the bus to come home at the end of the
show, the little, curly-haired mite would sit in intent silence
till, say, Ebley, when she would pronounce, in whispering,
lisping rapture: 'That's the *best* film I've *ever* seen'.

Anne did not, alas for actors and directors, become a film
critic but, like Clare, a nurse at Bart's, then midwife, health
visitor, senior sister and senior sixer – the lot; they both
now live in Cheltenham, each less than a mile from Mum,
surrounded by millions of their various and delightful kids,
all now leaving the nest. Whereas mine have just been
hatched, in almost my dotage. Wonderful. So wunderbar, I
feel like a song. How about one I've never forgotten from
those electrically exciting mornings at the Gaumont in
Stroud:

We Come Along
On Saturday Mornings
Greeting Everybody With a Smile.
We Come Along on Saturday Mornings
Knowing it's All Worthwhile.
As Members of the GB Club
We All Intend to be
Good Citizens When We Grow Up
The Champions of the FREE!

One Saturday, I remember, we all turned up, tingling with
anticipation, and a blackboard outside the cinema announced
with chalky severity: 'GB CLUB CANCELLED DUE TO

DEATH OF PRES. ROOSEVELT'. Gordon wanted to kick in the glass doors; till Peter explained patiently. We were none the wiser. 'The War' to us had really meant, or been no more than, blackout blinds; or our other-side neighbour Jean Pearce 'seeing Bristol burn, cross my heart' from Doverow that night; Dad being away a lot; Uncle John pumping up his tyres and priming his ancient cycle-lamp; or everyone cooing about me with only a reasonable confidence, 'daresay, he'll brighten up when it's all over and he gets a banana inside him'.

\* \* \*

Their convent motto was 'Veritas', so I had better admit that 'poor, pale little Francis' (as they called me) had a year or two being taught by the Dominican nuns at St Rose's in Stroud. Then there were a couple of miserable terms at the King's junior school in Gloucester while they worked out what to do for the best. Nevertheless, those Easter and Summer terms in the shadow of the cathedral at Gloucester were to be cataclysmic. I have looked up the dates, and in just five months between March 14 and August 16, 1946, I quite simply and irretrievably became hook, line, and sinkered on sport. All sport. It was Cheltenham that did for me. The King's school had a half-day each week. Dad had probably been at the cattle market, looking to flog his milking-machines, and turned up out of the blue – and took me to the Cheltenham Gold Cup. Five months later, I went to a day at Gloucestershire's cricket festival at the Cheltenham College ground. I was never the same again.

I was still daft about everything horsey – except, it goes without saying, the very idea of riding the beasts. I was still wasting hours of school holidays sitting mesmerized in the corner, just inside the door, of the Stonehouse village smithy's shop behind the Woolpack Inn – anvil-clanging, brazier-burning, singed-hoof heaven.

Only last year, pottering about near Chipping Sodbury (us Stroudites always referred to it as Soddin' Chipbury) I was led by the nose when I got the whiff again and, wearing the grin of a Bisto kid, I watched three smiths at work alongside three flanks, each bending to the task, and each between their knees the fetlock of a sleek, liveried hunter. That really is horsey country: Sodbury is near Badminton, the Duke of Beaufort's sensational Palladian pile. In a little over 40 years Badminton has become as much a proper noun as the name of the game which was 'invented' one wet afternoon in the 1860s by two great-aunts of the present duke in the mansion's entrance hall. Badminton means the Three-Day horse Event which – typically British – actually lasts four. I went to the very first Badminton in 1949, when Uncle John and I cycled up the long hill from Nailsworth and then, head down, into the rippling-gay south-westerlies as they bounced off the full length, high quiff of the Cotswold ridge. Below us to the west, the sun-glinting, widening Severn, and Berkeley Castle as sentinel to the rich, lush vale of meadows and blossoms and growth in the various shades of greens and browns and yellows that take the farmers' fancy as the seasons come and go and come again. Then the clay gives way to limestone and, in a line as straight and strict as parading soldiers, runs the proud ledge of the Cotswolds. And if we freewheeled a moment and turned our heads around to the north, we would see my dear and modest little Doverow kneeling bashfully in the front row. The great rolling glories of the Cotswolds (which tip their hat occasionally to Oxford and Northants, Warwickshire and Worcester) are very much Gloucestershire's. They can be bleak all right in the coffin-like days of mid-winter when hedgerows are as stiff as corpses and only snowdrops smile. In a dreamy summer's haze they can be perfection – though even then, most say, not quite as perfect as when spring is silver-fresh or in the gold of autumn. Now it was spring, and for horsy folk in the shires, Badminton hoorayingly greets the approaching summer as unfailingly as, for cricketers, the arrival in April of their primrose-jacketed Wisden.

Catholic Evidence Guild hikers: (*left*) Mum and Dad courting before
(*right*) he and his plus-fours go 'back to the land'.

First time 'up' – Little Birch, 1938, with Dad on Daisy.

A young, hooped 'Rodney', in the garden below the GWR line at Stonehouse.

Belmont Under-16s, 1950 – FK at 12, standing, far right.

Another puff of Sweet Afton for Dunstan Cammack OSB. (*Douai School*)

Douai, 1954, and still obsessively attempting to impersonate George Lambert's action.

The last Duke of Beaufort (hard-riding octogenarian and simply called 'Master' in our parts since he was a boy) dreamed up the annual four-footed festival – which now attracts the largest crowd to any sporting event in the world, bar the 'Indy 500' in America – when he was watching the Olympic Games equine cross-country event at Sandhurst in 1948. He was picknicking on a rug with his friend Colonel Trevor Horn, another leading light of England's bridle brigade.

'Another grape, Horn?'

'Not for me, Master. Perhaps a hunk of cheddar and a slug of port, what?'

'I say, Horn, I've been thinking: why don't we lay on one of these jamborees at Badders next year, what? Good wheeze, eh?'

'Absolutely spiffing, Master'.

'Good show, what? Begin work tomorrow, Horn'.

'You bet, Master. Absolutely top hole'.

Horn's first 'office' at Badminton was the top of the piano in the Music Room. The manageress of the village shop typed the first entry forms. The Colonel spent the previous winter riding over ploughed fields with a milometer on his bike. Within a year they had set up an institution. Many folk the world over, with straw in their hair and bow-legged jodhpurs, may not have a clue where Gloucestershire is but they all know what Badminton means.

Ditto the Cheltenham Gold Cup meeting. The thrill of that day in March 1946 when Dad, on a whim, arrived at the King's school and took me to the races, remains vividly bold in the memory. I have been countless times since, of course – from the days when it was little more than a sort of cavalry-twilled cup final for the point-to-pointers right up to present times when I have to go to work or, more often than not, get sponsored as a newt in the vast encampment of ruffled, candy-striped marquees which have, alas, almost taken over the famous field in the name of corporate hospitality. But, oh, the raging excitement of that first time! I am charged by it every March and the cockles are warmed. Prince Regent won on my début day; Tommy Hyde up, and trained in Ireland by Tom Dreaper.

> And one who rode on a dark brown steed,
> Clean jointed, sinewy, spare,
> And the resolute eye that loves the lead,
> And the quarters massive and spare,
> A tower of strength with a promise of speed
> (There was Celtic blood in the pair).
> [Adam Gordon, *The Legend of Cotteswold*, 1869]

I still sniff the air under Cleeve Hill each middle-March Thursday around St Patrick's Day – and, yes, apart from the traffic and overwhelming, profiteering, urban intensity and tenseness of the crowds crammed into those tented cities with waitress service, if you narrow the eye, nothing much has changed from that jingly-jangly, breathless boyhood day with Dad. The paddock grass has even more the gleam and wink of emeralds, and on it the horses prance in anticipation, or pose as if for a Munnings portrait, all burnished flanks, cool and sleek and serenely aware: swish of tail and sheen of silks. Then off they charge, just as they did nearly half a century ago – and five minutes later they return, heroic and knackered, clapped out, all in, and with steaming nostrils pumping like cartoon trumpets. And their toothless jockeys, still grabbing and gasping for air, touching, feudally, their hard-hats to their grateful, gentrified, unmuddied masters before slipping off, slapping nag's neck for a 'safe journey, thanks', and scurrying away to swap silks for 'the next' with their sweat-sodden tack.

Back at my first Cheltenham, I noticed Dad doffing his check-cap to the dog-collars. At this Gold Cup meeting in March you see more Irish priests in the square mile under Cleeve Hill than you might in a year in the Piazza S. Pietro in Rome. From over the pond their parishioners, too, pack out the morning Masses at St Gregory's down in the town –

and light candles, for guidance, to the statues of the Sacred Heart and Our Lady the Virgin ('Well, Holy Mother, can y'be seein' Beech Road having the legs of Morley Street in the Champion? What d'you fancy yourself, like, Blessed Mother? And how do you rate this Toby Tobias thing, or is Garrison Savannah the stayer? And generally, Mother of God, has Celtic Shot truly got what it takes if the going's fair to firm, like?')

Cheltenham and the Catholic Church have been saddled up a long time now. A lively colony of Irish settled in the burgeoning spa town after being thrown out of Paris during the Revolution. When Captain Berkeley founded the horserace meeting below the blissful ridge of Cleeve early last century the Irish, being naturals with nags, looked after the stabling and, in time, invited over their relatives to join in the fun. Many stayed. Indeed, 100 years ago Cheltenham parish church had to build a new cemetery, for, as the old refrain had it:

The churchyard's so small and the Irish so many
They ought to be pickled, sent back to Kilkenny.

One Gold Cup morning a few years back, I was waiting in St Gregory's for an Irish journo pal who needed to go to confession after Mass. A state of grace is important for winner-picking. He was kneeling, waiting his turn, with a few other like-minded and suddenly *mea-maxima-culpa* men. The amiable Benedictine parish priest, of Irish background himself, was getting quickly through the queue of penitents. In goes a ferrety, furtive little stable-lad type. 'Bless me, Father, for I have sinned', he begins in a quite audible mutter. Suddenly, from the priest's side of the confessional, a low wail comes, then an exasperated snort – then ripping sounds and a confetti of torn betting-slips is tossed through the curtain in fury. It had been plain to hear what words had preceded this storm: 'Forgive me, Father, I've nobbled the favourite for the big one this afternoon'.

For it is, in the end, simply the Innocent God-fearing versus the Flaming Bookie. Jeffrey Bernard, my esteemed if notorious colleague on *The Spectator*, tells the gloriously true tale of the time he saw an old Irish farmer put one hundred pounds on a horse at 7–1. The bookmaker's sign on his stand proclaimed him to be a Mr Finnegan. When the horse obliged and your farmer had his 700-odd counted into his gnarled palm he kept saying, 'Yes, you've heard of *Finnegans Wake* – well, this is your fockin' wake, Finnegan'.

A couple of weeks after this entranced little débutant's tumultuous introduction to the Cheltenham races, he fastened his ear to the battery-powered wireless in the corner of the kitchen in Stonehouse to see if that same 'sinewy spare' steed of dark brown, Prince Regent, could win the Grand National. The crackle and splutter, and gathering crescendo, from Aintree provided a different sort of tautness than he had experienced, for real, at Cheltenham; but potently dramatic, nevertheless. Prince Regent was a gallant third – behind the lovely-named Lovely Cottage, who had been bred in Cork. So doubtless Uncle John strolled down to pick up his bob or two from the one-legged village barber with the stabbing scissors, Mr Silvey.

\*      \*      \*

Suddenly, the wireless had opened horizons far beyond the view from the top of Doverow Hill. Only aural as yet, of course. Television would not begin to change every rooftop and chimneypiece with its forest of little wire H's till all of seven years later when, in 1953, advances in technology coincided with the midsummer Coronation of the young Queen. They built the transmitter in Sutton Coldfield, and its dying signals just reached down to us. In perfect time for the truly and (still) magically memorable 'Matthews' Cup final' at Wembley. Not forgetting the other Stan, Mortensen – comrade of 'Sir Twinkletoes' in the tangerine shirts of Blackpool. Not that the nation actually could see that the 'velvet' turf was green, that Matthews's hair was greying, or that his shirt was orange: the tiny screen was filled with flickeringly animated monochrome blobs – but the blazing black-and-white coruscations fair lit up the land.

Our patch's one Labour county councillor and devoted Tory basher was a concerned and delightful, pipe-spittled, tobacco-stained old cove called Bert Cole. Through the war, he had become best local friend of Dad and Uncle John as they chided and chivvied to keep the Socialists' end up in a very Conservative shire.

Mrs Pearce, next door, was soon to be the second, but it was Bert, ever the progressive, who installed Stonehouse's first television set in the spring of 1953. Not for June's (or rather, Lillibet's) Coronation – but for May's Cup final. The whole village was welcome, said Bert. He had a dinky-toy Cotswold cottage of mellow honeystone (it's a car-park and smelly white-tiled public loo now) just alongside the village green and Crown & Anchor pub. Bert made sure I was in early for the frontest seat in the house. Well before kick-off, the room was jammed, the LMS kids flattening their noses on the windows; with men, women, and children jostlingly filling the garden and blocking the road.

They stayed for the whole match, the continuing eruptions of sighs or cheers from inside Bert's parlour keeping them spellbound as the score (4–3, at the desperate finish, to Blackpool) was relayed out to them. Inside, the joint was jumping all around the best seat in the place. Which was mine, not Bert's. He had put his armchair exactly alongside the wondrous, flickering little box – and facing OUTWARDS. So there was no possible way he could see the minute – what? 10-inch square? – screen himself. For, as they say, the full 90 minutes, Bert sat watching *us* being enthralled, and I can see to this day his pipe-puffing, benign communal contentment, head and ear cocked and eyes moving from one of us to the other, simply witnessing our pleasure; rather like, I suppose, an olde tyme, loved and loving, village squire who received and graciously accepted his mellow kicks by generously providing brandy-buttered mince pies and steaming mulled wine when the choir with their lanterns and tone-deaf cohesion slogged up to the manor house to sing 'The Holly and the Ivy' and a few more of the same on long-ago Christmas Eves.

I still, nevertheless, reckon what exploded into my consciousness with even greater resonance had been seven years earlier, with the wireless and that 1946 final – Charlton Athletic against Derby County. In extra-time, Jack Stamps, of Derby, scored two palpitating (or so they sounded) late goals to settle the thing. I remember they had, around that time, decided that I would go as a boarder to Belmont Abbey, back in Hereford, at the start of the autumn term. This I was dreading – now even more desperately, for it was a damnable rugby-playing school. After that day, with Jack Stamps scoring and Raymond Glendenning bellowing, it was many years till I was to accept that rugby was remotely as good a game as soccer. (In fact, nearly half a century later, I still know it isn't. Still, it's a reasonable game when played well and imaginatively – which is not, alas, often).

Although I was not to meet him until 20 years later (at the Mexico World Cup in 1970), my very good friend John Moynihan (son of the artists Rodrigo and Elinor) was also entranced that Jack Stamps day. John was already at his prep school and, as he was to write in his classic *Soccer Syndrome* (1966): 'Perhaps soccer first attracted me – a weedy, unathletic, rugby-hating desperate – with that 1946 commentary by Raymond Glendenning on the wireless: an extraordinarily ministerial voice which moved from a bark to a gurgle into a squeak and back to a bark – 'Stamps has scored! *Stamps has scored*!'

Jack Stamps died just before Christmas 1991. He had been as blind as Pew for the last 20 years. I never met him, but I was glad *The Times* began his obit, 'A giant of a man. . . .' So most assuredly, in his way, was Raymond

Glendenning – town crier to a generation: rhythms and cadences of excitements and tensions; the voice of brown-windsor relayed through the soupstrainer moustache. Glendenning departed the scene long before my time, but a friend and contemporary with whom I was to work, briefly and happily, is Brian Moore, Independent Television's chief soccer commentator for the past two decades. (Brian, by the way, beat me to his Cup final television debut: his Gran in Kent installed a TV set in 1948, and the short-trousered sprog watched, entranced, another legendary final, between Man. United and Blackpool. 'I was fiercely smitten and bitten by the bug there and then', he says). One of Brian's first wireless commentary trials was at Fratton Park, Portsmouth. He was sent to 'help out' his hero, Glendenning. 'I was as nervous as a new-born kitten. Mr Glendenning was tremendously helpful and generous'. On his 90th birthday in 1991, I asked Rex Alston, another doyen of our long-ago wireless world, about Glendenning: 'Raymond was an amazing chap. Awfully nice fellow, you know. Great flying handlebar moustache, and 19 to the dozen with his delivery. But a very kindly man, and in many ways a most remarkably able chap, you know: could turn his hand to anything. Spoke languages, fluent French and Welsh and all that; and a really most amazingly good conjuror, you know'.

June, 1946, continued my crash-course crammer in the wonders of wireless. Another half-day at the King's school, and I hared across the bus-station and through the old market to the GWR station to make sure of being able to listen to the first Derby to be run at Epsom since the war. A mottled grey rank outsider named Airborne had been entered at 100–1, but on the eve of the race a flurry of bets by anyone who had anything to do with the RAF's airborne divisions, like the Parachute Corps, brought the no-hoper's price down to 66–1. Glendenning again added his frenziedly piquant breathlessness to the occasion in the corner of our kitchen.

Many years later, not long before he died, the legendary old war correspondent René Cutforth told me a tale of that very June 5. René himself had been among that large number who returned from the wartime fronts and suffered delayed shell-shock as soon as they were in their demob suits. A special nursing home was set up for just such cases. They were not deemed certifiable – until one benighted inmate in a parachutist's cherry-red beret announced that he was determined to plonk the whole of his newly issued prisoner of war's back-pay cheque – some £3,000 or so – on the mottled grey 66–1 shot named after his regiment in the next day's Derby. Nurses panicked for him; doctors were told; they *had* to save this lunatic's gratuity for him. Could, perhaps, the cheque be stopped till after the race? Whitehall was telephoned. Civil servants joined the race against time. Top brass at the War Office were contacted. If only someone could be found with enough stripes to certify the fellow and revoke the cheque, a tragedy would be avoided and the man would keep his money. But no soul was brave enough to make the decision without three memos in triplicate. Till it was too late. They were off at Epsom!

Airborne won, of course – and by teatime the 'nutter' parachutist had been discharged as totally sane. And very, very rich.

I see it was just two weekends after Airborne's Derby that the most memorable thing of my warm and cuddly boyhood happened. I went to see Gloucestershire play cricket. It must have been a labour of love for Dad, for of all sports he could see the least in cricket. For one thing, it needed the most time – thus the most time for a boy to waste away from his books. Poor Dad, having finished his rounds at Gloucester market and, on a whim, thinking he'd give me a treat for a couple of hours, could not possibly have known what he was introducing me to (or himself come to that) on Saturday lunchtime at Gloucester Wagon Works on the afternoon before midsummer's day. The cricketer's bible, *Wisden*, is invaluable for nostalgics. I see – dammit, I remember like it was last midsummer's eve – Jack Robertson and Bill Edrich were batting for Middlesex, and then craggy and tall Tom Goddard (as old as the century, born October 1), and young, placid Sam Cook got among the city slickers and spun them out for 150. I see Ian Peebles was last man in and 0 not out for Middlesex. I could not know that glorious and kindly man – who once got Bradman in a Test match – would, only a quarter of a century later, write for the same newspaper as me and be my guide and mentor.

Anyway, I was in love. At first sight Speared through the heart. Robin Bassett and I pitched stumps in our back garden – between the two apple trees and right under the bank below the Great Western line – and we batted and bowled the rest of the summer through. On Monday, August 16, Uncle John managed a day off from RAF Aston Down and with Bert Cole and Percy Horsham (a cheerful old boy who used to look after the village hall 'Subscription Room') took Robin and me on the bus to Cheltenham to see Gloucester play Surrey – and Charlie Barnett, from down the road at Chalford, hit 101 in next to no time and clocked big, young Alec Bedser, built like Bruce Woodcock, all over the shop. And we had a pound of Evesham plums for lunch. Afterwards Tom Goddard (he had taken six for 72 that first day I set eyes on him at Gloucester) skittled Surrey with an almost ridiculous nine for 84. The cup of Tizer runneth over.

Tom clean bowled the Surrey captain, N. H. Bennett first ball, to general mirth. At the time, of course, I did not understand why everyone was laughing – it was years later that good Jim Laker provided the explanation. Apparently, that spring of 1946 Surrey had been so busy getting their ground at The Oval ready for play (it had served in the war as a POW clearing camp) that they were still scratching around for a captain only a fortnight before the season began. In those days, of course, county captains had to be amateurs and gentlemen. They had in mind one A. C. L.

Bennett, a well known pre-war club cricketer in the county and a stalwart founder, too, of the BBC team. While they were enquiring what regiment he might have been in and how to contact him, news came through that a Major Bennett was in the downstairs office seeking club membership for the season. The committee invited him up at once and offered him the county captaincy. Yes, well, if they insisted, he would be delighted to accept the challenge. He thought he ought to point out, however, that his name was *Nigel* Bennett; he had just left the Army and was wondering what he might have a crack at in civvy street, and while waiting for something to turn up he might as well watch a bit of cricket at The Oval. He was hoping to continue playing for Wimbledon 2nd XI, for whom he had enjoyed the odd game before the war.

And so, on the resumption of first-class cricket, Major Bennett led out a side including such luminaries as Fishlock, Gover, Bedser, Laker, Lock and McIntyre. He got a duck against India in his first match and took it from there. But Jim, wincing as he remembered, said he had ruled with a rod of steel. Ducks quacked non-stop. It was his only season and, as *Wisden* next spring noted with exemplary tact, 'his want of knowledge of county cricket on the field presented an unconquerable hindrance to the satisfactory accomplishments of arduous duties, which prejudiced the general work of the side'.

In his final county innings, against the Combined Services, Major Bennett at least scored 2 – and Surrey pressed back into service Erroll Holmes, who had first captained them in 1934. Poor Major Bennett. But how was I to know? To me, his duck against my new god, Goddard, was absolute heaven. In five months my life had been changed irrevocably.

I was already aware of one sadness: 1946 was Wally Hammond's last summer in first-class cricket. Both at the Wagon Works ground in June and at Cheltenham in August, he was away at the Test match captaining England against India. After Sir Jack Hobbs and another Gloucestershire man, W. G. Grace, Hammond must be the game's most ruthlessly cold-eyed English batsman. So, by wretched chance, I was never once to see him play: I will die being sad about that. Still, that afternoon at Cheltenham, after Barnett and pint-pot Andy Wilson had put on 150, our first-wicket down was gentle Billy Neale, who was a farmer from near Thornbury way. Apparently Billy was the only man in the world to understand the black moods and dark depressions of the emperor, Hammond.

In the early 1920s Neale and Hammond had been best pals at Cirencester grammar school. At the height of his acknowledged resplendence, Wally would mooch and brood on days off around Billy's orchards at Breadstone Farm. Not far from the orchard where, a century before, Mrs Grace, a doctor's wife, taught cricket to her sons, one of whom became the very colossus of the game and, though always a Downend country doctor, introduced it to the world.

Another eminent Victorian left his mark on Gloucester- shire. Isambard Kingdom Brunel opened up the west when he built his famous 'billiard table' railway line from London (it is, to all intents, dead level for 85 miles from Paddington). The great terminus at Bristol Temple Meads and the magnificently zany Clifton Suspension Bridge remain monuments to his derring-do. Brunel has always been one of my heroes – non-sporting ones, that is. (Who else, non-sporting? Well, off the top of my head, how about the irascible old William Cobbett, Charles Dickens, Nye Bevan, Ben Parkin, John Arlott, John Osborne, Dirk Bogarde, Richard Ingrams for starters?)

Anyway, everything overlaps. When Brunel died in 1859, W. G. Grace was 11. The other day I came across a letter from Brunel written in the last year of his life. He was trying to persuade a Mr C. Richardson to become his engineer on his final project, the line north from Bristol through Ashley Down and Patchway. He offered £300 a year, rising to £450, and he wrote as bait: '. . . the country immediately north of the city I should think a delightful one to live in –

beautiful country – good society near Bristol, Clifton, etc – I can't vouch for any cricketing, but I should think it highly probable. . . .'

It was. He took the job and the 11-year-old W. G. more than likely watched Mr Richardson build his line; when he was not cricketing in his orchard, that is.

Only a mile or two away now is that breathtaking modern span of which Brunel would have mightily approved, the wondrous Severn Road Bridge. Mr Richardson's LMS line runs on to Gloucester, and just outside Stonehouse it is joined by my very own GWR from Stroud to Swindon. And alongside that railway now, in a kaleidoscope of sprayed-on primary colours, cars and lorries skim by on the great M5 motorway conveyor belt to north and south – and everywhere.

You can see it all from my slatted-iron bench on Doverow Hill.

# 3

When you return as a grown-up to the familiar landmarks of childhood they seem shrunken, midget things. I have not remotely found it the same when I re-meet those men who were the giants of my youth. Giants they remain. Even when my boyhood's callow, eyes-wide idol worship has been replaced – as now it has in many cases – with a fond and warm man-to-man friendship, I am still in awe of these cigarette-card heroes of my infancy. There was music in their names when I first heard them long ago; and a valorous chivalry in their deeds. The tunes still play. Many of these mellow, generous countrymen who made up those first Gloucestershire cricket teams of mine are dead. The remainder I cherish now as friends (some, glory be, seem to treat me like a favourite nephew). Yet even in their sometimes shuffling dotage, my sense of wonder in their presence remains, if different, certainly as potent as when I stared up balloon-eyed, with hesitant shyness and asked them to fill my books with their autographs.

Almost half a century on, their eyes (like those of all really good cricketers, have you noticed?) remain piercing bright and steady-gazed; their faces and forearms are still burnished with a sun-brown wash which tells of countless midsummers in the open air. The gnarled and knobbly twisted knuckles of their thumbs and fingers are proof and testament to the exacting trade and craft for which we loved them: a skill-based craft for sure – aye, and more, for it was one which from time to time allowed them to be uplifted into brief but very genuine realms of creative invention and authentic artistry.

Some know-all once said that the process of maturity into adulthood reduced giants to man-size. Not so with the officers and foot-sloggers – especially not the foot-sloggers – who trod the green turf of my favourite fields of childhood. If nothing else, these good men taught us urchins pride – for with all our youthful fibre, oh boy! what pride we had in them. They couldn't half play cricket, too. I'll give you 12 of my earliest time – and of that dozen, six played for England, some of them enchanting vast throngs of many thousands in grandiose concrete arenas in cities across the seas and far from distant, pastoral Gloucestershire: Barnett, Emmett, Crapp, Cook, Milton, and Goddard. And the other half, too, were all 'capped' for England in our interminable 'pick-up' games in the back garden between the apple trees, and the Stonehouse scorebook proves beyond doubt that Lambert, Monks, Cranfield, Scott, Wilson, and Wells also had glorious and prolific Test match careers the whole world over.

Although he did not play many games for the county – 100 innings and just one century, against the kids of Cambridge – notice that Clifford Monks regularly nudged the autocratic Stonehouse Test selectors (Messrs R. Bassett and F. Keating) as they ruthlessly picked their sides most summer holiday mornings. It was all because of The Catch. Monks was a chunky and soft-mannered stonemason (with forearms like Popeye's) from Coalpit Heath – and also the village organist and choirmaster. The Catch was the first single, wondrous, and palpitating heart-stopper I was in on. It remains up there on the pedestal with my all-time one-offers – like Beamon's jump in Mexico, Best's shimmying thrust against Benfica, the Lions' epic try at Potchefstroom, Coe's '1500' in Moscow, Bobby's Portuguese net bulger in 1966, McEnroe's tie-break, Montgomery's 1973 save, Dolly's Oval hundred, and Holding's six balls in Bridgetown. . . .

Context is all in sport, and The Catch was taken at an absolutely crucial moment in August 1947 at Cheltenham when – would you believe it? – Gloucestershire were effectively playing-off for the County Championship with mighty Middlesex in the London county's *annus mirabilis*. If it was that for them, what the heck is the Latin for what it was for us? Throughout the summer Gloucester had dogged them stride for stride. Now it was down to the wire. Winner take all.

Both days – it lasted only two – Robin and I had gone through what had already become our annual early morning ritual for the two luminous weeks of the August festival: the Western National from Stonehouse to Stroud at dawn; a queue outside Woolworths for the Cheltenham bus, then over the top past Painswick's yews and the Prinknash Pottery. We clutched our Mums' sandwiches in their greaseproof paper and I fingered my shilling for the bottle of Tizer and the pound of plums. All talk through the Woodbine smoke on top of the double-decker special was of 'the cricket'. We were plonked down outside the College and scurried to join another queue. Fifteen thousand of us were let in at last.

Men still speak of the match today. You meet people in pubs who can recite Gloucester's second innings scorecard. Only they don't weep at it any longer. We scored 100, needing 169. Bill Edrich's 50 was the top score of the match, and then lank, long Sims and tiny, trim Young bowled too well. Tom Goddard's fifteen wickets were not enough. But I still find myself holding my breath as I recall the boundary catch by the occasional first-time makeweight, Monks. He sprinted, memory insists, some 50 yards to catch R. W. V. Robins. Memory also insists that the ball would have hit me on the head had he not held it, but I've heard more than a dozen of men claim that over the years. It remains the finest catch I have ever seen. When Monks died 27 years later the *Cheltenham Echo* obituary was headlined simply 'The Man Who Made The Catch'.

*          *          *

Tom Goddard was my first idol. Huge cream tent of a shirt billowing out behind him, a couple of lollops to the wicket, he'd clear the air with a wipe of his left arm and over she'd come with his right. Huge hands, huge heart, he would wheel and deal for wickets all day long. He kept a furniture shop in Gloucester. Tom's appeal would reverberate round the ring of hills from Cleeve to Birdlip and out to Severn Sound. We called him 'Barnardo' because he'd appeal for anything. I don't think he ever knew the LBW Law. 'Eh, Ta-am! Whodabou'a bloke atop o' Leckhampton 'ill, then?' we would shout when he set his field. He took 2,979 wickets in his career. Only four men had more in the whole history of the game. Rhodes, Freeman, Hearne, and his own old pre-war mentor – born just up the road at Prestbury – Charlie Parker. Tom often took 200 wickets in a summer: now men are chaired off the field if they take 50, it seems. Once Basil Allen had to leave the field and put Goddard in charge. Over after over he bowled on, though it was not a day for spinners. Finally, Goddard, completely whacked, complained to stumper Wilson, 'Why don't the bugger take me off?' He had quite forgotten he was skipper for the day.

Goddard died in 1966. I went to visit his widow in Barton Street and she showed me his scrapbooks. Dog-eared cardboard treasures full of glued-in snapshots of cricket tourists looking like ordinary fellows in baggy sepia trousers: no names, just smiling faces of cigarette-smoking men, many of whom were going to die once their sun set on the cricket grounds of England. Like Tom Goddard, who played till well into his fifties, then had scarcely more than a dozen years of 'retirement'.

One of Tom's grandest of many notable deeds (although he wouldn't agree, by any means) was to save E. W. Swanton for the nation. England's tour to South Africa in 1938–39 was the first to be covered live by BBC wireless – young Swanton paying his own way by Union Castle line (return, first-class, £82.16s.0d.). The tyro was charged to cover, ball-by-ball, as they say, the last half-hour of play on each day of the series. The first Test, at Johannesburg, was played over Christmas, so a large audience was expected to be sniffing the ether, post prandially, back in Blighty. On the first day, England were batting 'for the morrow' with Paul Gibb, in painfully dreary mood, just patting back leg-breaks from Bruce Mitchell. Poor EWS had no scorer in the 'box' with him, so no access to reams of figures with which commentators now fill in time. The same happened for the last half-hour of the next day's play, another somnolent longueur, this time with South Africa's Mitchell yawningly blocking out Hedley Verity.

Swanton was in despair. He could sense not only the whole nation, but his bosses at the BBC (who had sanctioned the 'experiment' with weary suspicion in the first place) falling asleep over the Yule log. Then, for the last two overs, Hammond tossed the ball to Goddard.

I can imagine it. The great, reddish-turning southern sun over the yard-arm. Tom licking his right forefinger, then lolloping in. At once, he holds one back – bingo! Nourse caught-and-bowled in those huge farm-pail hands. Gordon, the night-watchman next: first ball, stretch him forward, Tom: exactly so, thanks very much and goodnight, sir: easily stumped; Wade in now, on the hat-trick, but a good bat; how about a faster yorker to greet him? Spear her into the blockhole – just like that. Middle-peg, too. And a hat-trick. There's something for that Swanton to talk about.

And how. Back home, the stultified England woke up at Swanton's thrilling gabble from the other side of the world. Here was a bit of history – and they were hearing it, uniquely, as it happened. Off the top of my head, I think only one Englishman has got a Test match hat-trick in the half-century since – Peter Loader. Certainly Swanton (85 in February 1992, our doyen and one who has always been so kind and encouraging to me: although I did not know him in his earlier, more, er, vibrant prime) has always reckoned Gloucester's Tom saved his broadcasting career at its infancy. The morning after the Johannesburg hat-trick, Swanton received a cable from his BBC boss, Michael Standing – 'Congratulations. Everybody pleased'. Standing might have sent a copy of the same to Tom Goddard.

For Gloucester, Goddard had already organized his successor. Can any county – man, women, and child – have been fond of a man as much as 'Glorse' was fond of Bomber Wells? He worked at Bellows' in Gloucester as a printing apprentice and his parents called him 'Brian'. On the eve of his first match, he had been to the pictures with his girlfriend, Pat, and they were strolling to the fish-and-chip shop in Park End Road when a big, black Austin Princess car drew up. It was Tom Goddard himself. 'Get to Bristol tomorrow by twenty-past 10, Bomber – you're in against Sussex.' So our bumper barrel of fun, with the hooter and a scarecrow-spiky hairstyle that made even gnarled old pros grin back, arrived on the bus from Gloucester with his sandwiches and whites borrowed from his future father-in-law. Gloucester fielded and for George Lambert's first ball they put him at gully. John Langridge cut delicately, the Bomber tubbily gave chase – and they ran five! He was at once moved to short-leg. At the moment Lambert was uncoiling the lovely action for his next ball, Bomber, to show he meant business, first spat in his hands and then smacked them loudly together. Langridge, distracted, pulled away complaining. Bomber was moved to deepish mid-on and there he stayed for the rest of a sublime career. When his turn came to bowl he at once bamboozled the Reverend Sheppard. By teatime his spinning-top off-breaks off a one-and-a-half pace run-up, had, incredibly, taken 6 for 47, and John Arlott looked for him in the pavilion, for he had been asked to broadcast an urgent radio interview with the young man who had become the hottest news of the day. He was told the boy was having a picnic with his Mum down on the grass by the sightscreen.

That evening, the county secretary gave him £20 and told him they had already telephoned his Gloucester boss, Mr Bellows, who had agreed 'Brian' could have his summers off playing cricket. He enchanted us for the next eight seasons and then had a second career at Trent Bridge. When he had taken 999 first-class wickets he called it a day – 'I'll only dial for the next one in an emergency', he joked. Once, on the players' dressing-room balcony at the 'holy-of-holies' at Lord's, Bomber and a few others were watching an allegedly promising young Middlesex leg-break bowler being given some terrible stick by George Emmett and Jack Crapp. The young bowler had not long left Eton and was already being talked of as an England bowler of the near future. George and Jack continued to clout him all over Marylebone. Bomber amiably nudged the stranger next to him on the balcony, 'Eh, I thought this poor young clown was meant to be a bowler?' Before withdrawing pronto, the stranger looked fiercely at Bomber and snapped, 'I never comment, sir, on my son's ability'. It was R. W. V. Robins, former Middlesex and England captain, father of young spinner Charles Robins, and the chairman of the Test selection committee. 'That's done it', said George Lambert, 'you'll never play for England now, Bomber'.

Though still with lashings of fun and laughter, few former players 'talk' cricket with such nous and insights as the Bomber, now living back in Gloucester after his enjoyable exile in Nottingham. Of the captains he played under in his travels, the Bomber thinks George Emmett far and away the best. 'He had forgotten more about the game than most of us were ever likely to know', says Wells. 'Us kids did not quite know how to take George. Oh, he could bat alright, sometimes breathtakingly. He was a tiny man, but perfectly proportioned. He looked like a sunburnt-brown Fred

Astaire, and had the footwork to match, twinkling from the crease with a chassé to turn the fastest full-pelter into a succulent half-volley to on-drive'.

Emmett had been born into an army family out East, and even as he impatiently lined kids up for autographs as he strolled round the ground by himself in his England blazer, there was something of the Sar'nt-Major about him. Many years later, I learned the youngsters in the team knew him (behind his back) as 'Cap'n Bligh'. In the car park opposite the College Chapel end, there was a roped-off square behind the marquees and a notice saying, 'Players And Officials Park Only'. One Vauxhall Velox was always, somehow, on its own, no other cars near. It was George Emmett's. For inevitably in it, bloodshot-eyed and permanently on a gnashing-toothed growl was George's ferocious dog, Kerry Blue. (Once, the Bomber told me, George's postman in Bristol, who would leave the mail outside the gate if the animal was lurking around the little garden, saw Blue was safely locked in behind the front-room window, so not only proceeded confidently up the garden path to the letterbox, but had the jaunty nerve to poke his tongue out at the jaw-snapping barker going berserk at the window. As he turned to go back down the garden path, Postman Pat merrily gave the beast a V-sign too. This last was too much for Baskerville Blue – it dived, a rocket-launched missile, straight through the plate-glass window like it was Mike Teague going for a scrum-half. And took most of the backside of poor Pat's blue serge trousers as well as a chunk of his left buttock.)

Emmett's most famous knocks seemed reserved for Bristol: people down there still say his big hundred against Kent and the clock in 1950 was Gloucester's all-time, post-Hammond gem of gems. There were 33 other centuries. Not one could have been remotely untidy. Funny, there might have been some insecurities (hence the beastly Blue) lurking around the seeming martinet – for he got out over 30 times in the 'nervous' 90s.

Emmett became, of course, one of our first professional captains. In my earliest days such a thing would have been unthinkable (Tom Dollery, of Warwickshire, was the first ever, in 1950). Basil Allen (Clifton, Cambridge, and for years Master of the Mendip Hunt) was 'my' first county captain. He was not on the autograph list. He looked as fierce as a few Latin masters I was to have. Like his immediate predecessor, Hammond, was said to have done, he went forth to toss for innings in a battered brown trilby. He blew his nose with a red-spotted snuff handkerchief. He scored a double-century once, against Hampshire, and Dad's old friend Percy Horsham said, 'Bloody hell, wonders'll never cease'.

Even Basil Allen's squirarchical swagger was upstaged by the skipper who was to follow. He used to take up three whole lines in the scorecard we'd buy for threepence from the tiny tent with the chuntering 'John Bull' press inside: Sir D. T. L. B. Bailey, Bt., DFC.

The funny thing is, from the very first moment we saw him, in 1950, every man Jack in the county began to have a warm affection for Sir Derrick. He was son and heir of Sir Abe Bailey, the South African diamond tycoon. After a dashing war as an RAF pilot he had enrolled for a course at Cirencester Agricultural College prior to, I suppose, going back to run the family ranches in the sun. The RAC have (or had) an annual match against 'a County XI'. In 1949, Tom Goddard played in it. In strides the young Baronet, unconcerned and with the clumping, heavy footed gait we were to become so fond of, and he proceeds to thump Tom hither and yon with the spin. Tom didn't like it, but when he got back he reported the 'find'. The committee followed it up – and a season later Sir Derrick was captaining the county. Everyone laughed and prepared for him to be out of his depth. And he was – but then again he wasn't, for what a fighter he turned out to be. Here he was, batting against some of the finest bowling attacks the game had known up and down the shires, but his sheer grit heroically overcame

his ungainly style time and again. In that first season he
made two centuries, and when he posted his 1,000 runs at
Cheltenham you could hear the hoorays in Hartpury.

Once, against Yorkshire, Sir D. was batting with Colin
Scott, he of the great 'large white loaf, please' boots always
splayed at 10-to-2 like Underwood's a quarter of a century
later. Bailey hoiked a ball high to deepest midwicket.
Lowson was at square-leg, Halliday at deep mid-on. They
both sprinted for the skier – which landed safely a moment
after the two fieldsmen had crashed, head bangingly, into
each other. They lay, stunned, on the ground, the ball next
to them forgotten as all the Yorkies, and the two umpires,
ran to tend to them. Bailey and Scott had run two as the ball
was in the air; then Scott had stopped, and looked to move
to join in the general ambulance kerfuffle around the
poleaxed, stricken couple at deep midwicket.

'Scott! Keep running!', ordered Sir Derrick. So they did, at
each turn of ends the captain loudly counting off the runs –
seven, eight, nine ... thirteen, fourteen, fifteen. ... At
which point one of the umpires, Fred Price, returned to the
square and ordered Bailey to desist. 'Alright, fair enough if
you say so,' said the captain, 'if you'll kindly inform the
scorers that the hit was worth 18 runs'. The umpires
conferred. Only two runs would be allowed, those taken
before the fieldsmen collided. Bailey batted on, seething with
furious indignation, and at close of play telephoned Lord's
at once for a ruling on his 16 disallowed runs.

We particularly sniggered and chortled – and loved – his
great booming voice with which he would move faraway
fieldsmen. Often with a matey swearword or two attached.
Or to a bowler. 'C'mon George [or Sam, or Bomber], get rid
of this bugger, I'm bored'. At close of play, when the rest of
the team, having changed, would come out in grey flannels
and their county or country's blazer, Sir Derrick would be in
khaki shorts and a moth-eaten old safari-jacket; and he
would sling his kit in the back and jump, without bothering
to open the door, into one of his racy, vintage tourers, and

off he'd rev in a din and a cloud of dust and grit. Arthur Milton once told me, 'He'd drive us kids who hadn't got cars to and from matches like a lunatic; weaving this way and that; horn going like Mister Toad on a spree, cussing and cursing to all and sundry who got in his way, and hail-fellowing everyone else he passed'.

Bailey bought a sublime estate and manor house, Brinsop Court, near Hereford, and apparently he liked nothing better than to pile a couple of the old pros into the tourer after a game and take them home to dine and talk about life and love and England and cricket. Jack Crapp told me, 'We'd sit at this great table and be waited on. As much to drink as we wanted; wine and everything. Then we'd stay the night, and after supper you'd go up and the clothes you'd brought for next day would all be washed and pressed and ironed. Then first thing in the morning, you'd wake up to hear him hollering and shouting at all the estate farmers and the like out in the courtyard; but all amiable enough, nothing nasty in it at all. Just like he used to holler around the field – at Lord's even, didn't make no difference to him. Oh yes, he was a one, that Sir Derrick, but a heart of gold, and a batsman full of courage and guts; at cricket, he had just about to teach himself everything as he went along, didn't he? But never once too proud not to ask one or two of us for advice'.

Sir Derrick is now in his middle-seventies and living in the Channel Islands. By fluke, only the other day in Hay-on-Wye, I happened upon a modest little paperback which turned out to be spectacularly unputdownable. It is called *A Funny Old Quist* (Eland Press, £4.95), the memoirs of a Herefordshire gamekeeper, Evan Rogers. He was gamekeeper to Sir Derrick at Brinsop Court. Another who loved 'the Skipper'. Wrote the enchanting Rogers in 1981:

'I can hear Sir Derrick's voice now ringing in my ears; he could put on a very loud voice. That's how he always acted but he was a dear good man, there's no mistake about it; he's one of the dearest gentlemen who ever broke a bit of bread. Even when my dear old Aunt as was blind, a stranger to him, died at 94 only a year after he come here, he said, "Oh, I'm so sorry to hear of your loss, Evan" he said, and he come upstairs and helped to carry her coffin down for me before it was taken to Brinsop churchyard. Mind you yet, I have seen Sir Derrick in a rage with some workers. I'm sorry to say he was also very fluent at swearing and of course it wasn't for me to tell him to stop.

'He's even swore when he's been out shooting and Lady Bailey was along. A pheasant fell in front of me and I was busy watching my dog to see as he didn't get too far away to flush too many birds, and Lady Bailey said to Sir Derrick, "I know exactly where it dropped, darling!" I remembers it quite clear. "Well," he says, "tell Evan where the bloody thing is then!" He said it to HER — to Lady Bailey! "BLOODY thing!" Well, you know, it was extraordinary. I couldn't believe my own ears to think that he would ever speak to a lady like Lady Bailey — his WIFE! — in those terms. I'd heard him swear at workmen, oh yes, but never to me, well, except once, when we were driving a patch of kale for pheasants about the end of one October . . . but all around, oh, he was a lovely gentleman, and I've never met his equal yet. I just don't know how to praise him enough. I'd like to put him up against that Colonel Astley, who was here before him, and gave me that tiny box of bloody fags for building up the whole shoot for him!'

Only two of those beloved salts of mine have so far stayed in to notch up 80. Andy Wilson and Charlie Barnett both serenely passed the mark in 1990. Both, aptly, in the summer, too. They had been the opening partners, with a century stand, the first time I went to the Cheltenham cricket in 1946. Forty-four years later I had to be at Wimbledon, but I rang the fish shop in Cirencester to wish the old, once-blazing batsman Barnett all ye best for his 4-score. His son, John, said Pa was still generally full of the joys, though some days were better than others. He gave up riding to hounds with the Berkeley only a couple of winters ago. He has moved, too, from the Chalford corner of our Stroud Valley and is now even higher up on the Cotswold ridge, where his wife keeps their herb nursery. I suppose Charlie was the first really ace-famous man I ever saw. Never having seen Hammond bat, for me Barnett was the next best thing.

I wrote a little *Spectator* tribute on his birthday, saying how he would open our batting, with just the same venomous splat he might plonk down a plaice or Dover sole on his fishmonger's slab. I was aware in doing so that I was letting myself in for a reply by return of post; severe, sharp, fountain-pen Quink: the name was, in fact, Charles; and it wasn't a 'fish shop' his family had run for four generations, but 'a high-class business' in both Cheltenham and 'Siren' which was 'licensed to sell game and poultry, sir. For years we supplied the Duke of Beaufort at Badminton House, sir'. So the old boy remains as scary-stern as he was to us village scallywags in the mid-1940s. Then, as now, the county cricket was hogged by Bristol in the south. Tom and Charlie, from the north, were our champions till the Bomber came. Barnett may have been a professional, but he batted with a patrician's disdainful swagger and crack. He had the Elastoplasted bat of an amateur, a fierce eye, and a businesslike kestrel's nose to match. His stomach for the fight unnerved the bowler, and the first (or last) ball of the day would readily fizz, frightened, to the ropes, or over them. Gusto personified. He scored 25,000 first-class runs, but was prouder of his 400 wickets which included those of Bradman, Headley, George Gunn, Worrell, Hutton, and Washbrook – and, he swears, Hobbs, plumb lbw at the Oval in 1928, though the umpire didn't agree.

Barnett averaged 35 in 20 matches for England. His first Test century was at Adelaide in 1936 – Gubby Allen's losing series. Cardus cabled back to the *Guardian* that day: 'Young Barnett's cricket suggests a standard-bearer has seized the bullet-ridden England colours and is determined to keep them aloft: his cricket appeals throughout to the

imagination, to our sense of cricket's art'. Only Charlie and
R. E. S. Wyatt survive from that team. The rest are all gone
– Verity, Hammond, Leyland, Ames, Hardstaff, Allen,
Robins, Voce, and Farnes. Hedley Verity was Charlie's
particular pal. They shared a cabin going over on the *Orion*,
and read *The Seven Pillars of Wisdom* aloud to each other,
and in the sultry moonlit evenings would stroll round and
round the promenade-deck together, Hedley with his
walking-stick showing Charlie how to play O'Reilly on a
sticky. Charlie, said Cardus, played 'the Tiger' (bouncy,
spitting leg-breaks) with consummate skill and counter-
attacking venom throughout the series – and the demon
O'Reilly copped it again in the first Test of 1938 at Trent
Bridge. Only three men, Bradman, Trumper, and Macartney,
have scored a century before lunch in an Ashes Test. Charlie
Barnett that morning at Nottingham carried in his bat for a
rasping, gloriously disdainful 99 – hit the first ball after
lunch for a savagely joyous four, and next morning opened
a letter from his mother, Muriel, posted back home in
Cirencester, which read, 'Heartiest congratulations. Everyone round about is delighted'.

Like most of this Pantheon of my boyhood's heroes,
Barnett sacrificed his cricketing prime to the war. One day,
soon after it, I cycled with Robin Bassett up that winding
hill above Chalford to get the very first signature in my
brand-new autograph book. I have the battered little thing
still. 'Best of luck, Francis . . . C. J. Barnett'. Still at the
wicket into the 1990s. Still socking it to them. Everyone
round about is delighted.

As, to be sure, they had been with another brand-new
octogenarian a couple of months earlier in 1990, this time at
the other side of the county, in Gloucestershire's north-west
corner at charming Redmarley d'Abitot, where Elgar did his
courting in the lee of the Malverns. Andy Wilson lives there
in warmly content retirement with his ever-bonny wife Liz.
Squint your eyes a moment and Andy scarcely looks a jot
changed since he came back to the pavilion – shyly flushed

but honestly satisfied – that first time I saw him after his century stand with Barnett against Gover and the Bedser twins in 1946. He was only an occasional, stand-in opener – in 'real' life he was our permanent fixture behind the stumps – a hale, jockey-squat, square-shouldered dumpling of 5ft 3in. Some of us village gawks were still nowhere near taking the 11-plus, but had nevertheless already outgrown Andy. But we were devoted to him and his strident shouts for lbw which, nevertheless, were invariably drowned by Tom's foghorn certainties from the bowler's end. Whosoever's turn it was to go behind the sticks in our get-up games would never so much as even begin to crouch till he (or she, for some sisters were besotted, too) had put on the school-cap and angled it, just so, to imitate exactly the jaunty, market-day, off-centre slant that Andy always put to the peak of his faded old blue one.

Can it really be – I suddenly wonder – over 40 years since I saw my first black man? What a truly mesmerizing day that was: I can still feel the spine riddled and griddled with the anticipation of it. Another day that they had to close the gates at the College ground in August. That West Indian touring side of 1950 – the 3-Ws, Worrell, Weekes, and Walcott; and 'those two little pals', Ramadhin and Valentine – must remain the best ever to come from the Caribbean (certainly the best balanced); and unquestionably the most exotically captivating to us who had been snuggled away in self-containment under Doverow Hill. Their caps of crimson-cherry, their smiles, their outrageous and natural cricketing, and their autograph-giving charm and generosity. They trounced us by an innings and a million or so – Glos skittled, all out for 69 and 96; West Indies something absolutely massive, with Walcott (especially, and with a bludgeon) and Weekes, with his rapier, just tuning up with a coruscating flow of strokes for the upcoming final Test at The Oval, in which they were also to beat England by an innings and almost as mercilessly. So the day was no particular disgrace to Glos as it turned out.

When Andy came in, mid-order, with Gloucester already 'Ramanvalled' and in total bemusement, we thought, 'Hey, if anyone can "read" this mesmerizing caboodle of "wrong-uns" from Ramadhin, it might just be our Andy: after all, he takes Tom and Sam all day long in his sleep'.

All these years later, Andy admits it: that is just what he was thinking, too, as he hurried to put his pads on as the collapse got under way out there: 'Not boastful, mind. But I did happen to mention I might be okay with Ramadhin before I went in. George [Emmett] chided and bet me a fiver I wouldn't last first ball from Ramadhin. Clunk – out – blimey! I pay George his fiver, suitably chastened. A lot of money then. Second innings, and Ramadhin's waiting again. First ball comes down. "Oh, no problem," I think, "this one's going the other way, leave it alone". So I shoulder arms. Clunk. Clean ruddy bowled again, bat in the air, my off stump reeling. What a fool. I felt terrible. In the dressing room they were all still rolling around the floor holding their sides, literally, a good five minutes after I'd come in and taken off my pads'.

Andy's career 10,000 runs, spanning three decades from 1936 to 1955, were a bonus: 416 catches and 168 stumpings were the bread-and-butter earnings. He was born in Paddington – though family lore had it that forebears were farming folk from Cirencester – and after a long apprenticeship on the Lord's ground staff (where he captained Denis Compton in his first match at Lord's for the Young Professionals) he spent two years qualifying for Gloucestershire. In 1938, by fluke, one of his first matches for his adopted county was back at Lord's, against Middlesex led by the Highgate patrician and Bomber Wells' brief balcony acquaintance, R. W. V. Robins. 'Snobby Robby' seems a popular and unlikely figure in this Western tale: just as the Gloucester rugby boys at Kingsholm have always enjoyed getting one across the Harlequins or the mandarins at Twickenham, same in the cricket with any snooty 'you-know-who' at Lord's. But Andy's memoir has an added piquancy for he was the adoptive West countryman back with the bullying boss of his apprentice years. He goes on with increasing relish:

'Robins was as naughty as ever that day. Out of order. I come in to bat down the order in my old Middlesex second XI cap. It was the only cap I had. He announces, sneeringly, to all and sundry, "Don't worry, chaps, we all know what this little rabbit is capable of". I'm nervous but I stay there somehow scratching and edging my way to 20; then 30; then 40. So Robins, exasperated, puts himself on. Now, he's the England leg-spinner, isn't he? But suddenly I'm relaxed and, first ball, just outside the off stump, I put the lap on him, boomph, and really get hold of it; it goes like a rocket straight up towards Father Time for a glorious six. I didn't dare look at Robins, but at first slip dear Denis [Compton] surreptitiously gave me the most delightful great wink you could ever imagine, as if to say, "Keep going, Andy, we're all loving it".' He kept going to 130, and it was Gloucestershire who were winking with glee for the next 15 years.

There was another famous innings in that débutant's year. Against Lancashire, the great Walter Hammond was fumingly left high and dry with the tail. The tyro tot was in at No. 9. 'As I reached the pitch, all Hammond said was, "Run when I tell you". He never said another word to me in over three hours. In the first six overs he never allowed me to face one ball. It was magnificent, almost heroic'. Wilson ended with 83 (Hammond 271) and their 239 remains the county's record eighth-wicket partnership.

Andy wishes he had been a bit taller. 'When Tom [Goddard] was round the wicket and biting, I was taking everything in my left armpit; it was murder'. Once he made himself a sort of tin 'breast-plate', tied on with string and inserted between his vest and shirt. Whenever a nippy one from George Lambert 'clanged' it, Arthur Milton, from short-leg, would say, 'Come in, Barrington Dalby!'

He thinks Jack Russell, his county heir and six inches

taller, is the ideal height for a keeper. 'I can't tell you how proud I am of Jack. I used to catch them if they came to me, but Jack "makes" many of his catches. And what a lovely young man with it: you can't fault him. He sent me a beautiful card for my 80th, didn't he?' Still, England's present wicket-keeper has yet to break the county record of 10 dismissals in a match, set by Wilson in 1953 against Sussex. For a dozen years it remained a world record, and the ball is proudly displayed in the sitting room of his handsome village home. When he retired – to work in journalism and, full-time, for the National Farmers' Union – John Arlott wrote: 'You learn a lot about a man when you are out in the field with him six hours a day all summers' long, and up and down England I do not believe you will find one cricketer who does not like Andy Wilson'.

He has kept his wicket-keeping gloves in his car-boot since the day he retired. 'Just in case', he laughs. Not that he drives too many miles these days. But he never misses at least a visit when the county play at Cheltenham, where Ramadhin's genius made his apple-cheeked face even rosier red all those years ago – and where he signed off almost 40 years ago with an innings against Worcestershire. 'I was nervous. Charlie [Barnett] says, "Go out and enjoy it". So I did. Golly, old Reg [Perks, Worcester and England opening bowler] was livid. Look, here's *Wisden*, read what it says: "Milton and Wilson put on 101 in 58 minutes, with Wilson's blazing 82 containing only six singles, and 76 in boundaries".

'Dear old days', he said, 'and dear old Arthur, too: just the same as ever. This winter the village got snowed in, no power, nothing. Do you know the very first phone call we got that terrible morning? It was young Arthur [Milton] from Bristol, asking were we all right and should he come and dig us out at once. He would have, too, if I'd given him half a chance. It would have taken him a day to fight his way up the lane to the village from the main road, but if we had asked Arthur to, he would have made it, no doubt about it'.

'Young' Arthur is in his middle-60s. The day in 1988 that Arthur Milton gently pushed the single to notch his three-score years, he had to retire from the job he loved as a Bristol postman. Being Arthur, in no time he had organized his same morning round to deliver newspapers for a local newsagent – 'So I'm still up on my bike on the Downs before dawn. Lovely. Perfection sometimes'. Then, with his greyhounds of an evening, and his *Guardian* crossword – he speaks of the paper's various conundrum-setters, Janus, Araucaria, Quantum and so on as personal, if infuriating, friends – through the day? 'Well, life couldn't be better, old friend, could it?' How we loved Arthur – placid at the crease, a genuine genius in the field, always a smile, the life and soul of comradeship. He is 11 years older than I am, so I was nine when I first saw him walk out to bat with that rolling footballer's gait.

Arthur is unique in British sport, unquestionably the last of an exceptional breed. Only 12 men have played full internationals for England at both cricket and soccer – Lyttleton, Gunn, Gay, Forster, Fry, Sharp, Makepeace, Hardinge, Ducat, Arnold, Watson and Milton. Only the last two are alive: Willie Watson, now 72, lives in South Africa. (Denis Compton's soccer caps were in unofficial wartime internationals.)

Sport is business now, and as business is business we can expect never to see Milton's like again. Why, League clubs are sometimes loath to release men to play even *soccer* for England these days! No soccer season seems to end till mid-July at least. Not like Arthur's day. Arsenal, he says, were a really decent club that bent over backwards to accommodate Gloucestershire cricket. 'Anyway, there were three teams at Arsenal in those days that could each have won the Championship'.

Thirty soccer seasons ago he won his one cap for England, on the right wing against Austria at Wembley. At cricket he scored a century against New Zealand in the first of his six Tests, and toured Australia under Peter May, but broke a finger after two Tests. His first innings for Gloucestershire was in 1948, his last in 1974. In those 26 years he scored 32,000 runs at 33 a go (56 centuries) and held 759 catches to underline his being not only his generation's but one of all history's finest fieldsmen – close to the bat, athletic, predatory, smiling.

Should just a sliver of nostalgia assail his contentment, he will readily admit to being lucky to be the last of the few. He had only played a dozen games for Arsenal. 'I still don't believe it. Finney was injured and Matthews out of favour – he'd probably only made three goals in the previous match instead of his usual six! There were a lot of good wingers around who were obviously better than me, like Peter Harris, of Portsmouth – he couldn't half play! – and a guy called Elliott at West Brom'. At Wembley he didn't do very well. For Arsenal he was used to Jimmy Logie carpeting passes into his sprinter's path. 'Now I had Ivor Broadis inside me and he didn't have a good game. Billy Wright was my half-back and he was one-footed on his right, so kept slinging out passes to the left, to Baily and Medley. After half an hour I was out of the game, and was too inexperienced to get back'.

In 1954 he went home to Bristol City where his dash outside John Atyeo helped win the Third Division South Championship at the first time of asking. Next morning he threw his old dubbined boots into a cupboard forever. But he continued to blanco his other pair for 20 more Aprils. As in soccer – where an Arsenal scout had seen him playing on the Downs – word about Arthur's cricket had preceded his leaving Cotham GS with his Higher School Certificate in maths, physics and chemistry. Basil Allen was his first county captain. 'No, I never once called him "Basil". It wasn't that my father worked in a packing factory and he was a hunting squire: not one of the players called him by his Christian name; except Charlie Barnett might have, I suppose'.

In a way, I fancy he has regrets about his misspent youth.

The Bomber, doughty Jack and crafty Sam — a trio of heroes: Wells, Crapp and Cook. (*Gloucestershire CCC Archive*)

Gloucestershire CCC at Cheltenham, 1950. *Back row*: Sam Cook, George Lambert, Tom Graveney, Monty Cranfield, Ken Graveney, Arthur Milton, Martin Young; *front*: Andy Wilson, Tom Goddard, Grahame Parker, Basil Allen, Lt. Col. Henson (secretary), Sir Derrick Bailey, George Emmett. Sam and George L doubtless had a foaming pint behind their backs; coltish Tom was 'to play for England within the twelvemonth'; Arthur looks unusually solemn and Mr Allen typically severe; Andy was already aged 40 and old Tom 50; Sir Derrick seems his benignly patrician self; and George E as fierce as his dog, if not Lt. Col. Henson. (*Gloucestershire Echo*)

On the night of the amazing Grace's favours, one of her fellow skaters supervises the slithering debut of the *Hereford Times* representative at the Kemble Theatre ice panto, 1958. (Note trousers already baggily inviting). (*Hereford Times*)

'Not for myself, mind you, but for the family it wasn't right. It took things away from my three boys. I was "away" even when Gloucester were at home. I didn't really see them grow up. Only the family really matters in life, don't you think?' In his sprightly London days long ago he had married Joan, the landlady's daughter from his Arsenal digs in Muswell Hill. Their eldest son got a First in Greek and a Second in Latin at St Andrews University; the middle one read Classics at Hull; the third is in the Civil Service. They have come back home to Bristol, married and prosperous, so their dear dad is positively revelling, he says, in 'retirement'. The whole family sit down to supper many an evening – 'all together at last, it's lovely!' Afterwards they might do the *Guardian* crossword together – 'see, it pays to have kids with a classical education!' Then early to bed, with the alarm set for dead of night, and cycle clips at the ready.

'Oh, it was wonderful last winter when it snowed. I got up there to the Downs somehow with my bag of papers. Total silence, everything pure white. Not one footprint, not a tyre tread, and then there was this great, huge, quiet, full moon. Perfection. Never seen anything like it in my life'. No wonder he shakes his head and smiles a contented smile these days when the boys in the newsagents say to him: 'Art, you could have made a fortune if you was playing today!' His Arsenal contract gave him £8.10s a week, his first at cricket came to £200 for a 5-months season. 'It's just a different game now,' he tells them. Sure is. For one thing, there'll never again be a double soccer and cricket England international.

In the all-time, worldwide history of the game, only seven men took more catches than Arthur's 758: Woolley, Grace, Lock, Hammond, Close, John Langridge, and Rhodes. Arthur never minded how they came – fizzers by the bucketful off the spinners, or raspers from the fast men. Most of the raspers were edged from the bowling of George Lambert. We were awestruck by George. Faster than Tyson?

No doubt about it. A more fearsome bumper than Lindwall's? No contest. Trueman should be in the England team ahead of George? Do us a favour. Us oiks would spend hour upon hour in the garden (or in the lunch intervals during matches behind the temporary scaffolding on the hospital side of the ground) attempting to emulate George's gathering, spring-heeled run-up and sudden, menacing, uncorked crescendo at the crease. His bowling action was as well oiled as the Sylvikrined gloss of his jet black hair and signwriter-straight parting. Uncle John (and even Dad knew enough to nod) agreed that handsome George deserved at least one chance for England. Like Andy, Lambert had come west from the Lord's ground staff before the war, and though he loved (and died in) Glos, he remained a Cockney to the end. He would holler '*Star, News 'n Standard!*' whenever something crucial seemed about to happen on the field, and his pronunciation of 'lye-siz' for the tapes that tied his boots — with the earth-scorched right toecap — never failed to draw a soft Wessex chuckle from Arthur's corner of the dressing-room.

Everyone else said Lambert should have gone with Freddie Brown's MCC team to Australia in 1950. But the county knew he hadn't a hope once he had ferociously bumped Gubby Allen (even more of an autocratic old boss at Lord's than R. W. V. Robins) in the Middlesex match at Cheltenham that summer. Frantically defending the target between his eyes, the chairman of selectors squirmingly leapt a mile in the air, dropped his bat, and gloved a sitter to Andy behind the sticks. There was much Gloucestershire mirth. Us kids hooted with glee. Allen picked up his bat, stared at Lambert and slowly marched off, seething. The whole ground knew George would never have an England cap to hang in his hall.

Sam Cook, the Tetbury plumber and slow left-armer, did at least get just one game for England. Sam was George's drinking buddy. Once when George was sent in as night-watchman to get a dose of his own medicine from Frank

Tyson at Northampton (he'd gone in saying 'No problem, Frank will be easy on a union member') he survived somehow but came back pallid and quivering. Sam was waiting at the pavilion gate with a pint and double-scotch chaser: 'Get this down you, George – he'll be twice as quick in the morning'. Another time, when Cook cut his cheek trying to hold on to a thick-edge in the gully and blood began to flow, George consoled his pal, 'Don't worry, Sam, it's not blood, it's Worthington E'. Lambert had five sons and a daughter (14 grandchildren were at his funeral in Bristol in 1991). A win bonus of an extra two pounds meant a lot to a family man; after any victory George would come in, flop down with his pint, and announce, 'Thanks boys, that's one more hundredweight of coal for the winter'.

His mate Sam was always called 'Cecil' in the Glos CCC Handbook. (Arthur, too, was always referred to in that annual volume by his first baptismal name 'Clement'). The young trainee plumber from the Wiltshire borders had arrived unannounced at the County Ground for the first net practice after the war. He asked which was Mr Hammond and introduced himself boldly: 'Cook from Tetbury, sir. Slow left arm, sir'. The great W R threw him a ball and faced him for an over. Then he walked up the pitch to him and said 'You'll play for England one day!' He did, almost within the twelve months. He took nought for 127, hit out of sight by the beastly South Africans at Trent Bridge on a featherbed in 1947's first Test, was never considered again, but touchingly continued to wear his brocaded international blazer until the day he retired 18 years later. Some said he bought a new one every spring.

We listened to that only Test of Sam's on the wireless – the first 'ball-by-ball' we'd ever heard. We were sad, not only for Sam but ourselves. I have since heard a crackly recording of John Arlott's voice in that match at Nottingham, and I wrote it down (read it in a youthfully spry Hampshire accent): 'Young Cook, I can tell you, now with a perpetually worried frown . . . perhaps he's trying to bowl too fast, too overcome with conviction that more urgency is needed on this bed-of-marble pitch . . . oh dear; well, I can tell you the young man today would be unrecognizable to those Gloucester folk who know how he can spin a ball so accurately'.

Placid Sam would spin webs for his wickets all summers long. He had an original, self-taught, meticulously stilted sort of action – like he'd picked it up from a heron on a day-trip to Slimbridge and the Wildfowl Trust. In all, he took 1,782 wickets (100 in a season nine times), so very nearly took more wickets than he scored first-class runs (1,965 at an average of 5). His only shot was his 'Tetbury Chop', which we loved and hollered for another one. He came downwards on the ball, two-handed, as it passed. It usually did. The players would call it Sam's 'killing-the-rat drive'. When he arrived at the wicket and took guard, the umpire would ask what he wanted. 'Gin-and-tonic, please', said Sam. Or, if he was feeling like middling a few, 'Scotch-and-soda'.

In his winters he plumbed on at Tetbury, as he still does. For 16 years till he had to retire at 65 in 1986 he was a first-class umpire, held in much affection all round the county circuit. With a nice touch of romance, Lord's gave him two matches, one after the other, at Cheltenham – against Notts and Middlesex – to bow out in August 1986. I rang him up and said, whatever happened, I'd get there at close of play to buy him a farewell drink. His first and last words to me that evening were, 'What you having then?' – and in between warm, contented ruminations on 'a lucky life' well spent. (For old times' sake, we began with a gin-and-tonic, and ended with a scotch-and-soda).

Six years later, apropos of nothing, I was chewing the fat after an Essex match with that county's delightful old scorer, Clem Driver. He nicely defined the appeal of the county game – and Sam's name came up. Said Driver: 'Cricket's enduring beauty is not only to do with its own character, but its characters. From the players – as a friend once explained to me, "county cricketers go through the mill as kids, so all the shits have left the game by 21" – to the umpires. Now there's a body of men. All truly marvellous blokes. Men like Sam Cook and Bill Alley, all of them.

'One day, against Notts, we were fielding. During the afternoon Sam called two umpires' conferences in mid-pitch with his confrère, Roy Palmer. Not Sam's style at all. He usually just believed in giving the bat either out or not out, and counting the balls up to six. After play that evening I asked Roy what the two earnest discussions had been about. "Well", he said, "Sam calls me over all concerned and says, why doesn't Fletcher put Ackers [David Acfield] on? I tell Sam, fair enough, but get back to square-leg 'cos it's none of our business. Sam mooches off, and sure enough Ackers comes on five minutes later. Sam calls me for another mid-pitch confab. "What's up now?" Sam said, "The bugger's put him on the wrong bloody end".'

Gloucester have always seemed to produce former players who continue in the game as expert, steady and patient umpires – David Shepherd and Barry Meyer are considered by many to be the best two in the world today. But none was better, in his time, than old Jack Crapp. At the beginning of that traumatic England tour of the West Indies in 1981, we heard that Jack's heart had finally given out and he had died just at the start of the first Test match in Trinidad. I was thankful at least that before we had left for the tour I had popped in to see him in the trim little Bristol council house where he lodged in an upstairs room with a fond and cheerfully fussy landlady. It was the day before he had a heart-pacemaker fitted and he was worried about it. Jack was a Cornishman, born in St Columb, and when his father was killed in the horrific trenches in France in 1917, his beloved mother walked six-year-old Jack and his sister 'right up the Devon and Somerset coast, to Bristol where we had relatives'.

He was late to cricket. His first Championship match was

in 1936 when he was 23, against Kent at Gravesend – b Titch Freeman 0. They put him at first-slip. He had never fielded there before. At once Frank Woolley edged him a fast chance. Jack held on to it. 'Woolley didn't go. He just unconcernedly started patting down non-existent divots on the wicket. He didn't even look round. "How's that?" I murmured, sheepish and feeling a fool. "Don't worry", said our wicket-keeper, "he'll go in his own good time, he always does".' And he did. After that Jack always fielded in the slips and he, too, became one of the world's finest snappers up of knick-knacks and trifles.

In any Gloucestershire innings of my boyhood we were always still OK if Jack was still there. He usually was. We knew he wouldn't let us down, so he seldom did. Always calm and watchful, he could suddenly break out and hit the thing with a clean and awesome ferocity, then lean placidly on his sword, the handle supporting his left buttock, while the ball was retrieved from miles away. 'Good ol' Jack! Give 'em another one, Jack!' we shouted. But he seldom did it twice in succession. Just once or thrice a session. Neville Cardus called him 'the most charming of all professionals'.

Had there been nationwide television coverage for that legendary series in 1948 when Crapp was called up to stand resolute against Australia's venomous attack it might have made him as much a national hero as when, in roughly similar circumstances, David Steele was beckoned from obscurity over a quarter of a century later. Not once did Jack flinch from Lindwall and Miller. He scored a famous century against them at Bristol and, with George Emmett, was summoned to save Britannia's sinking ship at Old Trafford. That is another story, the night I cried myself to sleep after George had failed. But I should have had faith in Jack; he batted with doughty courage for the remainder of the series, and the one which followed it to South Africa.

New, or passing, urchins on the Stonehouse cricket circuit would giggle at his name. We froze them with our stares. Jack didn't mind anyway, he'd just smile his sad, slow sort-of Buster Keaton smile and, later, tell the story of when he and Alec Bedser travelled together one time in South Africa. They reached their hotel apart from the rest of the team. They walked up to the reception-desk, Jack ahead. 'Bed, sir?' asked the hotel clerk, brightly. 'No, Crapp', said Jack. 'Oh, straight down the corridor, first door on the left', said the clerk.

In the late 1950s, a colleague who is now on the *Guardian* with me, our film critic Derek Malcolm, was on the *Cheltenham Echo*. One of the daily chores the sub-editors would take in turns was organizing the dreary Letters to the Editor page. The venerable editor, Cyril Hollinshead, was cricket mad. One day, Derek submitted to him his made-up letters page. He had led it with some local burgher's boring complaint about a by-pass for the town, or whatever. That's no good, said Hollinshead, why not lead on this letter – pointing to a downpage filler remarking on Gloucestershire's debt that season to Jack, the captain. So a furious Derek had to remake his page, getting some sort of pleasurable revenge on the editor by putting up, across eight columns, the banner headline, 'We Must All Take Off Our Hats to Crapp'.

Jack never married. 'Never got round to it. Not that I wasn't a bit of a jack-the-lad in my time'. Before I left for the West Indies that last day, he said someone had 'sent him something as a present: would I like to hear it?' He went up to his bed-sitting room, came down and beckoned me outside to his little car. We sat in the two front seats, doors closed. He put the cassette into a tape machine. The announcer said, 'One of England's famous Test victories abroad was at Port Elizabeth in the last match of that glorious 1948–49 series. England were set to make 174 to win in just 90 minutes. They lost seven wickets, but just made it thanks to an outstandingly fast and safe innings by Gloucester's Jack Crapp'. And, suddenly, there was Arlott's voice again, recorded over 30 years before, far away in the Empire, and very excited '. . . now Mann comes in, bowls to

Crapp who goes down the wicket, plays hard and high again, and that's the end of the game. [Excited applause]. It's won, and Jack Crapp takes all three stumps from the far end. The two batsmen embracing one another. I never thought this could happen. England win by three wickets. It's an incredible finish. They've done this with five minutes to spare. They've made 170 runs in ninety minutes. A rate of almost 120 an hour. On a turner with Athol Rowan and Tufty Mann, believe me, bowling very well indeed'.

I was next to him, in the passenger seat. But through the driving mirror, I caught a glance of my old friend's face. His eyes had come over misty. So had mine. We sat there in silence till the spell was broken. We sat going nowhere for a long time. Well, nowhere forwards. But, backwards both, a long, long, happy way. Or, as Thomas Moult's lovely poem had it

    ... did a young boy's worship think it so,
    And is it but his heart that's aching now?

# 4

Nye Bevan came to our house. So did Clem Attlee, the first post-war Labour Prime Minister. And Barbara Castle – 'oh, she was such a lovely, lively thing, bright red hair and a young, girlish figure', still recalls Mum. They are both in their eighties now, our Babs the younger by five years.

The endearingly fair-minded, Christian but crackpot 'back-to-the-land' Distributism had obviously been kyboshed by the war. So Dad and Uncle John went 'legit' and poured all their spare energies into the Stroud Labour Party. Dad took to the stump at weekends, and verbally taking on the supercilious fat-cat shire Tories must have been a doddle after an apprenticeship of jousting with the practised and devious heckling nutters of Hyde Park's Speakers' Corner. John's old boneshaker bike helped in the doling out of pamphlets and membership forms around the valleys and hills, the factories and mills. Old Bert Cole, our Labour county councillor, was the éminence-rouge, and other names I remember sitting around hatching the people's revolution were Pat Gamble (brother-in-law of my first love, bonny Betty, the dairymaid); Les Arrowsmith, the LMS signalman, and Bessie Brown, a rotund and rubicund Cotswold cottage-loaf, and lookalike of the Merseyside MP, beefy Bessie Braddock.

They wanted Dad to stand for the seat in the 1945 general election. He funked it. Well, he thought, (a) Stroud was not winnable – when it hadn't been Tory down the years it had been very conservative Liberal; (b) had he announced his candidature, the double-barrelled berks, two brothers for whom he worked at the Simplex Milking Machine Company, would have demanded his resignation on the spot ('Commie filth would upset our customers'); and (c) he had locked horns and now was fast falling out with the Labour wing on the Gloucester County Council over Catholic education. Come the revolution, the county socialists wanted comprehensive schooling for all and an immediate ban on exclusively religious as well as public schools. Dad was compromised: he wanted Catholics to have their own schools.

Then, out of the blue, a young teacher, just demobbed from the RAF, Ben Parkin, turned up to a meeting. His father, Capt. Parkin, a retired First War fellow whose hobby was meteorology, lived up above Whiteshill (and later, when I was on the *Stroud News*, he slung up his seaweed on the line and started doing weekly weather forecasts for the paper: oh yes, I was a talent spotter from the first).

Dad fell for Ben at once. He came home that night and said to Mum, 'We've found our candidate – and he's a Thomist [as in Aquinas], and not only that, a natural Distributist!'

The constituency was, in fact, Stroud and Thornbury, so it took in a big chunk of the south of the county. Suddenly it was realized the war had provided a great wodge of possible Labour voters from the aircraft workers who had settled in Patchway, north of Bristol. The seat was not really winnable – but, then again, you never knew. What about a landslide?

Attlee and Bevan spoke to a huge crowd from the balcony of the Stroud Subscription Rooms. Dad, as local chairman, had introduced them. Afterwards, as they dispersed, we heard a chap say to his pal, 'Didn't think much of that Attlee myself – but that Farmer Keating talked a lot of sense'. Next, the little Stonehouse 'Sub Rooms' were rafter-packed. Nye turned on the spellbinding stuff – but as he was leaving the hall and through the jostling crowd outside (just like Jack Ruby leaping out for Lee Harvey that day in Dallas), the wife of Dr Murray-Brown, the snooty old village quack, took two steps forward and spat a real splatting gob of the stuff to bullseye Nye's cheek. He turned the other one, smiled slightly and proceeded to supper with Dad and Ben, while the doc's venomous old bag was cheered and jeered in turn. Great stuff at the hustings.

And the landslide, of course, duly slid. Ben went to Westminster – lost the seat five years later after three palpitating recounts, but was soon back in the smokerooms of SW1 as member for North Paddington, where I revelled in seeing a lot of him, and which constituency he served till his death in the 1970s.

\* \* \*

Dad proved that his quandaries and inner turmoils about both Catholic and private boarding education had contentedly been resolved in his breast by sending me at once for a ruddy great dose of the whole works. They packed a trunk and escorted me back to Hereford, to the black-cowled Benedictines at Belmont.

If I had not realized there had been a war on during the war – now it was over, it felt like, well, that there *was* a war on. There were about 60 boys in the Belmont senior school, and some couple of dozen of us under-12 waifs alongside them in the preparatory classes. To a boy, we were famished – as, I suppose, the rest of the country was in those first austere days of the late 1940s after the awful conflict. Not that it was a Dickens' workhouse job, for the monks were obviously just as famished as we were; they ate what we ate, there was no Beadles' common-room where they fed their faces at our expense. For breakfast, after Mass at crack of dawn, we'd have powdered milk submerging a dollop of glutinous porridge, which you had to bend and snap at quickly else it stuck like Bostic to your spoon; for lunch, a potato or two (which for some arcane reason we were not allowed to mash with our forks: very common) and gravy with a few slivers of meat greasing about; for tea, a rock-bun and a pat of margarine. We had to provide our own jam, Marmite, marmalade, whatever, and the frosty old white-haired matron, never seen in anything but her crisply starched full rigout (some of the old monks doubtless lit many a candle to her after Vespers) would write labels for each jar and stick them on with your name and number – 'KEATING, BELMONT 48', or in the case of one family of three brothers, 'LOESCHER MAJOR MINOR AND MINIMUS'.

On Sundays, before the interminable High Mass, it would be scrambled egg made with an obnoxious yellow powder from a huge tin. At home (from Dunkirk to Hiroshima, you might say) I had eaten like a trooper; when I see those colour-supplement pictures now of a plateful of wartime Britain's allowed rations for each week – you know, a finger-length of bacon, a thumbnail-square of butter, one and a half eggs, a thimbleful of sugar, and a chipolata – I realize what Mum, Dad and Uncle John must have given up for us three kids. Mind you, we were luckier than most: Dad's round of the farms brought us back more than our fair share of such as rabbit, wood-pigeon and, certainly, eggs.

For all that, looking back, I think I survived Belmont better than I might have hoped in those first two frightening, igloo-winter terms. The freeze-up of 1947 is still, I understand, in the records as the most severe and prolonged of the century. What with no food, no radiators that worked – well, no wonder I wet the bed in protest most nights. Mind you, Father Hilary had an infallible way of warming up the bed-wetters (there were quite a few of us); I suppose, in fairness, he thought it the best way of curing us as well as warming us. We had to report to him each morning if we'd 'weed the deed', shivering like so many pathetic little Cap'n Oateses in a wretched queue outside his room and, one by one, we would go in to be given at least four strokes, 'of the best', as they say, and still in wet pyjamas. And when he beat you, Father Hilary beat you – with a great blacksmith's forearm of a swish, bending back to give himself room like Gatting going for a military-medium long-hop outside the off-stump.

At least half a dozen boys tried to run away, off to home and happiness: a couple mooched back within hours, tail between their legs; a couple more were returned by cruel fathers, and promptly beaten to set an example; two others were never seen again, lucky sods.

Every Sunday evening, after Benediction, we had to sit down and write our weekly letter home. Mine never varied those first few terms: DEAR MUM AND DAD, HOPE YOU ARE WELL. I AM. PLEASE SEND MORE JAM. YOUR LOVING SON, FRANCIS. No, sorry, it did vary sometimes: DEAR MUM AND DAD, I HOPE YOU ARE WELL. I AM. PLEASE SEND SOME APPLES. YOUR LOVING SON, FRANCIS.

Of course, in those first two, horrendous and frozen-up terms there had been no opportunity even to explore the presumed horrors of rugby. Slithering cross-country runs over the huge, banked, ice-armoured snow-drifts was all the exercise possible.

Then somebody let in the sunshine. The summer did, that's who. All those hours the summer before with Robin in the back garden were now put to the real 'Test' on a real field with ten real fielders. The inspiration of Barnett and Emmett and Crapp, too. And I found I was middling everything, even from over-armers much older. Dad brought a Gunn & Moore 'Autograph Junior' at half-term. It was as whippy as Father Hilary's cane, with a sugar-plum of a sweet spot, and it remains to this day the best bat I ever had.

He also gave me the 1947 *Wisden* so I could check that I did actually recall every leg-bye that had been signalled at the previous year's Cheltenham festival matches.

And out of the now unfrozen monastery cloisters emerged a more gentle, languorous, loved and loving bunch of men who, in their different ways, actually seemed to like little boys. Father Fabian, a handsome loose-limbed smiler, took the cricket. Father Bruno took over as the senior prep school housemaster; he was a tiny, enthusing little chap, buzzing with the vitality of an Arthur Askey and always sad to ring down the final curtain on every day. Father Bruno knew things, and was just dying to impart them to us; he was not just a ventriloquist and conjuror himself, his mission was to teach us to be ventriloquists and conjurors; he wanted to share everything. If other more sombre, bored, and screwed-up monks sent us to Father Bruno for a beating, he'd just say, 'OK, message received and if he asks you tell him I gave you "four". . . . Now look here, Francis, I think we should organize a cubs' athletics match against Hereford cubs, don't you?' Or, 'Look here, old chap, why don't a few of us start a weekly house magazine – Reid and Holmes can lay it out and stuff it with those mazy Meccano drawings they keep swopping with each other during prep (they think I don't know), and you can do some drawings of your cricketers or write up reports of house matches. What d'you think, eh, old chap?'

In 1991, just before he died – in fact, I suspect he had been brought back from his long illness at a convent sanatorium just to die at Belmont – after Mass one Sunday I wandered up to the monks' dormitory cloister wondering if I could find his 'cell'. There he was, a tiny, frail figure shuffling along to the loo, holding the wall for balance, and in the same moth-eaten dressing-gown I remember he wore when he used to wake me softly at midnight to have a pee and so enable me to keep (literally) what Peter Shilton calls 'a clean sheet'. Bruno had not set eyes on me for 40 years. 'Hello, Francis', he said, the old, sickly moist eyes suddenly twinkling again, 'how are you getting on, old chap – haven't seen you for ages?' Talk about Mr Chips and 40 years on. I wanted to weep.

Then there was Brother James, a portly, insecure Friar Tuck who loved taking us on long walks and reading to us even longer reams of his homemade poetry – but wonderful, 'primitive', straightforward stuff about the change of seasons, larks on the wing and larks in the dorm. He drew and painted an intricate, illustrated, 'tableau' map of the area, say, five miles around Belmont, working at it day and night like a roly-poly Michelangelo. Did I imagine then it was about the size of a squash-court's side wall? It isn't, but it is still there at Belmont, I'm pleased to say. He was a 'primitive' alright, Bro. James, but a primitive genius in his way, and like Fr Bruno and Fr Fabian, a dear good man who stood out like an Armada beacon.

One or two of the other monks may have seemed to be bullies, but they had nothing on the older boys, of course – as at any school, and especially at Belmont in my time, when our ages ranged from eight to 18.

Many and varied were the forms of torture. You had done well if you survived a day with only an ear twisted off in the boot room, or a bottom blackened with a scrubbing brush and Cherry Blossom. Most horrendous was the collective gang bang, and that meant 'The Tower' – so awful that even the leading sadists only summoned the courage to inflict it once or twice a year. I heard the dreaded words 'Keating for The Tower tonight; pass it round', whispered through the school on three occasions. The school's church tower was more squat Saxon than tall and fluted Norman. But it was high enough to be absolutely petrifying when you were dangling over its edge, held, only by the ankles, by two other boys. The rest of the school would watch the fun from below. I'm still surprised no child ever fell to his death. I seldom have nightmares, but when I do they invariably churn up my fear of heights. (I can never look out of an aeroplane till it is in the clouds).

To be 'Towered' was by no means necessarily a mark of general unpopularity. (One senior God, the 1st XV captain, was 'Towered' after the team lost a match against the 'yobs' of Ross Grammar School, who were usually beaten 40–nil at least. No, some boys even earned a 'Towering' for quite jolly reasons – as Betjeman remembers the 'treacling' in the common-room wastepaper basket at Marlborough, a terrible lynching: 'We didn't mind the cause; perhaps he sported coloured socks too soon, perhaps he smeared his hair with scented oil'. Whatever; suddenly the word went round and in no time sentence had been passed by that collective judge and jury that only schoolboys know.

Twice I was 'Towered' for 'family connections'. Every other short-trousered prig in the place was, of course, a Conservative, so when I boasted about my father's political affiliations, I did so with my heart in my mouth. I cannot remember exactly why, but I was possibly sent to The Tower when the Labour Party nationalized steel and when they 'sold out' the Indian Empire to the 'wogs'.

The third time was altogether different. In the midsummer of 1948, the triumphant march of Bradman's Australian cricketers had the English selectors in all sorts of panic. For the third Test match at Old Trafford, out of the blue, they picked two Gloucestershire players. I would have got away with it had the only selection been Jack Crapp, our doughty left-hander who had scored a century against the tourists in the county fixture at Bristol. But the sprog, George Emmett, was another matter altogether, for he was chosen to replace Len Hutton, revered both in the school and the land as a national institution. So my one-man Gloucester gloat at Emmett's selection had its comeuppance at once. In a seething fury the word went round. 'Keating for The Tower tonight'. Hey, I was hung as a martyr for wee Georgie Emmett! (When he failed in both innings – it was to be his only Test match – there were threats that I should be 'done' again).

\*     \*     \*

As I dangled up there, petrified, little did I know that my sacrifice for Gloucestershire cricket was, in fact, heralding a glorious chapter for my adopted county – and for the game of cricket itself. For if George Emmett had not been picked for that one solitary Test match, it is quite possible that the world would never have seen Tom Graveney bat. After Bristol Grammar School and National Service in the Army, young Graveney had seemed to have fluffed his apprenticeship as a Gloucestershire cricketer. At the time of that Manchester Test match, which began on July 8, 1948, his 'career' seemed to have ended before it began. On his first-class début he had made a duck, and followed that with just over 200 runs in 20-odd innings. He was seriously thinking of re-signing for the Army, which he had enjoyed, and taking a PT instructor's course. He had been demoted to the Gloucester Second XI, and looked an unlikely bet for re-engagement.

Then, out of the blue, Crapp and Emmett were selected for England. Graveney was hastily despatched to Bournemouth for the First XI fixture against Hampshire. He made a precocious and calm 47 against the spinners, Knott and Bailey, on a spiteful wicket. In the following match against Somerset at Bristol he scored an undefeated 81. By the time I got home for the holidays, my Stonehouse chums, Peter Beard and Robin Bassett, were filling me in with details of his maiden century, against the Combined Services at Gloucester Wagon Works. It had, they said, been amazingly wizard-prang.

We hurried to Cheltenham in August. The first time I saw him, Tom made a silky half-century – all coltish, gangly, upright youthfulness, with a high, twirly, backlift and a stirring, bold, flourishing signature in the follow-through – and he came back blushing at the applause, and signed my book before he went in to lunch: T. W. Graveney, neat, joined-up, surprisingly adult. In the following spring, the last sentence of *Wisden*'s Gloucestershire notes said: 'A pleasant feature of the season was the form of a newcomer, T. W. Graveney, a product of Bristol club cricket, who showed graceful right-handed stroke play'.

Tom became more thrillingly the real thing every time I saw him bat. Funny, as dear old T. W. Goddard at last realized that a man in his fifties should think of giving up childish games for a living, another T. W. G. had shyly grabbed the reins to lead our grand parade. When the West Indies came that famous day to rout us at Cheltenham, only Graveney made double figures, poring over Ramadhin's intricacies for over an hour, and a man next to me said, 'Our Tom'll be servin' England this side o'twelvemonth'. And he was. When Denis Compton was injured, Freddie Brown blooded him against the South Africans at Old Trafford in 1951, and on a real sticky he made 15 against Athol Rowan ('every run full of cultured promise', said John Arlott on the wireless).

Tom served England for the next 10 years. When George was still King he was taking 175 from the Indians at Bombay; when Lindwall and Miller were still lethal in 1953 he matched Hutton stroke for stroke in a partnership of 168 at Lord's; and a couple of years later he collected a century at Sydney with three successive boundaries. Onwards to 1957, and his massively flamboyant 258 at Trent Bridge blew away forever the wispy mystique of Ramadhin and Valentine, after May and Cowdrey had done the tedious, pad-prod spadework earlier in the month at Edgbaston.

Yet while these, and even the shortest innings, were a delight, word was going about that he lacked the cruel competitive edge to take a game and an attack by the throat; he was getting out when the very critical need was just to stay in. He was, horror! playing festival cricket instead of Test match cricket. Never the twain must meet, and he was dropped for, as someone said, 'being happy only to present his ability, but not to enforce it ruthlessly'.

He had moved from Gloucestershire now. But so had we.

And wherever I was in the world, I daresay I wasn't the only Gloucester man to sneak a look first at the Worcester scores to see how Tom had done. For it was soon apparent that there, under the old Norman shadow that matched the mellow architecture of his strokes, his batsmanship had actually become even better. It was still joyous and free of care, but now it was more stable, more serene, more certain. The England selectors, of course, seemed oblivious to the fact, and though century followed century and Championship followed Championship, not even the wildest betting man would have wagered on a recall by England. But at last they had to. After his four years in the pleasant backwaters alongside the Severn came an almost tangible rumbling of public demand for Graveney's Test match place to be restored, following another woeful England start to the West Indian series of 1966. They turned to Tom, now in his 40th year.

At Lord's too! The full-house standing ovation startled him as he made his way through the Long Room once again. Hall and Griffith and Sobers and Gibbs. . . . He returned to grandstand applause after a magnificent 96. 'It's like a dream come true', he said as he passed me in the pavilion before making his way back up the stairs, eyes moist with tears. In the next match, at Trent Bridge, England were 13 for 3, Hall's Larry Holmes and Griffith's Joe Frazier both murderously, cruelly, hostile. Graveney and Cowdrey alone had the technique and fearlessness to stand unflinchingly firm. Tom finished with 109, and many still shake their heads in wonder and insist it must have been his very best innings. It wasn't. There were more gems in the old man's kitbag.

I was working for television in 1966 and was briefly (violins, please) engaged to be married – to my secretary, a freckled fizzpot of personality, a convent-reared redhead with a delectable figure-of-8 contour and a technicolour temper quick on the draw. She did not – and does not – suffer fools gladly, so I reckon I did exceeding well to have

warmly nestled my hand inside her bra for six months or so
of that celebrated sporting summer, before she danced off
on a myriad of other adventures which ended with her being
a wealthy and spiky columnist, a disc-jockey, and a high-
octane flasher of eyelashes each week on BBC TV.

Darling Annie. We had been working that summer on the
soccer World Cup and recuperated with a holiday in Malta,
borrowing a friend's beach-hut, swimming off rocks, eating
fish in the evenings, and having a flaming row at least once a
day. What else is there to do in Malta? Well, listen to the
BBC World Service, that's what. Halfway through the hol,
on Friday, August 19, in fact (*Wisden* is so useful for
logging precisely all the finer details of life, isn't it?), the
transistor by the rock-pool was lullingly telling pastoral
tales from home, and Annie and I were affably snorkeling
about in the water with nothing on, when John Arlott (for it
was he, pronouncing poems from The Oval) announced that
John Murray, Middlesex's wicket-keeper-batsman of considerable poise and nous, had joined Tom Graveney at the
wicket towards close of play. England were in desperate
trouble against Hall, Griffith, Gibbs and Sobers – 166 for
seven – but an optimistically reassuring Arlott sensed he
could see the siege being raised if Murray could just stay
with Tom for the morrow. He did, and so the eighth wicket
stand would be continued the following morning, Saturday
– always a lovely day at The Oval. All of a sudden, in white-
hot Malta, I felt overwhelming pangs for England's softer
evening sun, reflecting, as it would now be doing, a rich and
rose-pink wash on the gasometers' gentle west-facing curves.

'Sod this for a lark, woman!' or words to that effect, I
announced. 'If I do nothing else in my little life, I'm going to
be at The Oval tomorrow to see Tom face the opening over
and then take it from there'.

Give her her due, Annie came, too (Naunton Wayne to
my Basil Radford). We were at Heathrow by 9 am. 'The
Oval, and step on it, cabbie!' There was already a queue
snaking round the Harleyford Road. We were almost the

last in. We sat, holding hands, at deep backward third-man when the bowling was at the Pavilion end. Graveney and Murray went on till mid-afternoon. Murray finished with 112, Tom with 165. They put on 217 for England's eighth wicket. No two have done better before – or since. For obvious reasons it remains my favourite Graveney knock of all.

The following summer, against India at Lord's, Tom beguilingly unrolled another masterpiece – 'superb', said *Wisden*, 'the day belonged entirely to Graveney and his elegance'. His 118 against the West Indies at Port-of-Spain, in the New Year of 1968 was the definitive and comprehensive retrospective.

'Any art gallery in the world would have bought that innings', wrote Henry Blofeld, who was there. Tom overflowed with fluent strokes and quite outplayed the 1968 Australians, as he did the Pakistanis in the winter, when Karachi saw his last Test match century. When the West Indies rejoined battle next summer he scored 75 in the first Test then, on the free Sunday of the match, played in his own benefit game at Luton. It was against the rules and Lord's banned him for three Tests – in effect forever. But Our Tom of Gloucester had become Worcester's Tom, then England's, then the world's. After that final Test a panegyric was written by that most caring of men, J. M. Kilburn, who was for 40 diligent and creative years the correspondent of the *Yorkshire Post*: 'Graveney may have disappointed some cricketers by playing in Graveney's way, but he has adorned cricket. In an age preoccupied with accountancy he has given the game warmth and colour and inspiration beyond the tally of the score-book. He has been of the orchard rather than the forest, blossom susceptible to frost but breathing in the sunshine. . . . Taking enjoyment as it came, he has given enjoyment that will warm the winters of memory'.

Yet it might never have happened had George Emmett not been picked for his solitary Test match in the midsummer of

1948. The very same day that Tom was despatched to
Bournemouth and I was dangled, head first, from the top of
a church tower in Hereford. Whenever I see Tom now, I still
have momentary feelings of vertigo, not entirely caused by
hero worship.

\*     \*     \*

In the first couple of summer prize-days at Belmont, my
mother remembers me collecting the swag as an academic
clever-clogs. Then, as sport took over, any book became,
well, a closed book, and I unconcernedly sank like a stone
to the bottom of every class. But I was rattling up the 50s
with my Gunn & Moore – my best was 75 out of 93 all out
in a house match – and was such a swanky little prodigy
that at 12 I was even picked for the senior school's 1st XI
against Monmouth School. I was bowled first ball and took
my pads off, apparently muttering, 'I must really work on
my big-match temperament'.

Dad wanted work of a different sort. It was time for a
change. He plugged into his old boys' Chesterbelloc.
network. I suppose you'd call Dad progressive. He gave me
a final choice after he'd conned three schools into agreeing
to sort out this dunce: the fearsome Christian Brothers in
Prior Park who, by all accounts, thrashed the curriculum
into you; the philosophical Jesuits at Beaumont; or Douai,
where, Dad said, his friend the headmaster Fr Ignatius had
actually played cricket for Warwickshire. That was the
clincher – though I might have thought differently had I had
the 1920 *Wisden* to hand then: *Warwickshire 1920*. Also
batted, Rev. W. I. Rice – Inns. 4, No 0, Runs 15, Av 3.75.

Not very distinguished, but it was nevertheless the sole
reason I chose the Benedictines at Douai, a soft-breezed and
friendly place of rosy Berkshire brick perched high on a
pastoral ledge in the hills between Reading and Newbury.
Alas for Dad, I immediately found my own level, in the
unacademic, lazy-flowing 'C' stream, and never swam out of
it. To be sure, the major triumph of my five-year span was

my nurdling through three O-Levels when the clever money was on a resounding nil in that department.

Fr Ignatius was soon to retire and in fact spoke directly to me only twice. 'Do not, my dear boy', he said with a pained cast in his soft-boiled eyes, 'copy the others and go round calling the maids "skivvies" '. (That's nothing: the Matron, an unsympathetic, no-nonsense, long-serving Nightingale of indeterminate years was addressed by both priests and boys alike – and to her face – as 'The Bitch', as in, 'Keating, you've come out in spots, report to the Bitch at once'). One afternoon under the summer's sun, Father Ignatius said, 'Like cricket, so with life: play yourself in a bit, to be sure, but then start getting onto the front foot at every opportunity. You'll have more fun that way'.

I began to enjoy rugby and changed from a non-tackling full-back to a ditto scrum-half in the creative, Onlwyn Brace mode. Amazingly, I played two seasons in the 1st XV, slinging out reverse passes all over the shop, but funking even more tackles. I was one of a clique which gathered around Father Dunstan's wireless at 5 o'clock on winter Saturdays to listen to the soccer results on Eamonn Andrews's 'Sports Report'.... De-dum, de-dum, de-dum, de-da, de-diddly-dum, de-*dah*. Father Dunstan was taking a chance. At Douai, generally, soccer was taboo.

Dad and Uncle John had taken me once to watch Aston Villa play at Villa Park in the early 1950s. Uncle Vincent in London took me to Fulham against Liverpool at Craven Cottage. At home during the Christmas holidays I badgered them, on one of our twice-yearly visits for tea and Swiss-rolls-in-silver-paper with Auntie Mabel at Clifton, to take me to Bristol City. The first Cup tie I saw was a third round replay when Swindon Town beat the comparatively formidable Cardiff City. Norman Uprichard, Swindon's Irish goalie, played an absolute blinder in a green jersey. The place was packed, and Dad and I, for some reason, were allowed to sit on the touchline alongside the wheelchairs. The massed ecstasy when Swindon scored the winner in extra time was something I had never been exposed to before.

So why didn't I support Swindon Town thereafter and for evermore? Or one of the 'local' Bristol teams, more like? Or even Aston Villa, which was the first side I saw in the flesh. Or Hereford United? (I had been born in Edgar Street, after all). A thesis is crying out to be written why those of us not born to any bias or given any lead by family or geographical affiliation should harbour an unswaying devotion for one football team and not another. I suppose I support Fulham with some modicum of reason: they were playing, remember, that first time I went to Villa Park. Stan Lynn, of Villa, missed a penalty, which prospective heroes shouldn't, and I was much taken with the magisterial hooked nose and confidence of Joe Bacuzzi, of Fulham, who Dad said had been born, like him, in Pimlico. It couldn't have been long afterwards, on a week's holiday in London, that Uncle Vincent took me to see his team play Liverpool at Craven Cottage and I was stretchered down over the flat caps of cheery Cockneys to the very front row, right on the corner flag. I remember vividly blushing in turmoil when Billy Liddell (winger for Liddellpool, of course!) winked at me as he turned round after placing the ball for a corner. And with all the other boys I touched the hem of his shorts as he ran up to take it. In the second half I saw Arthur Rowley biff and barge and snort about the Liverpool penalty area and quite fell for him – and Fulham. Then, much later, when I first came to work in London, I lived in Earls Court and everyone else was supporting trendy Chelsea – but I went back to Fulham for old times' sake. And there was Rodney Marsh.

At Douai there was a housemaster called Father Norbert, doubtless a pious priest. But he had a manic fixation about the evils of association football. (We were allowed a jokey Ireland v England soccer match on St Patrick's Day, but otherwise associating with association was a capital offence.) One Easter term I brought from home my Christmas present

– a real leather soccer ball, one of those romantic old hand-stitched panel jobs with an inner tube and a leather lace that could cut your forehead if you fancied a bit of the Tommy Lawton or Nat Lofthouse. We were blowing it up in the locker-room on our first night back when 'Nobby' Norbert came in and went berserk. 'It's only for water polo, honest, Father!' I pleaded. He essayed a stamping, rotating Dervish jig in his long black habit, ran to his cell and was back inside a minute attacking my lovely Christmas present with a geometry compass as if – bang! – he was casting out the devil and all his works and pomps. Stab! Stab! Stab! He made sure the poor deflated carcass would be used no more, then took me upstairs for the bendover business. I got six of the best, too – and in wet shorts – when he caught a handful of us conspirators committing high treason in the drizzly dusk after rugby on one of the pitches far away from the monastery: Ginger Morgan in goal; his brother Bernie, a wizard of the dribble; Jimmy Murphy and Aubrey Bal-hatchet our canny inside forwards, John Moriarty bullock-ing about in the No 9, me and a lovely Cornish boy called Whetter vying as midfield supremos ... when suddenly through the murk this devout monk was upon us, cursing in Latin, swishing his cane in all directions and causing one hell of a sting around our centre circles. No red cards in those days. Forgive them, Father, for they know not what they do.

I've just emerged, grimy as a coalface worker, from the loft, having scrambled around on all-fours looking for the bag with old Douai mags inside. Here they are – 1st XV Rugby, 1955: 'With a stream of long accurate passes from F. Keating at scrum-half, the fly-half position should easily have been filled all term. But nobody came forward confident enough to take advantage of this Tanner-like service'. 1st XI Cricket, 1954: 'Keating, though unorthodox, displayed a commendable spirit of aggression at the wicket'. And 1955: 'Keating had a light-hearted approach, made a reasonable quota of runs, proved an excellent cover-point

... and, later in the summer, his bowling developed a considerable nip off the pitch'. Ah me, haven't read that for 35 years. My first ever mention in print! Makes me blush all over again. Those school magazine notes were written by our coach, and Old Dowegian, Charlie Cuddon, who came back to the school for two or three summers and invested us all with our first glimpse of the real world out there. He was a scholar and gent, a writer who actually had articles printed in the *Manchester Guardian*. He treated us sprogs like men, expected us to stand our round in The Rowbarge, down the hill, and to hit back fast half-volleys with double vengeance, aiming if poss to crack mid-on between the eyes. He himself bowled like a demented Dennis Lillee, all venom and aggro and flying jet-black hair.

'Shippy' was groundsman and umpire; by my day he had become too arthritic to coach. He swore by Nottingham marl on the sanctum. In I'd come, at No 7 or 8, a hundred-odd still needed by Douai with only a couple of wickets left. First ball, you might desperately dap a one-bouncer into the tennis courts then, at the end of the over, Shippy would saunter gingerly in on his wonky pins, white coat flapping, to the bowler's end – and look at you sadly with those old pro's spaniel eyes, and whisper despairingly, 'What's roosh, lad? Joost stay out 'ere, an' roons'll coom, you see, roons'll coom!' Not for me, they didn't. I was invariably out before the 6 o'clock angelus rang down from the school chapel tower. I always let old Shippy down terribly, I'm afraid. Sometimes, when rain stopped play or whatever, he would roll up a fag and sit in the pav near Miss Crook's tea-room door, sipping indescribably delicious powdered lemonade and munching a ditto sandwich-spread sarnie, and tell me how he used to play with the young Harold Larwood at Trent Bridge. 'Ooh, 'e were fa-ast, even as a lad; 'e 'ad this three-speed boomper, y'know, an' Australians joost couldn't 'andle him, y'know. . .'. And off he'd go into his sublime reverie; sometimes a tear or two would help the tale as it trickled down the nut-brown, sun-battered old face. I've just looked up Shippy in *Wisden*. Shipston, F. W. joined Notts in 1925, the same year as Larwood, and played 72 games in all, averaging just 18.48. They never gave him a bowl once.

Most of the monks were amiable, gentle souls. One or two were undoubted sadists and took obvious pleasure in administering beatings. A new headmaster, an affable chuckler called Father Alphonsus, had some success in rooting out most of those monks who could not teach for toffee – which was quite a few of them. Three lay masters, bearded Oliver Welch, studious Joe Greer, and batty William Bell – 'Ollie Hardy', 'Cheesey', and 'Ding-Dong' – were signed to improve the academics, which they did, spectacularly apparently. But they had no luck with me at all.

Our distrust of each other was mutually wary. Then Father Dunstan, a tiny, round, plum-duff of a dumpy priest, his habit flecked permanently white with cigarette ash and uncontrollable dandruff, was made my housemaster. Things at once looked up. When he died, some dozen years after I left the school, I was working in France on a film, but was delighted – honoured, rather – that Father Alphonsus contacted me, through ITV, and asked me to write his obituary for the school magazine. I dashed this off by return of post:

'DUNSTAN CAMMACK: a memoir

'Fr Dunstan never liked to follow the syllabus too closely. While it was John Moriarty who may have taught me to blow smoke-rings (on the bus back from cricket at St George's, Weybridge) it was Fr Dunstan who had taught me to smoke in the first place. Dunstan Cammack, in truth, taught me just about everything. There was English Lit, and Divinity, of course, but they were just the official starters: for free he taught me to give up gambling (having earlier encouraged me to get hooked on the Sport of Kings); he taught me, unknowingly but so naturally, about the Brotherhood of Man, erroneously that Gilbert and Sullivan represented the ultimate in British drama, rightly that

Graveney represented the ultimate in British batsmanship. He taught me that two 'O'-levels were better than none and, anyway, were two more than I deserved. As a teacher Dunstan Cammack was the personification of the Benedictine education: anyone, he argued, born with even a fractional streak of the dramatic must necessarily be encouraged to have an interest in prize-fighting as much as academic prize-winning.

'I first saw Dunstan, I suppose, in 1951 when he used to hold those furtive little lunchtime conversations in the Court of Arches with that marvellously nice Baddie of the Fourth, Oily Andrews, as they checked their ante-post hunches against *The Sporting Life* know-alls. Otherwise, in that bewildering first year of the Junior Dorm, one never really came across Dunstan except, I remember, one Saturday morning when we craned to see the limousine, rumoured to be Vincent O'Brien's, as it purred round the Sixth Form lawn with Dunstan in the back, off for lunch at The Feathers and a day at the Newbury races.

'When his predecessor, Father Norbert – a nice guy but with a phobia about soccer and its sinful sullying of the Twickers' traditions of our famous second Division public school – caned a few of us for daring to play soccer (even with a rugby ball), Dunstan sought us out to sympathize. "Don't worry", he said, "it is a great game. And that man can sometimes be a bit of a bully". One of Them was actually on Our side! Two terms later, hooray, Dunstan became the Faringdon [the school's three houses were named after martyred bishops, wouldn't you know] housemaster and it was all plain sailing from then on.

' "Smokes" were instituted in his room. An hour a night. And while (we imagined) the Sampson and Walmesleyites, straight backed and prissy, were discussing the sayings of Baden-Powell or whatever, we Segals and Moriartys and Prices and O'Farrells would be lollingly passing round our packets of Woods, our hero chainsmoking his Sweet Afton in his armchair, telling us hilarious tales of his beloved theatre and his favourite Sport of Kings. He encouraged "Nanny" Norman to play the cello, and John Barnsley and a few more of us to start a jazz club.

'Dunstan instituted, and worked the projector for, the weekly film nights in the gym. We'd choose the films with him. I had a craze for a Hollywood bio of the captain of the hornblowers, Bix Beiderbecke. It was called *Young Man of Music* with a cleft-jawed Kirk Douglas miming the famous jazzman. Dunstan indulged me and put the film on at least once a term – for about five times, till I let slip my real reason was the crush I had on Miss Doris Day, who gets her Kirk in the end. Dunstan was furious. How could you possibly fall for Doris Day, he said, when the same film includes Lauren Bacall?

'Over a decade later and roles reversed at London suppers, for which he always called on his way to take various convents of nuns in retreat – his holiday hobby – he would want to know one's weedy opinion ("what is the thinking", he would say) on the Vatican Council, on Finnegan's world title chances, on violence in TV drama, on Brigadier Gerard's stamina, on the Rhodesia sell-out, on The Pill, on John Osborne's relevance, on the modern Mass, on Close's captaincy, on permissiveness, on the virtues of Barry Richards' off-drive, Neville's OZ or Gielgud's diction. Not for himself, he would say, but for the nuns in retreat. They demanded to know everything. And he was going to tell them. Everything. Just like, dear Dunstan, you'd tell us schoolboys all those years ago.

'And having been given his beaming, welcoming entrée by St Peter on that happy-sad day when he died, one of his first requests was surely for a visit to the celestial gallops: must see what sort of shape St Paddy's in. That is, one of Lester's Derby winners.'

FRANK KEATING (1950–56)

\* \* \*

There were about 230 boys at our placid, pubescent prison in the Berkshire hills. About 50 of us were raving sports fanatics who never voluntarily opened a book from one year to the next. Another 150-odd had been brainwashed into thinking 'O'-levels vaguely important, and they included twerpy little swots who actually bagged desks at the front of class and some who, when the post was doled out in the refectory at breakfast, blubbed on receipt of the daily letter from their maters.

The final 30 lived for just one night in the whole year: the annual Christmas dance. These 30 never got their knees dirty at rugger nor perspired one bead in the groves of academe. They were the Smoothies, sons of South American diplomats and suchlike, who brazenly smoked Black Russian or Passing Cloud in front of the pav, not behind it, and could afford a weekly subscription to *Picturegoer*. The Smoothies came back from the holidays with wondrous tales of successful fornications with girls who actually liked it and begged for more – and in term-time, to prove it, they got letters from them, steamy stuff sometimes, and they would read to us choice sentences and we would think, blooming heck, if only that could happen to us one day.

The week before the Christmas term ended the Smoothies had the one day of the year in which they became Gods and us flannelled fools cringingly kept our heads below the parapet. (The only girls I'd ever met, anyway, were friends of my sisters; and of course, for friends, my sisters chose only a rigidly decent type of gel who all had ambitions – as indeed did my darling elder sister Clare – to become 'cook-nuns', serving God and the Convent community in equal measure).

So the week before we broke up for Christmas 30 real live unadulterated virgins were bussed in from a posh convent school near Reading. The gym was decorated by simpering new boys under orders from the 30 Smoothies. There was lots of mistletoe.

A live band was hired from Newbury. The MC was my teacher of Latin and Greek, Oliver Welch, the bearded scholarship whizz who utterly loathed me for the single-minded sports slob that I was. Not one miserable, quaking, cringing Mon.-Wed.-Fri. morning lesson passed without him skulling me in class with venom and a wooden-backed blackboard duster.

At the end of Christmas terms, alternately home and away, we would play a rugby match with Ampleforth, in Yorkshire. Ampleforth and Downside were (are) the two jewels in the crown of Benedictine education. They always licked us hollow up there (well, we always got off the train drunk on brown ale, didn't we), but it was always a closer match at Douai − although they still won − because they had been supping in the buffet-car. Anyway, in my last rugby term we were determined to give Ampleforth a real game. That is why, I think, diabolically sly Ollie Welch picked me for The Dance. My rugger-bugger mates were astounded. Quickstep-wise, I had nudged the selectors. I can still recall the paralysing fear that numbed the back of my grubby neck like a karate-chop when I read on the notice-board − 'The following 30 have been chosen to represent the school at the annual dance in the gymnasium. . . .' After the names of 28 Smoothies, most with hyphens and an army of initials, came a pal of mine, Paul 'Polly' Breen, who stuttered particularly badly but played a mean game at wing-forward and was going to be crucial in the Ampleforth match. And then, last on the list, was me, just above the order. 'Black Ties Will Be Worn'. Welch, we decided, had chosen me because I was thick and Polly because he stuttered.

Dancing Day dawned and as I woke in my freezing cubicle, it was utter panic that made me shiver the more. Dear stuttering Polly found us a b-b-bow tie apiece in Father Dunstan's d-d-drama-club hamper of tat, and we took an age to tie them round our cricket shirt collars. An hour before the 'off' had the two of us embracing in the cavernous, white-tiled school loo, taking it in turns to be 'the girl', and with a gaudy, yellow-covered book between us. It was called *Teach Yourself Ballroom Dancing* by

Victor Sylvester, and consisted of a text of utterly incomprehensible gibberish illustrated with a meaningless series of black footprints and demented dots and arrows. For all we twigged, Victor's footsteps looked like Captain Scott's on his last, staggering stroll in the Antarctic.

Across the Sixth Form lawn came the strains of Newbury's maestros tuning up. Overture and rank beginners, please! We both, I said to Polly as we walked, scared stiff, across to the decked-out gym, had big-match temperament. This was the biggest one of all – Us v Girls. Not to mention that even more devilish opponent, Ollie Welch.

Welch inspected his line-up like a visiting general at Sandhurst: 28 of his hand-picked young Smoothies gleamed with Brylcreem and Cherry Blossom. He looked at Polly and me, grunting with distaste, as though a captive elephant had farted, and pointing his beard at us like it was a firing-squad revolver and he was Jimmy Hill on TV and England had just missed an open goal. The convent school bus decanted the goodies, plus two chaperoning nuns. Our head Smoothie – was it D. W. B. Buxton-Hopkin that year? Certainly something double-barrelled – shook hands with their head girl, Delia Fortescue. Now here was a mountain of an early-developed lass, with shot-putter's shoulders, a potatoey face and a long dress of pink taffeta. She was high and wide, and handsomely heavy. Also, just slightly, hairy lipped. Miss Delia Fortescue was already famed in local education circles. Her reputation preceded her even more dramatically than the storm-tossed ship's prow thrust of her gigantic bust. She already had more A-levels than anyone had ever heard of in the county. She had won the Berks schools debating cup single-handed, and had captained the Southern Schools at lacrosse. She was a very, very, big girl in every sense. She spoke Greek and Latin, was sailing into Oxford, and Ollie Welch thought she was the absolute 'it'.

Sherry or cider was served and the band struck up. Dumpy debs in party frocks were twirled and swirled by Douai Smoothies; or gawky gels stood around, gigglingly

onny, beloved Beryl on the pole at Leominster fête, 1959.

Maria on the castanets, South Africa, 1962.

Ken Tynan' of the *Surrey Times* – pstaged by famous jacket and nuse sodden' cigarette smoke. (*Surrey Times*)

Two cubs in Kenya; the more literary of the lions en route for his tryst with Maria.

Another hard day at the office for ITV's OB stalwarts – the effervescent worrypot, Grahame Turner, is on the left; the two girls (centre) are Suzanne and Maggie, both long in leg and wisdom; with Steve Minchin sippin' the soda, Jim Pople perfecting his David Lean stuff and FK looking for once as if the night had yet to begin.

Golf with Barry John, prince of fly-halves. (*Jeff Goddard*)

Commiserating with 'Sir Geoffrey' – c Murray b Garner 40 Jamaica Test 1981.

chatting, and preening their buttons and beaux. All to the manor – and the manner – born. Except me.

I had two large slugs of Cyprus communion sherry and looked round for Polly Breen. The swine! One of the girls had got off the bus with a hockey-playing leg in plaster. Polly had made a b-b-brilliant b-b-beeline. He sat stammering at her throughout the evening. He didn't have to dance. He matily winked a V-sign signed to me. I was on my own.

Although I say it myself, I was masterly for half an hour, pretending to be quite at home, edging in and out of knots of Girl-Smoothie chatter as if I was part of each group. I beamed and I mingled and I nodded and I smiled. Suddenly, the clamp of steely fingers, wickedly strong from a lifetime of writing with black-board chalk, grabbed my bicep. It was Welch. He thrust his beard in my ear. 'I've been watching you, Keating. Isn't it time you danced, laddie?'

'Just eyeing up the crumpet first, sir'.

'That one guttersnipe sentence has cost you six-of-the-best tomorrow morning', he promised with relish, 'but meanwhile I suggest you ask the head girl, Miss Delia Fortescue over there, to take the floor. Nobody has obliged her since I did the honours at the opening waltz'. The iron grip launched me across the gymnasium floor. The famous Miss Fortescue was sitting, lumpenly huge, next to the two chaperoning nuns. A dance finished. I held my hand towards her and muttered some sort of invitation. What would it be? A waltz or a quickstep? I hadn't even read the tango stuff in that flaming book of Victor's. Pray it's not the mambo. The Newbury band-leader burred, 'Laydeez n'gennlemen, take y' partners please for – a Jive!'

Merciful God in heaven, I was saved! I'd seen the 'jive' on television in the common room. A cinch! Just jiggle about, holding hands and occasionally twirling your arms over your head or hers. Any twit could do it.

I have to say, Delia not only seemed delighted to be asked to dance. She was delighted with it. Daunting her reputation may have been, but I hoped the sneering Welch was watching with what sudden devotion she pulled me to the floor. It was only for this new-fangled jitterbug jive, no problem, so Welch's ploy had been stifled at birth. Delia and I jigged about, holding hands, arms pumping rhythmically backwards and forwards like oarsmen in a small pond. No more to it than that. A doddle! After a minute or so, unsaid, we came to the instinctive mutual decision to copy the practised Smoothies around us and have a go at the twiddly bit over the head. That's Jive, Man. Her great fist was clenched tight in mine. Over went our two arms in unison. First time, it is obviously more difficult than it seems. Simultaneously, the two clenched fists of ours tumultuously hit Miss Fortescue's left temple like it was a right cross from Ali in his prime. She took off backwards. Up first, then backwards if I am honest. The back of her head hit the parquet floor like Dave Boy Green's when Sugar rayed him. Dave was out cold for five full minutes. So was Delia.

The band ground to a reedy, shocked silence. Everyone rushed to the stricken hulk in taffeta. A beached whale in a party frock. I was petrified. Welch, luckily, didn't have a black-board duster handy, else he would have killed me with it. 'To your room at once!' he snarled, pointing his chin at me like a revolver.

For hours I sat in my freezing cubicle. They would surely expel me. What would I tell Dad? And worse, I would miss the end-of-term match against Ampleforth. Welch burst in, still enraged, his beard dripping with foaming spittle. Miss Fortescue had been carried to the sanatorium. Matron was still with her. We would never have a dancing fixture again. I had ruined it for generations to come. Did I want my 'six' now, in my pyjamas, or at least a dozen from the headmaster himself tomorrow. 'But before we do anything else, laddie, write an abject letter of apology to Miss Fortescue, and I'll deliver it before she is carried to the bus tonight'.

I wrote the abject note at his dictation. 'Dear Miss Fortescue, I apologise most sincerely for my gauche performance which resulted in your inability to give the vote of thanks, as Head Girl, to Mr Welch and all at Douai who had made the Dance this year the best we have ever had. . . .' Then the brutal bendover business. Eight vicious strokes. Next morning I was 'gated' – confined to barracks – for the whole of the following term.

Even best rugger friends agreed I was an absolute disgrace. I was shunned. Until, three days later, the very last day of term and the morning of the Ampleforth match, the breakfast post was doled out. On the envelope was written SWALK (sealed with a loving kiss). The letter said: 'Dear Francis, Thank you for your letter of apology. It is warm and snug in my brassiere. I saw you the moment I stepped off the bus. When you strode across so manfully, so swaggeringly, to ask me to dance, I was so happy I could have burst. I will think of you all through the holidays. It was my fault totally. You see, I have never done the Jive before . . . PS. On the first Wednesday of next term (January 20) I will wait for you all afternoon at the Palomino Coffee Bar. Bridge Street, Reading'.

I never turned up: I was 'gated'. For months I bathed in glory. My love letter was, at various times, read in awe by the whole school. And, for some reason, the feared Greek and Latin guy, Ollie Welch, never ever again, in my last two terms, skulled me with his blackboard duster. Delia's letter had done for him.

# 5

Dad had big plans when I left school with my three 'O'-levels. First, I had to get out of the still compulsory National Service. He solved that one with ease. 'Mum tells me you're still prone to the odd Jimmy Riddle after a night out at the Woolpack. When you go for your medical, tell the Army things aren't too good dry-sheet-wise – look pained about it, don't let them think you're lead-swinging – but say your ambition is to serve your Queen and country in khaki and that the occasional night-time Jimmy Riddle wouldn't even be noticed on manoeuvres as long as they provide you with a decent groundsheet and always ensure you have the bottom bunk'. Good old Dad: they fell for it totally and marked me down as unfit, lowest grade of all with the lunatics and convicted homosexuals.

Next immediate problem: to get two more 'O'-levels, including Maths. A couple of terms at the Stroud technical college (where the teaching was far more enthusiastic than Douai's) got two more certificates in the bag – but not Maths, which remains a total non-starter for me. After Delia and the double right-hook, the 'Tech' also served as a crash course in the first principles of Boy meets Girl. I was briefly besotted by classy Emma Alford from Chalford, so much so that when she finally interpreted my quivering mumblings as an invitation to come for a walk with me, I was so swoonily bemused I couldn't think of anything to say. Not a word. We walked round and round the hillocky old town and had tea-and-cakes in the Cadena. When I left her at the Chalford bus-stop, she said, puzzled but chirpily enough, 'You're a dark one, aren't you?', which I took as a parting shot meaning 'get lost'. Which I did, cursing myself for weeks.

I asked sensuous, sly-smiling Jill Creedy to the film *Oklahoma*, and when that song came up, 'I'm Just a Girl Who Can't Say No', I thought she pointedly squeezed my hand. I was wrong, and again was mortified at my utter gaucherie and uselessness. I snogged with Jane England and the breathless abandon of innocence (and actually, if momentarily, touched the buckle where the top of her stockings were attached to those dangling bits of elastic) in a bunker on the golf course at Minchinhampton Common; Jane's brother was a good pal of mine, but as their mother was a bigwig in the local Tory party I treated that touch of suspender-belt, however fleeting, as a triumph for the proletariat over capitalism.

Two other new friends from the grammar school, Mike Barnes and Tony Reeve, had steady girlfriends, which I envied terribly – not only the fact that they had them, but that Sally Holland and Pam Angus were such humdinging smashers. (Tony married Pam, and went on to a knighthood as Her Majesty's Ambassador to South Africa.) Things looked up more than somewhat when, out of the blue, I almost fell off the wall around the Amberley village hall when I was given my first kiss *à la française* at the end of a Saturday night square-dance: the generous tongue-in-cheek donor was Shirl Brown, squat and blonde baker's daughter – and I jumped on my bike and freewheeled all the way down to the Cairnscross Road and home, singing 'The Yellow Rose of Texas is the Only Girl For Me'.

In summer 1956, I hitch-hiked around France for a month with my Douai mate, John Moriarty, and returned sporting a crew-cut. Dad went berserk and smeared a whole tub of Brylcreem over my head in an effort to re-locate the parting; he had arranged for me to begin my first job the following morning as a trainee estate agent with the snooty Cheltenham firm of G. H. Bailey & Son. I lasted a few miserable weeks. I had to be up at dawn to catch the bus – the same route I took when going to the cricket, but without the fizz of anticipation. Every morning, my first chore was to polish the big brass plate outside the office, which was in the Promenade, opposite Cavendish House, the swanky 'county' store. Then I had to carry the great leather-bound ledgers up two winding flights to a crotchety old bag in the accounts department.

G. H. Bailey was a friendly old boy, but the '& Son' was a stern, humourless man; he looked like the great Leonard Rossiter but without an ounce of wit: Rossiter could have modelled his part as the lugubrious undertaker, Mr Shadrake, in the film *Billy Liar*, on Bailey's 'Mister John'. I was the one who had to man the office alone on Saturday mornings. This ruined my sporting arrangements. One Saturday, young Bailey popped in and found me smoking. He went bonkers. I don't know what came over me: I got out my packet of Senior Service, and offered *him* one. He went even more bonkers. Okay, he could stick his job up his jumper, I said, and I went home to face poor Dad, who had paid £500 for the privilege of my being 'articled' to this creep.

Thus it was that on a whim and my nineteenth birthday – the feast of St Francis, 1956 – I presented myself to the editor of the *Stroud News*, clutching the copy of an article I had written on that summer's hitch-hike tour of France, plus a flowery longhand report of the previous week's local soccer match in Stonehouse. It was mid-morning. Geoffrey Saunders was bloodshot-gruff in his tiny downstairs office. His breath carried the tang of the golden brew. He glanced at my two epics. 'Piffle!' he announced, tossing them away, 'But at least you can effing spell'. 'Oh yes, sir', I primmed, 'it was my best subject at school'. 'More than those effers can do upstairs!' he said. Dear Geoffrey, my first and probably best boss and the pride of Bisley and the Stroud Constitutional and Conservative Club. He gave me a month's trial at £2.19s. a week as a general reporter, plus an extra 10s. for the all-night shift on Thursdays when Vi, the tea-lady and proof-reader, would feed the sheets from on high into the clanging old flatbed press while we kids below would string the paper into quires and then vroom down the valleys in vans tossing the bundles into newsagents' doorways at dawn. I have always kept that unprinted Stonehouse versus Welton Rovers match report. It is even worse than some of my stuff now. It was embroidering the first preliminary round of the FA Cup. I headlined it 'The Magpies Set Off On Wembley Trail'.

It was a long, long time before I was to do any more sports writing. My early pretensions did not sink so low. From that first day on the *Stroud News* – when a breezy young smiler from Selsey, John Hamshire (ace tabloid crime reporter now) gave me a driving lesson in the paper's clapped-out van – I was aware that 'this is the life'. Even the sack did not matter. The land was teeming with local rags in those days – even Stroud boasted two, the *News* and the *Journal*. The *World's Press News* each week carried page after page of job offers, and the younger and less experienced you were the better – because they could pay the basic minimum. This was nevertheless ample for a bachelor boy they still called 'Scruff'.

In half a dozen years 'on the road', after Stroud, I had a series of sublime little adventures in Hereford, Guildford, Bristol and Slough. I ended up in Africa. And from day one on any paper you were at the hub of the community's high life and low life. Within a week or two of my starting out, our beloved, bloodshot-eyed editor was charged in the magistrates' court with being in charge of a car on Bisley Hill while under the influence. I was 'observing' in court with our demon shorthander, the voluptuous Wendy Lewis.

When Geoffrey stood up boldly in the dock and said 'there must be some mistake, your worships, the only drink that had passed my lips all week were two small sherries before choir practice', Wendy and I collapsed in a fit of the giggles and had to be removed from the courthouse.

Once I presented to Geoffrey for publication a glowing profile of the Painswick squire, Jonathan Blow, full of the generosity he was displaying to some old tenant crone on his estate. Geoffrey exploded, spiked it, threw me out, and called to Vi for hot tea and whisky. Unknown to me, Squire Blow was Geoffrey's deadliest enemy. On the Friday, Blow telephoned to ask me what had happened to the promised Page One spread. I explained Geoffrey had suppressed it. 'Saddle up Maisie', I heard him roar to a Painswick minion before he slammed down the receiver – and within 20 minutes sparks were flying up the hill past the clock-tower and Squire Blow had ridden his massive hunter into the *News* front office. There it stood, snorting and crapping, outside Geoffrey's room – Blow in the saddle, demanding that Geoffrey come out and fight. Like a scene from Fielding. Geoffrey didn't see it that way, and stayed most of the day silent behind his locked door, under the table, his bottle in quivering hand.

After about six months, we finished a Thursday night delivery run in the van, and Geoffrey summoned us all. He picked up a paper from the pile. This, he said, sobbing, was the last ever edition of the *News* which his great-grandfather had founded. There was no more loot in the kitty. The hated, wealthy, *Dursley Gazette* group had swallowed us up and next week the *News* would be merged with the *Journal*. The tears wouldn't stop. Vi passed him a large slug in a cracked mug. 'It would break my heart if any of you were so treacherous as to even enquire about a position on the newly merged paper established by these vile, carnivorous business predators'. We all agreed. He paid us four weeks' money in lieu of notice and, perking up noticeably, took us along to his Constitutional and Conservative Club, where we stayed all day excitedly wondering about the future.

Our future had obviously been a part of the deal. The following Friday's brand-new merged and re-styled paper, the *News & Journal*, announced on Page One: 'None of the editorial staff of the former *News* have been retained, except for Mr Geoffrey Saunders, who has been delighted to accept the post of Editor-in-Chief'.

He kept the job till he retired, bless him, and right up to his death in the 1980s he would occasionally drop me a cheery note telling me to keep going, 'But, boy, be more sparing with your exclamation marks'.

So from Stroud I reached out for the big-time: I joined the *Hereford Times* in 1957. In that old scuffed-brown-lino-ed office behind the Covered Market there were two other cub reporters – Eric Toplis, a long, larky know-all, a sort of Borders' Billy Liar in a brass-buttoned Burton's blazer who had a way with girls and actually greeted some of the Hereford United footballers by their nick-names; and Leslie Watkinson, a refreshingly dotty, bespectacled worrier from Anglesey who could do shorthand and saw a scoop in everything. On whatever subject you passed the time of day with him in Bassi's Wye Cafe, he'd twitchingly react with: 'Good story that, boy!'

Watkinson joined a week or two after me and shared my attic digs – no meals – on the edge of town up Whitecross way. (Our landlady was an amiable old duck called Mrs Millichamps; Watkinson never understood why I called her 'Mrs Thousands-of-Fields', and he soon left, saying, 'sorry, I need a cooked breakfast every morning'.). On Watkinson's first night I was woken to find him furiously pulling on his trousers. There was frenzied excitement in his Menai lilt. 'The big one! I saw it first! It's my story!'

'What is?' I mumbled from my concave and pungent pit.

'The city's ablaze! I'm going to beat the Fire Brigade to it! What a break on my first day!' I raised a hungover head to the window – then pillowed back to explain to the tyro from Anglesey that in England even small cities ran to glowing, fluorescent, orange-pink street lamps.

Grand days. Three yobs with their pencils at flower shows, hunt balls and gymkhanas; the Mother's Union, the Round Table and the Rotary even welcomed us. We were the very prophets of hatchery, matchery and dispatchery. When the Duke of Edinburgh came to visit Bulmers works I wrote my first ever unspiked colour story. When Hereford formed a CND committee, I not only reported it but joined it.

That didn't go down well. The *HT* was a mouthpiece for Mr Gibson-Watt, MP. Our chief reporter, Tubby Court, a charming old bull of a man with a spaniel's sad eyes who doubled as agricultural correspondent, could not care either way about CND. But my sympathetic treatment of the story sent the news editor, a Welsh horror-comic called Lewis, into furies of rage. He pared the piece down to a single paragraph, and thereafter he treated me as scum and scornfully gave me every possible menial job when he marked the diary of a morning. But we three little bears were in awe of him: everyone knew he had been something dashed brave in the RAF, and hadn't he once actually done a casual subbing shift on the Manchester night desk of the *Daily Mail*? What glory!

Girl-watching in the evenings offered compensation for Lewis's sarcasm by day. Toplis played the field and Watkinson and I seethed at the beauteous string of High School girls he'd bring into the pub. Watkinson flirted with – but never dared to speak to – a flighty confectioner's assistant in Widemarsh Street. By jove, the Bounty bars he bought with a blush! He obviously fancied the retail trade for I heard, years later, that he was walking out with a real cracker from the Leominster bakery.

No crumpet to help pull my crackers as yet, alas. But the possibilities looked up considerably when the wife of Peter Brown, a delightful and generously encouraging senior reporter, had a baby and Pete happily bequeathed me occasional evenings at the theatre. Bodenham Brownies' ballet exhibitions, sure, or the WI madrigals at Marden –

both doubtless butchered by this fearless new critic – but also the real pro stuff, weekly or fortnightly at the Kemble Theatre in Broad Street. An Arts Council touring production of *Look Back in Anger* arrived for a week and, like the rest of my generation was said to be, I was also comprehensively kayoed (Osborne has been at the top of my flagpole ever since: what a sportswriter he would have made). The representative of the *Hereford Times* was asked to the first-night chat-and-grin party backstage. Suddenly, tremulously, he found himself daring to ask the actress who played Helena if she would 'care for a coffee' the following morning at nearby (still there) Ascari's snack bar. Cor, she was the real London goods. With thespian disdain, she strobed me up and down with her false eyelashes, and said, 'Coffee at Ascari's? No change, my funny little fellow', and I felt an absolute clot till she added, with expertly trained timing, 'but you can buy me the largest drink you can afford at lunchtime in the Green Dragon if you'd so care to, big boy'.

I didn't sleep a wink in Mrs Millichamp's attic. What should I wear? – oh, bugger that, what should I *say*? It came to nowt, of course. Lewis had put me down for a 2.30 funeral in Lugwardine, so I was watching the clock for the bus – and Helena spent the whole half-hour listening, with a perplexed smile, to my elementary and nervously prattish chat, and punctuating it with occasional sniggering giggles at herself, doubtless for lumbering herself with such a bumpkin. Still, what could she expect in Hereford – and I consoled myself on the bus to Lugwardine that the length of her leg, the pointed twin thrust of her expensive cashmere jumper, the classy swish of her skirt, and the whole, general metropolitan Max Factor aura (and a few London Maxes doubtless had), had placed me up a peg or three with my regular enemy, the surly and suspicious head waiter at the Green Dragon.

For that at least, Helena got the rave notice in the *HT*, 'outplaying' the female lead, Allison, 'in both depth of

characterization and that indefinable stage quality "Attack",'
and I dropped off a Thursday 'Market Edition' at the
Kemble's stage door. It was not acknowledged, and the
company moved on to set up for the following week at
Wrexham. But I was smug. The daunting date with Helena
had not only given me something to boast about to
Watkinson and Toplis in the office, but it had established
my own Green Dragon 'green room' without too many
sneers from the staff. And why not, for if Hereford now
might be a cultural backwater, had it not been, less than
two centuries before, downstage and in the light of the lime,
like no other provincial town in the land. Did not Roger
Kemble, actor-manager, produce two of his twelve children
here – John Kemble and Sarah, who changed her name for
immortality when she married another actor, Bill Siddons?
And a blue-tin plaque just three windows along from my
*Hereford Times* offices in Maylord Street, announces,
'David Garrick, Actor, Was Born Here, 1713'. (Lichfield
claims him too). But there's no doubt that Nell Gwyn –
born in that little twitchel opposite the front of the
Cathedral – was the city's most talented tart. Was Nell the
first chorus-girl to be mistress to a King? I doubt it, come to
think of it; and certainly she was not the last.

All such stuff I learned from my landlady in the
Whitecross Road, game old Mrs Millichamps. Thousands-
of-Fields and thousands of stories. She could tell me a
stream of them about Welsh comedians, whom at one time
she would board for the annual panto. She had closed her
books a decade before to the panto, 'because I'm not one for
*smut*, Master Frank, unless of course it's absolutely crucial
to the play. Now if Shakespeare himself was to set
something in a nudist colony, then of course I wouldn't
mind seeing naked bodies all over the stage, would I? Your
John Osborne, too, I dare say. I don't go for him and his
"angry young men" myself – I'm too old for that sort of
thing – but I grant him he's a serious writer of plays, and if
*he* wants to put in some smut – which I hear he does a bit

too often – then I think he's got to be allowed; if it moves the play along. No, I say anything goes – as long as it's not gratuitous, if you get my meaning. "Gratuitous" is the trouble, right'.

Like many of that dying (dead?) breed of old theatrical landladies, Mrs Millichamps ate, slept, and breathed the traditions of 'the Theat-ah, my deah', more than most actors. She steeped herself in theatrical biogs, and was proud that her Hereford had such an ancient stage background. She was full of tales about that celebrated troupe of Hereford actors of three centuries and more ago. Before King Charles 'had' her, according to Pepys, Nell Gwyn 'was first got away from Drury Lane by Lord Buckhurst, who lies with her and gives her £100 a year as long as she hath sent back all her parts to the Lane and will act no more'. According to Mrs M, David Garrick had a long affair with an actress, Peggy Woffington, who was extremely free with her favours, especially with the powerful and powdered aristocracy. One night, Garrick and Peg were in bed together when her maid burst in to say that the actress's regular beau at the time, a grand nobleman, had arrived and was at this minute ascending the stairs to the boudoir. Garrick clambered out of the window, holding his clothes, and made good his escape. But he left his wig on the floor. When the suspicious lover saw it, he fell into a jealous rage, till softly calmed by Ms Woffington who convinced him she had been in the process of rehearsing, solo, her next role – a 'breeches part' – as Sir Harry Wildair in Farquhar's *The Constant Couple*.

Of old Mrs Millichamps's heap of yarns concerning John Kemble, the one I remember best was when the great man was in full flow with his torrents of declamation as Othello. A crying baby in the audience kept trying to complete with him. Finally Kemble gave in, halted, and solemnly approached the footlights: in his measured tragedian's tones he announced: 'Ladies and Gentlemen, unless the play is stopped, the child cannot possibly go on'.

Life doodled on contentedly enough, just as Hereford itself has done through the centuries. My home-made hieroglyphics, mercifully, were too unsafe for me to be let loose in most of the tedious and pompous council chambers, so Tubby and Peter took me as leg man to the agricultural shows. And there was the 1959 General Election. Not too many years before, a local-boy-made-good and a Beaverbrook journalist, Frank Owen, had won the South Hereford seat for the Liberals, and with no Labour traditions in the area the Libs remained the only party with any chance of unseating the Tories. Robin Day – yes, him! – was the Liberal candidate in South Hereford but, from the first, seemed to me to be too detached and disdainfully lofty a smart-arse to have the slightest chance; but up in North Hereford, young Grenville Jones, a local laddo working on the *Sunday Express* Crossbencher column, was giving it a real fizzing go. He clandestinely took me aboard and called me 'campaign manager'. The *HT* would have fired me on the spot had they known. I did all I could to pack the paper with 'news bites' for Grenville. Even a routine visit to Leominster market to report a sale of Hereford cattle would have me inventing quotes of farmers making complimentary references to young Jones, 'who seems just the man to get us farmers back on our feet'.

The Tory agent was a typical Lord Snooty who went by the name of Allcock. Reporting a public meeting in High Town, I 'quoted' Grenville as calling him 'the most aptly named man in Hereford', and successfully smuggled it into the paper when the sharp-eyed old sub, Ray Goulding, was out at lunch. So when Allcock steamed in to complain, Ray got far more blame than me for letting it through. It didn't do much good, of course. It was Macmillan's 'You've-never-had-it-so-good' election, and the Tories sailed in all over.

The Kemble Theatre decided to get 'with it': for Christmas they announced an ice panto. These were all the rage on television, but the old Kemble was not built for such novelties, and all it could manage was to fill the little stage with two encased blocks of ice – each as large as, say, two double beds – on which the chorus-line of four girls would gormlessly and grinningly gyrate on skates for a few setpieces.

I had made the acquaintance of the troupe's desperately dreary leader and pantomime dame at the press conference during rehearsals. On the first night he recognized me at the end of the front row scribbling my notes. Presuming a personal on-stage performance by 'the gentleman of the press' might jolly things along as well as improve the tenor of my review, he made a point of coming down and, as they do in panto, dragging me onto the stage and attempting to skate.

The fullest-chested, longest-legged and most toothsome of the chorus-line quartet – they all came from Blackpool and were in a 'proper' ice show in the summers – fixed my skates and took charge of my slithering routine to general hilarity, and that was that. But the buxom bint and I had, so to say, made our introductions, so at the first-night party thrown after the show by the Mayor and corporation, the skating lass and I took it from there without my usual nervous umming and aahing. Her name was Grace and she was reet lanky in both leg and county. I suggested a drink in the Green Dragon the following morning. 'Tomorrow!' she scoffed, 'What you up to tonight, lad?' Er, going home. 'Well, why don't a nice boy like you ask a nice girl like me home to have a drink with him, then?'

Blimey, I think she fancies me. Bloody heck, I think she fancies IT.

We each whipped a bottle of the Mayor's plonk and set off through the wintry slush of the Whitecross road. I was nervously full of anticipation. Our Gracie seemed the same, without the nerves. My attic in the high, thin house was one floor above Mrs Millichamps's room, and we crept by on the stairs, and into my rank, dank hovel. But who cares: booze and a bed and a Blackpool belle: what more does a bloke want?

I tiptoed across the landing to rinse out the tooth-mug in the bathroom and, on my return, had scarcely closed the door when Grace – already down to her pearl-white bulbous bra – was tearing off my coat and then, not bothering with my shirt, urgently attacking the buckle of my belt. Now my trouser buttons – no zips in those days – were pinging off and machine-gunning the wall. I can remember my shock – my fright – to this day over 30 years later. What the hell was this hefty brute doing to me? Had she gone potty or something?

Amazing Grace was now on her knees, and making friendly, desperate Lancastrian noises, which I gathered, roughly translated, to mean, 'Cor, c'mon lad, let's be 'aving yer!' My trousers were at my ankles. My underpants followed. She buried her buck-teeth into my innocent, hitherto untouched member – and I screamed. Loudly. She gobbled at my groin, and gasped and gyrated and wouldn't let go. I let fly another screeching howl as I unbalanced, and toppled to the floor as heavily as Foreman in the 'rumble in the jungle'. The fall at least detached her. A contented doe eye looked at me, 'Ee, lad', she whispered, licking her saliva-soaked chops with a satisfied grin, 'I don't think you've had that done to you before, have you? Great, ain't it?'

There was a knock on the door. 'Master Frank, is that you? What were those screams?'

The door-knob twisted. I struggled to my feet to try and save my good old landlady from a trauma of the one thing she detested: gratuitous smut. My trousers were still around my hush-puppies – and as I shuffled to greet her at the door, miraculously, I thought of Mrs M's tale about Peg Woffington and David Garrick's wig.

So as the dressing-gowned old landlady surveyed the tawdry scene – me trouserless and drooping membered, our chops-soaked gobbler, Gracie, supine in the full twin-towered glory of her Bristol City strip – I explained, innocent as you like, 'Sorry about the screams, dear, we were just rehearsing for Grace's next part after the panto has finished. I was just hearing her lines'.

'Oh well, that's alright then, dears', said Mrs Millichamps, relieved and suddenly unconcerned, 'but try and be a bit quieter'. As she turned to go, her parting line, however, was tinged with disapproval. 'Pity. By the state of you both, it's obviously one of those new "angry young man" plays'.

Whether so shamedly (and so uncertainly?) losing my virginity had anything to do with it I do not know – but within a week I got my hands on my blissful, bonny Beryl. Now that was some lady. I come over all gooey as I write well over thirty years later. She was a sultry blonde Janet Leigh with a dash of Doris Day's delicious pertness. (I was still besotted by DD). I met Beryl when covering the heats of the YFC Dairy Queen contest. She was runner-up to some blousy Bo-Peep from Bredwardine – a travesty that inspired from me a major policy piece for the next Friday's paper (spiked again by the sneering Lewis).

What was this thing called lur-ve? I'd hum Dean Martin songs in the evenings when we walked back from the flicks across Castle Green. We'd lean over the bridge and stare at the sunsetty, salmony river – and I'd make my plans, our plans. A world trip to start with, my dwarlin'. Perhaps I'll edit that English paper in Brazil. Then perhaps a spot of the *Sydney Sun* would do us good. Back, via say the *Times of India*, my sweetheart, to edit *Punch*. I think. A pity the *Manchester Guardian* didn't print in London. . . .

We held hands and the long evenings shortened. Golden leaves rocked gently down like crisp little cradles to die in the Wye. Beryl and I snuggled deeper into my duffel. Arms entwined, we even watched United having a good run on Southern League Saturdays – which mornings would be spent with noses pressed to Samuel's window and the engagement ring tray next to the Everite watches. There was a teeny glitterer that Beryl had set her heart on. It cost all of £9.19s.11d.

On Saturday I arrived in the office to find the smug and accursed Lewis had put me down to cover some afternoon memorial service in the cathedral of an Archdeacon's wife or somesuch, some local benefactress of long standing and now long lying. It was just a question of taking the names of the mourners at the door, then knocking them up for the paper in some sort of order of civic seniority. And no matter, really, for United were away that week anyway.

Around noon I met Beryl in the City Arms, our pub which was opposite the Vanity Fair hair salon where she was receptionist. The day before, my little brown Friday envelope had bulged with the Christmas bonus of an extra week's pay and I said to Beryl I was going to treat myself to that plum waistcoat in Colliers. It was only £1.15s. She looked sad. She looked almost more beautiful when she was sad.

'Alright, dwarlin',' I said. 'Let's do it!' We got to Samuels just as they were closing for lunch. I counted out ten one-pound notes. Beryl asked if she could keep the penny change – for ever. Fourth finger on the left. And in the middle of High Town, the boy with the water-combed medium-Tony Curtis kissed with tight-closed mouth his beloved Janet Leigh.

Back in the City Arms the ring dazzled the whole bar. Watkinson bought pints instead of halves and cross-examined us for a good Timesman's Diary angle. Toplis bought show-off's whisky chasers and even let one of his High School harem give me a kiss and lick my ear in congratulations. It was a very good session.

At closing time the happy couple staggered to the cinema by the bus station and saw *Bell, Book and Candle*. We paid extra for a back-row double. I kept whispering to Beryl that she was far more scrumptious than Kim Novak. It was one of those fleapits with pretensions and a Cadena Café upstairs, and afterwards – tea and toast 1s 9d – we held hands and hummed together softly 'Tea for Two, 'n' Me for You. . . .'

Of a sudden, a terrible panic slapped my face. I'd totally forgotten the flaming Archdeacon's wife's flaming memorial service! Shh-ugar!

No sooner had the fright welled up, it abated. Hadn't Lewis put only me down for the job. Of course. Easy! I'd say that I'd stood there taking names at the West door, but had packed up as soon as I realized they'd opened the South door too. It had been a two-man job and it would be Lewis's fault he'd only sent one. He'd never bother to check up. I never gave it another thought, and Beryl and I caught the bus to Berrington village hall and danced last waltzes all night.

On Monday morning Lewis was barring my way to the reporters' room. He wore a twisted grin above his clip-on bow tie. He was bristling with bully-boy bravado like he was apprehending one of his hated Eyetie PoWs. 'What's your excuse?' he spat. I already sensed the game was up.

'Well, sir, I was at the West door. . . .' I began.

'Liar!' he shrieked and with sadistic steely fingers he grabbed my ear, twisted it, and marched me, bent and screaming, into his own office down the corridor. He threw me inside. And then he closed the door. 'Er', he began, stroking the sides of his evil grin, 'er, I think you'd better take one moment's notice, hadn't you? I realized they'd probably open both doors at about lunchtime, didn't I? I had to give up my own family Christmas shopping, didn't I? I stood taking names at the West door for freezing hours, didn't I? And when I came to collect your lot at the South door, you weren't there, were you? I didn't get where I am today by missing important funerals, laddie'.

He wouldn't even let me say goodbye to Watkinson. I met Beryl in Bassi's Café. She cried. Don't worry, dwarlin', there's absolutely no doubt I'm going to get that job in Buenos Aires. If not, what about the *Straits Times*? You'd love Malaysia, my sweet. Even if I have to settle for being star writer on the *Manchester Guardian*, we could stick the north for a few months, couldn't we? Don't worry, I'll line everything up and send for you. They pay the fares for wives. I think.

Tearfully she waved me away on the bus to Gloucester to spend a mizz Chrizz with my pained and shocked parents. I answered every possible ad in the *World's Press News*. I started hitch-hiking around England attending the measly interviews I had conned. Some six weeks later my parents forwarded on a bundle of letters from Beryl. The envelopes were all marked with a smudged inscription S.W.A.L.K. and they bore the order 'PLEASE FORWARD TO ARGEN-TINA'.

Sorry, Beryl, my dwarling, I was too ashamed to reply, for Dad had only had to forward them to the Reporters' Room, *Guildford and Godalming Times*.

# 6

The ad. in the *World's Press News* had read: SMART cub reporter wanted. 80wpm shorthand essential; some interest in theatre an advantage. Apply, *Surrey Times*, Guildford.

The grey, flakey-frail and kindly old editor, Tom White, noticeably winced as he read the overblown adjectival gush and critical gore in the handful of *HT* theatre-review cuttings I had proudly offered him. He looked up at me, his eye lingering with distaste on my 'interview' suit – a baggy, tweedy old thing of Uncle John's which Mum had heaved about and hemmed in a gallant effort to achieve some semblance of fit. Things had not started well.

'Mmm', he sighed, sadly, 'I'm afraid we aim to be less, er, provocative here, and certainly not so, er, mannered and, if I may say so, boy, er, egotistical. I've many more applicants to see, of course, but while you're here I'd better just see if your shorthand is up to the mark'. He nodded towards a pencil and notebook on his desk in front of me, and reached for a nearby *Surrey Times* to dictate at random (and at 80 words a flipping minute) a couple of pars. Crunchtime for Francis. I primly flittered my eyes like goodie-goodies do.

'Certainly, sir', and I reached with confident assurance to pick up the pad and pencil – then, with by now practised

111

(and, dare I say it, exquisitely perfected) timing. 'Er, sir, I think I should tell you I've had to turn down three job offers in only the last fortnight because the papers concerned did not seem to run a satisfactory, er, company pension scheme, sir'.

His eyes glazed just for a split second, and he looked up from the two paragraphs he had just selected for the shorthand test. I went on, 'Your advertisement for this job, sir, had no mention of a company pension scheme. I presume you have one, sir? It may seem a silly question to you at this time, sir, but it is an important matter for me: you see, sir [lowering eyelids shyly], at this present moment in time I am contemplating, er, marriage, sir, and we are very keen to start a family.'

I could tell without looking he was feeling a sudden, almost fatherly, new warmth towards me. His veined old hand replaced the newspaper on his desk and – 'It so happens', he said – and he began rootling and riffling in one of the drawers alongside him. 'I can see, boy', he went on, 'you've more sense than many, and more sense than I might have given you credit for. . . . Ah, here we are'. And he handed over a crisp white pamphlet, The Surrey Times Group Pension Scheme. 'I think you will find, when you've studied it at your leisure, my boy, that it most favourably compares with any similar scheme in the country. You will notice there is even a very decent opt-out clause should you decide to take a slightly earlier retirement, at 60 instead of 65. Our former chief reporter did that only last year and bought himself a gift-shop in Haslemere. He enjoyed the theatre, like you, by the way. Anyway, my boy, study it, and if you've any queries. . . .'

Editors want a stable team and a quiet life. They like men's men, like them: steady men who like pension schemes. Local editors want unexciting people to work for unexciting papers. Local editors are proud to be Rotarians, delighted to be on the permanent list for sherry parties in the Mayor's parlour. They do not want reporters who might enquire about the Mayor's hospitality budget. Local editors' wives are friends with local Tory councillors' wives. Local editors' wives do not want local editors to employ snotty, long-snouted, ambitious-for-Fleet-Street 'investigative' journos. Local editors want to employ Safe, Married, Dull Family Men whose priority is studying details of the Company Pension Scheme.

I pored over, with a swot's furrowed brow, the totally meaningless forms he had given me, interposing a few appreciative mmms and aahs as though I could have been a surprised and too-good-to-be-true winner reading a letter from Littlewoods. It was with a fond tone that the old man interrupted my retirement-home reverie. 'What are your hobbies? Not by any chance campanology, eh?' (Now at least I knew what the word meant: I'd been sent by the accursed Lewis to cover tons – or rather, *dins* – of excruciating Sunday night bell-tower competitions and 'concerts' in just about every rickety, wooden-laddered, bat-crapped tower in Hereford).

I grinned at the editor and mimed with my hands a momentary, extravagant sort of bellrope hornpipe.

'Oh sir, what a coincidence', I gushed. 'How could you possibly tell I loved bell-ringing? I could have shown you no end of cuttings of my campanology reports in Hereford. I'm still terribly green about the techniques, of course, sir – but once I manage to get a settled job I'm determined to start lessons on the jolly old ropes and changes'.

The grizzled greybeard's grin was beatific. It turned out the *Surrey Times* Group printed the national weekly magazine, *The Bellringer* – Ed-in-Chief, T. White – my own brand-new Editor himself.

Home and dry. I was now officially a 'critic of the drama'. I was 22.

I still missed Beryl. But knew there was no going back to Hereford and its musty-pink, cosy cathedral, or to 'our' bench on Castle Green where first-love's fingers had excitingly explored and strayed. I would miss Edgar Street, and summer tennis with Toplis, and cricket on Fownhope's fields, or Marden's meadows. (I would not, however, miss my 'green room' soirées in the Green Dragon Hotel. On the night before I left 'for Argentina', I had misbehaved by getting blotto in their posh 'Shires Cocktail Bar'. By all accounts, as I toppled over I had 'yawned' rather colourfully all over the carpet. As Watkinson carried me out, my loathed and loathing long-time enemy, the Head Waiter, had gleefully pronounced my lifetime's ban. Some dozen or so years later, United had one of their FA Cup runs and the *Guardian* sent me down to cover it. I said to my mate, John Moynihan of *The Sunday Telegraph*, 'Let's get an early train and I'll buy you a slap-up in the old city of my youth'. We had no sooner been given the great, pretentious, leather-bound menus to examine by the waitress when, across the cavernous, carpeted salle-à-manger, dashed my hated adversary in the black tie: 'Not him, Miriam, not him – he's barred for life!' We grabbed a sandwich at Ascari's).

Guildford had a respectable, solid, professional weekly rep company. The theatre then was in the very centre of town (the plush modern riverside building dedicated to Yvonne Arnaud was still on the council's drawing board). In the late 1950s, the nearness to London – half an hour on the Waterloo express – made it appealing for a string of guest stars to visit and there was always a West End buzz about the place. As well, the permanent company was made up of some of the brightest probables and possibles in the British theatre. London agents beat a path to their door each week. They all lived in digs in a high and handsome warren of a house on the hilly, northern, side of town. Their landlady was called Mrs Pharoh-Band, a dear and as theatre-loving as my Mrs Millichamps had been. I contrived to get a bedsit just down the road with a Mrs Rosenburg, much sterner but also in 'the trade' (she claimed to be related to Flora Robson). In short, nothing but the best connections for the new critic of the *Surrey Times*.

The next thing, of course, was to dress the part. Wasn't

Kenneth Tynan's middle name 'Peacock?' Hadn't he owned only two suits at Oxford, one Lincoln green, the other cherry-blossom pink? It so happened that 'Haybag' Hepworths, the chainstore tailors of taste in Guildford High Street, had in their 1959 New Year Sale just one daring signpost to the liberated decade to come – a magnificently garish, almost fluorescent jacket in purply-mauve houndstooth check. It cost £11.19s.11d. – half the advance on my first week's wages. It was worth every penny.

It only came out, of course, at nights. For, by day, there was more humdrum hay to mow, and I had to doodle around the routine cub reporter's beat. I wrote up yawningly tedious wedding reports from the reams of forms sent in ('. . . the bride, given away by her father, wore primrose organza net over cerise taffeta, and the honeymoon will be spent touring the West Country'), and collected and collated columns of mourners' names at funerals ('. . . the coffin was topped by a single floral tribute of white irises and primroses, inscribed "From your ever-faithful chihuahua, Candy-Poo" '). Or I had to listen to local councillors' endless bombast and drivel, have parleys in the Mayor's parlour, or report poor sods being nabbed by the local cops for riding bikes without lights, or exposing themselves when the High School bus went by.

At nights, I would re-sleek my hair with water, then don my houndstooth jacket with the solemnity of a Roman priest in his vestry, or Lee Marvin dressing for the gunfight in *Cat Balou*. Next to the theatre was the Surrey Arms pub. I'd be waiting in the lounge bar to chat with the stars when the show came down. Just Shaftesbury Avenue gossip, dahlin'. I was the Kenny Tynan of southern Surrey.

Tynan, of course, was the coruscating young critic of the *Observer* who had, to all intents, discovered Osborne. Weekly and gloriously he axed away at the twin pillars of the proscenium-arch which for years had framed 'well-made' plays in which chaps and gels bounded through french-windows fluting, 'Anyone for tennis?'

I soon became a mate of a charming young actor in the permanent company, Sebastian Breaks, beefily handsome and bright as new blazer-buttons. (I wonder what happened to him? To me at Guildford – as well as to himself, it must be said – he looked booked for stardom). He kept me tumbling off my Surrey Arms bar stool in gleeful mirth, or over the Nescafé in one of the warren of Mrs P-B's bedsits, with his theatrical tales. I have heard them since as the hoariest of chestnuts; but to me then, an innocent in a new, magical world of footlights and literary allusion (and one in which, because of my 'critic's' role, I found myself flatteringly courted), the yarns broke me up with delight.

There was the one about Sir Donald Wolfit in the sword fight at the end of *Macbeth*. He goes for his sword in its scabbard, shouting 'Lay on, Macduff!' – and then realizes poor Macduff's sword is unaccountably NOT in its scabbard. So Wolfit, slashing air the while at a bemused and weaponless Macduff, who can only think of dodging and weaving like a boxer, whispers to the hapless knight, 'Kick me!'. So he boots him in the shin, and with a blood-curdling groan and rolling of eyes, Wolfit falls, and expires, shouting, 'The cur hath foiled me with his poisoned boot!'

Or Robert Atkins, another grand Shakespearean whose language was full and frank and who ran the Regent's Park Open Air Theatre for years. He was Caliban in *The Tempest* one heat-wave summer's night in London, so hot that one of the nymph-spirits failed to come in on cue. She had fainted. He strode from the stage and came across the poor girl squatting on the grass in the wings, her head deep in her lap. He kicked her softly, but barked loudly, 'By *examining* y'entrance, dear, you've *missed* it!'

And when he was running the Shakespeare Theatre at Stratford, the chairman and chief benefactor was Sir Fordham Flower, owner of the local brewery. Atkins's fruity and unchristian language was deemed too risky to be chanced at reading the lesson at the service in Holy Trinity church on Shakespeare's birthday, traditionally the theatre director's role. On hearing of the snub, Atkins angrily invaded the meek Sir Fordham's office. 'That you, of all fuckers, sir, should believe this scurrilous fucking tittle-tattle going around about my vocabulary. I take the dimmest fucking view, sir, of your fucking accusations about my fucking language!' 'Point made, I think', said Sir Fordham, waving him out of his office. Atkins went, but turned at the door and in his most booming, back-of-the-stalls declamation, announced, '*Flowers's bitter is piss!*'

Sebastian even had a tale of Peg Woffington – you remember, the 'breeches-part' actress whose quick thinking saved David Garrick's reputation all those years ago, as well as mine at Mrs Millichamps'. Apparently Peggy was so famed for her 'man's' role as Farquhar's Sir Harry Wildair that as she came off stage one night to another rousing ovation, she said to one of her envious girl-friends, 'I have played the part so well and so often that half the city believes me to be a man'. Said her bitchy pal, 'And the other half, my dear, *knows* you to be a woman!'

Weekly Rep, first night première Monday. I'd have Tuesday morning off to write my review. The paper came out on Thursday. Sometimes they would put my photograph on the front page, billing 'FVK at the Theatre, page 14'. The byline pic had itself been quite a production. I told the paper's hardbitten old snapshot Sid to try to emulate Tynan's classic mugshot in the *Observer* – the artist staring, muse-sodden and mystical, into the distance and holding his smoke-billowing Capstan Full-Strength thoughtfully between his third and fourth fingers. The *Surrey Times*'s Armstrong-Jones grumpily pointed out that the particular pose would tend to emphasize my most unaesthetically bitten fingernails. So I settled for the conventional forefinger cig-grip, as long as he could portray the smoke wafting around me in wistful, theatrical symbolism. The jacket came out well too.

It was one thing to pose like Tynan, but altogether more of a strain to write like him. In the end, I coped pretty well. Easy-peasy – what he wrote in the *Observer* one month, I

wrote in the *Surrey Times* the next. It was shameless
cribbing: metaphor for metaphor, allusion for allusion,
whiplash phrase for whiplash phrase. What Chelsea or
Hampstead relished in February, so Guildford and Godalming read in March. You just kept his cuttings and, in time,
you just milked the master. Nobody twigged. Suburban
Surrey was (and is) sublimely unaware of any frontier
beyond its own. (There wasn't even a titter in the house at
the first night of Christopher Guinee's Hamlet. The chap
playing the Ghost, who appears as soon as the play opens,
was a very good stick called Denzil Ellis. Coming down
from London, he had found his half of the train uncoupled
at Woking — as sometimes happened — and diverted to
military-only stations up past Farnham. When the train
stopped at last, Denzil frantically rang the theatre and its
pleasant but always harassed manager, a soft Lancastrian
called Eric Longworth. Denzil told Eric he had already
bagged a cab and would be leaving post-haste. Curtain-up
was at 7 o'clock — in five minutes. At which time, bow-tied
Eric eased himself, embarrassed, in front of the drapes,
cleared his throat and announced in his most apologetically
cringing Lanky to the Mayor and the packed house:

'Mr Mayor, your worship: ladies and gentlemen. I am sorry
to inform you that the show will be delayed a quarter of an
hour owing to the unforeseen and unlikely circumstance of the
Royal Ghost of Prince 'Amlet's Father being unavoidably and
most unfortunately detained in the military sidings and
shunting yards in the general area of Camberley'.

Now in any previous incarnation I would have made a
nice gossip col par or two of such stuff, or done a jokey
front-pager with poor Denzil. But such stuff was far beneath
the dandy suburban 'Ken T' in his sharpest of sharp
houndstooth.

Word for word, if not play for play or part for part. If,
one Sunday, Tynan sneered that John Neville's Hamlet at
the Old Vic 'resists agony with lips so prefectorially stiff
that he simply cannot let go of his voice', the very same

description would be attached by me to an actor playing, perhaps, a farce at the Guildford Theatre some six weeks hence. If Alan Badel's London Hamlet was 'like a restless marmoset' one Sunday in May, or Ralph Richardson's Macbeth had a 'Robeyesque, comic cheese-face', then so exactly similarly might a Guildford player strike the *Surrey Times* critic in July. I was especially good on actresses. Just like Mr Tynan, in fact; word for word, bitchy and bullish in turn. If Dorothy Tutin was 'like a mouse on the rack' in some West End production one month, then so was some innocent actress in Guildford the next.

It was all so easy. Indeed 'FVK' was making a local name for himself; a colourful, bracing wit, over and above the famous dayglo brightness of his houndstooth check jacket. It was a good life.

But I'd walk back to my bunk at Mrs Rosenburg's after late-night coffees with the kids, humming Radio Lux's latest most longingly – Bobby Darin's 'Dream Lover' . . . jingle, jangle, jongle, 'I-wanna-Dream-Lover-so's-I-donna-have-to-dream-alone. . . .' And just like the man sang, she came. Miss Beronice Barron joined the company from Oldham Rep. She had all the pert, confiding, humorous charm of Miss Dora Bryan; though not so spiky with it and, certainly, far better legs; not to mention a complexion of porcelain, and the loveliest, liquid, upturned eyes of puppyish trusting brown. An absolute A1 smasher.

Beronice was in the permanent company, and moved into Mrs P-B's. One week she'd play a minor walk-on as she rehearsed the following week's starring role. It was all the same to the critic of the *Surrey Times*. Every entrance had me (and of course Mr Tynan's cribs) drooling over Miss Barron. As Juliet, in the balcony scene, she had 'a quiet candour as still as a smoke-ring, and as lovely'. As a maid in a drawing-room comedy with a two line part she still stole the show for the *Surrey Times* to the exclusion of every other – 'in her tiny cameo as Hetty, Miss Barron was impatient and mettlesome, proud and vehement, and never a blindfold skivvy of milk and water: alas, she lit up the stage for only two minutes in each act. What *is* the management doing, casting her in such insulting roles?'

If Tynan one week called Joan Plowright 'a budding Meggie Albanesi', then that would be FVK's Miss Barron the next. When Frances Cuka was 'an embryonic Anna Magnani' in London, then, sooner rather than later, ditto my beloved Miss B in Guildford.

In *Peg o' My Heart*, Beronice out-Hepburned Hepburn (both of them at one and the same time) with her 'controlled pathos; trusting rag-doll eyes, cheeky mould of nose, rosebud pout . . . long auburn hair and 8 o'clock Sunday Mass hat'.

Cinderella at Christmas was the last time I saw her. Hers had been 'a glass-slippered performance, as sharply crisp and joyous as crystal'. After the last-night party, as I had contrived to do most every night, I waited in the pub to see if I could walk her home. Certainly I could, for she had something to tell me, something important, something she'd been daring herself to mention for weeks.

Bliss! Did she feel the same as me? Was love as many splendoured a thing for her? She loves me, she loves me not? I had never so much as held her hand, for all the nights I'd walked her up the long hill to her home. In spite of December, I was junily, moonily, warmly in love, my spirit palpitating, my jacket strobing even more madly, it seemed, as we passed beneath the street lamps. Now, as the wintry snowflakes softly, soundlessly, feather-flaked down, Cinderella let me put an arm tenderly across the back of her delicious shoulders. It was a silent, soulful stroll. As I remember, I can smell again her delicate perfume in the clean, sharp, wintry air. I could hardly wait. What, as Bogie would say, is on your lovely mind, kid?

At her garden gate, lo and behold, she kissed me – just a sudden, darting fond-enough peck with pursed, sisterly lips. Not the smacker I had my mouth open and eyes closed for. Then she stood back and spoke firmly. I had been kind, said

the Beloved, but much too kind. It had to stop. My weekly
drools in print were making her a public laughing stock. She
hoped she was quite good, but knew she was not as good as
the *Surrey Times* said. Would I please desist?

Also, she said – now coy, the firm tone gone – there was
something else, 'but I don't quite know how to tell you, you
dear funny boy'.

So I was right! Hooray, hooray, what rapture! She *was*
crazy about me. It's just that I'm 23, and she's nearly 25.
'What is it, darling Beronice?' 'No', she said, 'it's very
difficult, you don't understand'.

'I do, I do. Just say it. Please'.

'Alright, I will . . . Sebastian has been keeping all the
cuttings of your notices about me and sticking them on the
dressing-room noticeboard exactly next to various old
reviews of Kenneth Tynan. They have all been laughing at
you for months. I'm sorry, Frank, but I really think it's time
for you to leave Guildford.'

Not only jilted by his Cinderella, but rumbled as well, this
shattered Buttons was, within five minutes, lying in rueful
contemplation on his lonely bed. He was still wearing his
houndstooth jacket. In the darkened, smelly room, you
could see just a pinprick of red fire as he dragged long on his
Capstan Full-Strength. He held the cigarette thoughtfully
between his third and fourth fingers.

Perhaps she was right, perhaps it was time to move on.
New years, new pastures.

\*     \*     \*

The young man went West again. To Bristol. Where Glorse
plays cricket. And, hey, it would soon be summer. And
Graveney's in his glory. And, if truth was told, I never did
*really* go all that much for poncing, preening acting anyway.

Mind you, I was lucky to get the job. I slunk back to the
old folks at home – Mum and Dad had moved to
Cheltenham – and presented myself to Mr Hollinshead,
editor of the *Cheltenham Echo*. (He was the cricket nut for

whom Derek Malcolm, remember, had put up the headline,
'We Must All Take Off Our Hats to Crapp'). Once or twice
in local games at Stroud, or when I was home for the
weekend, I had lofted Mr H's nippy but telegraphed off-
cutters over square-leg or midwicket, then talked in the
evenings of the great men of Gloucester. If he liked me it
was certainly mutual.

'No jobs here, m'boy', he said, 'but they are looking for a
sub on the sister rag at Bristol, the *Evening World*. Have a
go'.

This time, for the big time, Dad – bless him – kitted me
out with a realistic 'interview suit' from The Famous. The
chief sub-editor, Ernie Averis, looked bustlingly fierce, his
questions rat-tat-tatting like a Desmond Douglas ping-pong
rally. Except there was no one at the other side of the net.
What had I subbed before? How was my layout? Any
examples? Could I cast off? What type-faces did I most
enjoy? Was I a fan of Gill? When was Bodoni's boldest
used? Was I a serif fellow or a sans? Anyroad, all the
gobbledygook that born subs took in with their mother's
milk.

I knew I had just one desperate flail in my locker –
knowing just enough about it from my mate and our junior
sub on the old *HT*, Ian Bowman. From him (a born sub
who can write – he is now ace-man at the *Guardian* – but
who has always, and voluntarily, submerged his writing
talent simply because he *prefers* subbing), I had learned
early that subs, however careworn, take a kindlier view of
anyone who says, as boldly as Bodoni did, 'Look here, sir, I
know you know I know nothing about subbing because *I*
know I know nothing about subbing. I am pig ignorant of
typefaces, layout, captioning and, especially, casting-off, I
think a 'stick' grows on a tree, a 'banner' goes on a march,
and a 'splash' is a swimming-pool or puddle job.

'But, sir, you see, I don't *like* writing; I *hate* writing; I
have no remote ambition to write. I don't want to be a nosy
investigator like Duncan Webb; I have no ambition to be

On a Sussex seashore a year before he died in 1986, Tommy Farr demonstrates to FK how he kept Joe Louis at bay for 'the full 15'. (*Jeff Goddard*)

World Cup, 1970. Two groupies — but who's the blonde? The other one is Bobby Moore, England's best captain of England's best team.

Pat Ward-Thomas — 'Smarten up, lad, we're dining with Jack tonight'. (*World Golf Hall of Fame, North Carolina*)

'What the Papers Say' award from Prime Minister, James Callaghan, in 1978. 'Stoker Jim' was no sports buff. On the way to the Savoy an aide had obviously referred him to my piece of waffle that morning in which I had quoted Milton. In his speech, the PM gushingly mentioned my Eng.Lit. pretensions – oblivious to the fact that I had been quoting, not crusty and declaiming John, but good ol' Arthur of Arsenal, Glos and England. (*Granada TV*)

Sir Neville – 'Get on the front foot, boy'. (*Guardian*)

Glos *v* New Zealand, Bristol, 1949. A youthful John Arlott being given his production orders by telegram. (*Hulton-Deutsch*)

Sefton Delmer, René Cutforth, or this new twerp, Bernard Levin; let alone James Cameron. As for that Neville Cardus, Geoffrey Green, or John Arlott, well, don't push me, sir. I do not want to be a crime reporter, a feature writer, a cartoonist's caption writer, an industrial correspondent, or even a co-respondent correspondent on William Hickey's Diary. And whatever you do, sir, *don't* mention that dandy and dolt, Kenneth Tynan, to me. Simply, sir, I feel, in my bones and my spirit, that I'm a natural-born sub-editor. Give me a chance, sir!'

Good old Ian: it worked. And good old Ernie, too. Because all 'natural' sub-editors hate writers – almost as much as all 'natural' writers despise sub-editors – he gave me a month's trial. He was a sensational teacher, ruthlessly, overbearingly brash and bossy, but within one harrowing week he was beloved by me. God knows how I passed the test – on his advice, I gave up beer for a month and took to black coffee – but I did. And, thanks only to Ernie, I learned to love the arts and craft-versed skills and sciences of the 'bench' and the 'stone'. Still do: although, alas, I would not have a clue how to sub now after Mr Murdoch's print revolution and the new ghostly-green screens. I'm forever a Caxton (and Ernie Averis) man myself. (Our Saturday afternoon 'Pink 'Un' football-special copy boy then was Ernie's 13-year-old son Mike. 'Copy, boy!' I'd shout, having subbed, say, Stonehouse's Western League runner drama with Cashes Green for the northern slip edition. 'Copy, boy!' is what Mike shouts to me now: he's my Sports Editor on the *Guardian*. One could not have a better.)

So Bristol was my first *real* newspaper. I cannot describe the palpitating frenzy of that weekly six-day war – 10 editions and as many 'slips' to the districts. Ernie organized us, and through the glass partition Reg Eason sent the front-line troops into battle. Reg was the reporters' News Editor. Kindly, fussing, only frantically urgent when necessary (which, come to think of it, was always), he and Ernie would shout and hate and love; shake fists and growl and despair at each other behind that glass partition. I learned there that Writers, with a capital W, can make newspapers very good, but that News and Sub-Editors can make them absolutely brilliant. Ernie and Reg, a team less smoothly, slidingly serene, shall we say, than Torvill-and-Dean (or even Pearl-and-Dean) made those final months on the *Evening World* perhaps my finest finishing school. (All right, then — apprenticeship.)

I had only been there a year — black-coffee-ing as Ernie insisted I did, till at least the 2.30 'almost Final' slip editions had gone to Minchinhampton, Minehead, and Minetey — when it was announced the paper was to close. I thought, dear old Geoffrey Saunders strikes again, and got out while the going was good. I thought Africa was the best place to lie low for a bit.

# 7

Bristol had broadened ambitions in all directions. Ernie and Reg had trained up a crack team. The skilful young sub who taught me to make up the weather-page was Brian Barron, now BBC TV's Far East correspondent. David Foot showed how a writer could be equally original, fluent and fast whether covering Bristol City at Ashton Gate for the Saturday Pink 'Un or, in midweek, an Old Vic first night (where young Peter O'Toole was the company's leading light). Foot is now a colleague on the *Guardian*, as is Keith Harper, the Labour Editor, with whom I merrily shared a rickety, cold flat in Clifton and who remains a dear friend. Keith took out a string of girls, each of whom, mysteriously, farted more explosively and pungently than the one before.

Once, on a whim dreamed up the night before in the old Gaiety pub that folk weren't as thick about current affairs as they seemed, Keith tried a 'vox pop' canvass in Park Street in the morning rush-hour. The question we selected was, 'Who is John Osborne?' A dozen were sampled. Two knew he was the current bête-noire of the English stage establishment; nine had not the remotest clue; and one typist pondered long, with the answer on the tip of her tongue, till she finally cracked it: 'Yeah, 'course, he works down Fry's in packagin', don't 'ee?' (Fry's was the big local chocolate factory.)

Another general reporter, who doubled as film critic and gave us coruscating flashes of what was to come, was Tom Stoppard. Years later, in his play *Professional Foul*, Tom managed a marvellous send-up of tabloid sports reporters. He was the Colmans-keen wicket-keeper of our *Evening World*'s midweek XI, and I am always pleased when he tosses cricket metaphors into his plays. When the *World* folded, Tom was interviewed for a job by Charles Wintour, editor of the London *Evening Standard*. What were his special interests, asked Wintour. 'Politics', said Tom. 'Okay: who,' asked Wintour, 'is the current Home Secretary?' Said Tom, 'I said I was interested; I didn't say I was obsessed'. He didn't get the job.

Not unlike that story of another old friend, Andy Mulligan. When Andy, already scrum-half for Ireland and the British Lions, came over to London to get a job, one interviewing chairman in the City asked Andy at the end of their chat: 'By the way, what religion are you, Mulligan?' Andy smiled sweetly at the chairman: 'That depends, sir', he said, 'on what religion you have in mind'.

Another Bristol buddy from those thirsty recuperative evenings at the Gaiety was Charlie Wilson, a Scot who was the West Country stringer for the *News Chronicle*. Even then Charlie knew the business inside out, and was as brusquely kind and encouraging to me then as he was to be when editor, successively, of the *Daily Mail*, the Scottish *Sunday Standard* and – no less – *The Times*.

One day-off from Ernie's paper-swamped sweatshop of a subs' table, Charlie suggested I accompany him and our 'crime' man, George Gordon (now the *Daily Mail*'s US correspondent) to cover a suspected murder over Bath way. Apparently, the teenage daughter of a gardener at some big country-house institution had been missing for a few days and the police, fearing foul play, were dragging the lake. At Stroud, Hereford, or Guildford, a real murder had not entered my ken. The scene was morbidly exciting, and I looked on as my two seniors interviewed various people, from chief suspects to Chief Constables. The frogmen bobbed up for lunch with no clues, let alone bodies. George said he had telephoned through his piece for our lunchtime edition, and that he and Charlie were going down to the pub. If I wanted, I could hold the fort at the scene and, if any further statements or developments popped up, I could phone the office from the big house for the 2pm edition. 'Sure, any colour, anything new. . .,' said George, and he and Charlie sloped off. This was too good a chance to miss. I sat in the sun in Capability Brown's parkland and let it flow. My first murder story. . . .

At 1.50, I picked up the phone in the hall of the mansion, asked for 'Copy', and prepared to dictate a new intro to the 'Bath Murder story. . . .' I had no sooner been connected to the copytakers, when George came back, breathless. 'Are you through to the office?' 'Yes.' He snatched the phone and began dictation, 'Bath Murder. New Intro. This supersedes all previous copy, right? Begins, "Somerset Police this afternoon called off their two-day murder enquiries when missing 17-year old schoolgirl, Carla Kington, was found safe and well in the London flat of a former school-friend. . .".'

George expertly finished topping and tailing the story and hung up. I was still holding my notebook and my 'colour' story for the 2pm edition. 'What were you going to put over?' said George, grabbing it, and reading: 'In my opinion, there is no doubt at all that the gardener did it. . . .'

It really was time to go to Africa.

\*     \*     \*

Only Africa would do on account of the unvirginal Virginia. I had met her in London on occasional sorties when I had slept on the floor of the ground-floor bedsit rented by two pals from Stroud days, Mike Barnes and John England.

Virginia was a white-tribeswoman from what was then still racist Southern Rhodesia. So she was dominant with it. She had a bonily welcoming, slender figure and a bob of corn-coloured hair which she washed unfailingly twice a day to rinse clear the grime of London. She looked like Hollywood's June Allyson. She was over for a year 'doing Europe' but would soon be going back to 'Godzone country', and she couldn't wait. She had none of the voluptuous 'give' and generosity of my gentle Beryl, but her own hard-edged perception of her worldly-wise, white colonial worth had me obsessed, and straining with a starting-gate eagerness for more of the sexual favours she rationed with prim relish. Although, in fairness, when she did decide, very occasionally and probably after too many Babychams, to ignore the ration-coupons 'just this once, Frankie, so don't take advantage', she undid her own bra in a businesslike way and proved to be as enthusiastic a learner as I was. She came down to Bristol a few times as the day approached when she was due to sail home. And on the last occasion she promised that she would marry me if I proved my passion by turning up on her father's doorstep in Africa.

It must have been the autumn of 1961 when I saw her off at Southampton on a Union Castle liner. I said I'd see her in Rhodesia. She gave me a dismissive look and said she didn't believe a word of it. But as it happened, I had already planned it, accepting a free flight in return for a job on the Salisbury evening paper, *The Standard*.

My headlong determination over Virginia would certainly have been extra-charged by the rumours that the *Evening World* was to close shortly, and also because at this time Uncle John was killed in a road accident. The shock of it threw me completely. He was working then at the RAF station at Hartlebury in Worcestershire. He was waiting by a bus-stop just outside the camp, when a friend's car stopped on the opposite side of the road and offered him a lift. Without a thought he dashed across and – whoomph! – straight into an oncoming car. It was instantaneous, and almost as stunning to everyone else. Mum and Dad were still tearful when they bought me a farewell supper at the Cumberland, Marble Arch, and next morning saw me off from the couple of Nissen huts which then comprised Heathrow airport. I arrived in Salisbury in good time to catch a train to the coastal port of Beira in Mozambique to await Virginia's arrival. Christmas was coming. We would have a white wedding to celebrate it.

As she walked, laughingly and lovingly, down the gangplank on the arm of a uniformed purser-type of berk, she saw me and the colonial porcelain of her face assumed a sneer. 'I'm in love. Get lost', she said.

Lost I had certainly got. Percy the Purser drove her off in something swish, and I caught the train back inland to begin my subbing shift in Salisbury. It was my first Christmas away from home. I had pledged two more, the length of contract − at the end of which I would be deemed to have paid back my free fare. I was determined not to stay that long. I immediately fell into what officialdom is pleased to call 'wrong company'.

White Rhodesians lived the selfish life of Reilly in a beguilingly perfect climate. They did not know it then, but they had just been rumbled by the world − as South Africa, their jackbooted neighbours, were to be after them. The lazy, leisure, houseboy-bullying, sun-blessed suburban whites of Salisbury's residential areas like Avondale, Borrowdale, and Preston Park gave themselves a string of public holidays through the year. The particularly long weekend after Christmas coincided with festivities to mark the reopening of two or three 'public' swimming pools in the city suburbs after their closure for a couple of months for cleaning and repainting. Tradition was for the pools to be re-opened on the bank holiday at midnight, for which all the young white bloods would queue with jostling jollity after their breifleis barbecues to see who would be first in the water. The *Rhodesia Herald* always front-paged the pic of the opening dive.

I had soon made, for me, a daring contact with a small,

multi-racial band of (theoretically, at least) furtive freedom-fighting students from the local university who sat at the feet of the courageous and honest lecturer in English, Dr Terence Ranger. He read the *Guardian Weekly*, and so the establishment thought him a Red. One student, pottering in the Government records office, came across a Thirties bylaw which stated that only residents of two years' standing could use the pools. Of course, that assumed white residents only – an assumption so obvious that the bylaw neglected to say so. Aye aye, we thought – and lobbied a handful of brave black houseboys, nannies, and gardeners who had lived for more than two years in their shaming little dog-kennel huts at the bottom of the garden in each of the whites' lush, lawned bungalows. They agreed to get early in the front of each queue at the midnight swimming pool revels. It was extremely brave and I wondered if their nerve would hold.

Earlier that evening I had a job. As well as my contracted subbing shifts, I was getting some pin money whenever possible by writing bits for the local daily, *The Herald*. I had also begun sending the occasional bits of unprintable, anarchistic waffle back to Fleet Street in airmail envelopes. I saw myself as the conscience of Sir Roy Welensky, the white Prime Minister. He was not aware of it. I earned enough to get some business cards printed – 'Francis V. Keating: African Affairs Specialist'.

Anyway, that night a European touring company was playing a few days at the city's biggest cinema: Luisillo and his Spanish Dance Theatre. The *Herald* booked me to do a par or two for their gossip column. There were about 20 of them – a handful of sallow, tight-trousered men, including the disdainful, pouting, small-arsed leader, Luisillo, and a chorus of twirling, skirt-swirling, sole-stamping, soulful Latin lovelies. Sensational stuff.

By the end of her first number, I was irretrievably in love with the lead singer, Maria Vivo. Tall, haughty, noble nosed, kestrel eyed, spark-heeled, finger-clicking good. After the show, this tremulous colonial Dempster conned an introduction – for an interview – with this celestial, castaneting crumpet. And later, si, si, she would come for a midnight swim, if some of the other members of the troupe would like to accompany her. The interview was conducted through a wardrobe mistress interpreter.

We got late-ish to the local pool. The African houseboys had done their stuff. The white laddies had gone potty at kaffirs' cheek. Fights broke out. We recited the bylaw to the police. They promptly reclosed the pool. A taxi was called for Maria and her friends. Before I, among others, was carted off to the cells for the night, Maria kissed me for being so brave or something – a whacking great, gargling, gum biting, tongue twirling, earth moving, Latin job which was overwhelmingly, mouth-wateringly pleasant, and must have helped me no end through the next day's hoohah. The upshot was that they threatened to revoke my work-permit if there was a repeat of such 'incitement to riot'. The bastards then kept the pools closed till they could write in a new 'whites-only' statute. The long-faced bores at the *Rhodesia Herald* said I could use their crayons again only if I took a Siberian attachment to the *Bulawayo Chronicle* to sub the weather forecast and fatstock prices.

But 'Maria, Maria, I've just met a girl named Maria'. The lovesick drooler went down the Gwelo road to Bulawayo with a grin. After Salisbury, Luisillo's next stop was the quaint little two-horse town. Each night I sat in the stalls, captivated by Maria. Stagedoor Frankie would send in a posy, his card arranged in the leaves. She certainly recognized me, and seemed to enjoy the attentions in a distant sort of way. When she saw me in the foyer of her hotel, she and her chattering mates would giggle at me and wave; I left letters in the reception pigeonhole where she kept her hotel key. When I saw the coach off to continue their tour in South Africa, Maria made a point of coming across to give me another sensational kiss.

So I robbed a bank. I had £87 in my account at the

Standard Bank. For £5 each I bribed two fellow bums on the *Chronicle*, and at precisely the same time in the next day's lunch-hour we each presented a cheque to different tellers for £85. It worked. Eighty-five times three, minus 10 equals £245. I sold my Burton's suit and set off next day, thumbing down the Johannesburg road. I arrived to see Maria's last show, and then I hitched on to Durban. She looked worried for me when I presented myself outside the stage door in West Street. But she took my posy and kissed my cheek. I made Cape Town in time for their first night. I saw every show, including matinées. The other dancers, as they stamped and skirled, would look out for me and sometimes, laughingly and brazenly, shout 'Franco! Franco!' in time to their heel stamping.

At the time a groupie's life seems one of bliss. I would follow Maria on her daytime shopping expeditions. If she caught my eye, she would wave, or sometimes tantalizingly shake her head. I was also humming the Carmen Jones number 'You go for me and I'm taboo, But if you're hard t'get I go for you'. By the telescope on top of Table Mountain, Luisillo looked at me with scorn – but, behind his back, Maria winked and blew me a kiss. Oh, rapture!

I went to the docks to say goodbye. I muttered something about seeing her in Madrid. The company's number had been printed in the programme. 'Si, si, Franco,' she said, and, laughing still, she wheeled away.

Cape Town, and the money was getting low. I set out for Cairo that very afternoon. I went back through Rhodesia in disguise, furtively sold a watch and camera and all my other odds and ends. Then, a final V-sign to the *Rhodesia Herald*, and the Great North Road by rule of thumb.

I was beaten up by a black man in Lusaka; had a crewcut in Broken Hill; saw a leopard near Tunduma and just stood stock still, petrified, as it loped past; stayed with the White Fathers in Serenje, and did some gardening jobs for the nuns in Dar-es-Salaam. I sold a few bits of 'sources-close-to-Westminster' piffle in Nairobi; perched on the back of a lorry through Garissa; and got a lift on a camel to Beles Gogani.

I had £39 left when the rains of 1963 cut me off at Kismayu on the coast of Somalia. I kept humming 'Maria, Maria', as well as that defiant number from Carmen Jones. Rico's Bar, where I had a mattress on the roof, needed their money. I found myself playing chess with someone in the Italian consulate, and the good soul wangled me an appointment with the chief engineer of an Eyetie boat, the *Frigo Afrique*, which was being laden to the gunwales with green, hard bananas. They took every penny and agreed to take me back to Europe.

I ran down the gangplank at Civitavecchia, the port for Rome, and kissed the ground like a Pope. The Catholic Murphia can be useful. I went at once to the English College where an old school friend was studying theology, but was not too honest to deny me a furtive free phone call. Long distance to Madrid, and pronto! This is an emergency. 'Ello darlin, I'm back and on my way!' Soon afterwards I was kneeling in front of Our Lady's statue in the basilica of Santa Maria Maggiore and weeping real whopping, cheek-sopping tears. Maria had handed the phone to someone who spoke English. 'Maria thinks you should know', said the cold, precise voice, 'that she has been married for years to Luisillo'.

# 8

The *Guardian* had moved from Manchester to London, and while not for a moment admitting the drivel I had sent them from Africa in those flimsy airmail envelopes had been any good, they hinted that if I hung around there might be a desk job in London, if and when the foreign desk moved from the north. Once I had paid back £25 to the Foreign Office (for which I had hocked my passport in order to get home from Rome), I was thinking I might become the next James Cameron or René Cutforth.

As it happened, no immediate call came from the *Guardian*. I had a summer doing holiday shifts on the *Gloucester Citizen*, living with Mum and Dad and playing a great deal of cricket on every mown plateau above and below the nooks of my blissful Stroud valleys. Then, for a soccer season I was, grandly, Sports Editor of the *Slough Observer*. I enjoyed it all right but sports writing did not seem 'me', even though I wrote massively long critiques every week about the chronic lack of peripheral vision and the wall-pass ineptitude of Slough Town FC, which toiled away in the Athenian League.

The *Guardian*, bless them, had not forgotten me, and I joined their London subs' table at last and at £25 a week, rising by a guinea after a year's satisfactory service. At once I felt part of a family. We were a happy group of late-night laddoes. I stayed long enough, just, to get my extra guinea – and then, out of the blue, having with ludicrous optimism answered a fancy, half-page advertisement in the *Telegraph* for a producer in ITV's Outside Broadcasts department, I was called for interview next morning. Late-night sub-editors cannot readily knock-off and go straight to bed unless they get drunk very fast; they are too hyped up. So one knew the gentle unwinding of the early hours. I spent it that night before the interview in the *Guardian* office cobbling together a learned treatise on The Future of Television and Sports and Live Outside Broadcasts.

When I entered the boardroom for the interview, I handed the pretentious piffle to the panel chairman (who turned out to be the splendid, matey Ray Dicks) and boldly asked if he could get copies made for the rest of the interviewing bods. The long and the short is that it worked. At over three times the loot, I was suddenly ITV-Associated-Rediffusion's newly created Editor of Outside Broadcasts. With an office – and a secretary in an outer office. In fact, every corridor was positively frothing with crumpet. We were in the old Air Ministry building at the bottom of Kingsway, and my third-floor office was alongside the Heads of Drama and Light Entertainment, two marvellous old long-lunching coves. The former was Peter Willes, as camp as a bottle of coffee and with hilarious 'theat-ah' yarns coming out of his ears. The latter, Eric Maschwitz, wrote the wartime favourites: 'A Nightingale Sang in Berkeley Square' and 'These Foolish Things', and was married to Hermione Gingold. Eric wrote no end of musicals and revues. One nice little earner was *Goodnight Vienna*. Having finished in the West End it went on tour. Eric was driving up to town from his suburban mansion one evening when he noticed his play was on at the Lewisham Hippodrome. He popped in and asked the manager what business was like. 'About as well as you'd expect "Goodnight Lewisham" to be doing in Vienna', was the deadpan reply.

It was said that Eric had been known to visit his other plays just as the curtain was about to come down, stand at the back of the stalls and start cheering and shouting 'Author! Author!' so enthusiastically that the audience would take it up – at which Eric would whip down to the stage and take a bow. I've no evidence for that myself – but certainly have for the similar habit of my immediate boss and executive producer, Elkan Allan (who was very kind to me, when he could have fired me daily as a nincompoop when I first arrived). When there was a lull in conversation in his office, Elkan would blithely pick up his telephone and call, say, the VIP Lounge at Heathrow, or Earls Court if there was an important show on, or the Ritz – and ask, 'Could you please urgently page Mr Elkan Allan, the TV producer, and ask him to telephone his office most urgently'. Said Elkan, 'It pays to get your name about in this game'.

The man who nursed me best and most generously, however, was the Outside Broadcasts senior director, Grahame Turner, an exhilarating worrypot driven by his manifest insecurities. He was a darer, too, and an enemy of the dreary conformity which, often with good reason, he sensed all around him. His two favourite phrases, which he alternated almost on principle, were 'Let's have a ruddy go, boy!' and 'You don't think you can possibly get away with that, do you?' We laughed together round the world, crazy journeys punctuated by gloriously blazing rows.

Grahame had started at 15 as a BBC teaboy. On his first day, at Bush House, he was in a small studio clearing up some cups when the wall began to talk, as they do in wireless studios. 'Is the announcer there?' the voice boomingly enquired from Control somewhere in the bowels of the building. 'Is anybody there?' asked the fretful voice. Grahame tremulously murmered, 'Yes, sir, me'. 'Well, see that bulb on the table next to the microphone?' 'Yes, sir', quavered the kid. 'Well, when the bulb turns red, I want you to say into the microphone, "This is the General Overseas

Service of the BBC", right?' 'Right, sir'. And, Grahame swears, he did, too. No wonder he sailed up the ladder from then on.

Which is more than I looked like doing. 'Right, lad', said crisp, businesslike Commander Robert Everett, Head of Programme Planning, 'the Olympic Games are coming up in a few weeks, right? Why don't you and Turner cover 'em, what?' The Tokyo Olympics of 1964 were the pioneering 'Satellite Olympics'. I knew nothing about satellites. The first had winged into space only months before. We had to make do.

Us v the BBC. It was no contest. We were given a matchbox-tiny dungeon near the Middlesex Hospital. There were about 20 of us, mostly light-entertainment bods whistling Russ Conway and very browned off. We had even less clue than budget. In fact, we began breakfast television. Though no one had made the remotest plans for relaying the results across the world. I suppose it was my job. The Games began. 'Give me some results of the heats of the 100 yards', shouted Turner. I put my raincoat on and belted 100 metres to the Cleveland Street corner up the road and jogged desperately on the spot waiting for the first edition of the *Evening Standard*. Then I hared back, shamelessly ripping out the stop-press tabulated, early-morning results, and plonked them breathlessly in front of our long-suffering genius presenter, Kent Walton.

How he put up with it I will never know, but Kent has ever remained, for me, the most troubadorious old trouper of all time. After that he stuck to wrestling commentaries, and who can blame him?

We worked manically round the clock, and slept on the floor. We would watch the suave BBC transmissions and swoon at their competence and calm. Peter Dimmock was arrogantly twirling his moustache, Coleman was beginning his years of pioneering brilliance. We hadn't a hope.

At dead of night, before dawn on October 14, 1964, I blearily opened one eye as I lay there on the floor; slowly it

panned upwards – ever upwards – the full length of the
longest legs in ITV. Under her new-fangled mini-skirt pelmet
Suzanne's little V of her knicker-crotch looked as high and
distant as a crow's nest ensign atop the mainsail. Suzanne
was Turner's PA, and she was waking me up. She and
Graham had been listening to the BBC World Service.
'C'mon, get up! She's done it, Mary's gone and bloody well
done it! Get up!'

So I sat up, lit a Gauloise, and said 'Hooray – let's think
what we do now!' Certainly something big. For Mary Rand
had not only won the long jump, but had broken the world
record.

We were on the air in just an hour or two. We had no
sound commentary, just a few fuzzy monochrome pictures.
What the ruddy hell do we do? Coleman and Co. would
have it taped.

We hired a car and sent it into the Home Counties to
fetch Mary's infant daughter, Alison, who was being baby-
sat for the month by the former Olympic athlete Diane
Leather. Reluctantly, Diane agreed to come to the studio.
To this day I send her kisses.

What an Olympics that was. We did the same sort of
stuntish thing when Lynn leapt, when Mrs Ken Matthews
tumbled on to the track to greet her walking chap, and
when Ann Packer fell into Robbie Brightwell's arms at the
end of the mesmerizing, first-ever women's 800 metres final.
But we ITV-ites were first with Alison Rand. Oh no, you
can't take that away from me.

Diane and the mewling Alison came out of the panting
minicab. The show was almost over. The BBC had done a
sterling job from Tokyo. But an engineering genius had
somehow kept us in landline contact. We put a mike to the
mite. 'Hello, Alison', squeaked a breathless Mary far away.
'Hello, mummy', mumbled the woebegone tot in Diane's
arms. The hundred or so ITV viewers had only time for a
sigh before the pips went and Alison bawled.

Mary and Tokyo were cut off – and we still had at least

two minutes to the end of the programme. The beaming, brilliant, Kent was doing his best above the bawls to pour balm and for the umpteenth time brag about another British gold medal. But even he was stretching things. I carefully placed the braying brat on the concrete floor. In the excitement of the morning I had forgotten to purloin the *Evening Standard* stop-press results. On my knees in the tiny studio space, amid near-panic, I scribbled out a note to Kent on a piece of paper and thrust it under his nose as he played for time.

It was a good wheeze – especially as I was throttle-stifling young Alison Rand at the time, rolling her over on the floor to keep her quiet. My note to Kent said: 'Two minutes to titles. Close the show by pacing out – VERY SLOWLY – Mary's new world record of 22ft 2¼in across the studio floor, to give the folks some idea of what she has achieved – i.e. walk 22-and-a-bit paces'.

Good old Kent, ever the pro, got up from his desk. As if we'd rehearsed it for a week, the grand old trouper slid into the routine, smiling and fluently waffling about the great feat (while the tyro producer and the babe writhed at his feet) that had been logged in all-time history that very morning.

I grabbed dear, darling little Alison and rolled over on the concrete floor like I was a scrum-half waiting for my forwards to come and save me with the ball embraced lovingly. Kent stepped adroitly over me as he continued his crablike shuffle sideways, his beetle-browed gaze never shifting from the tracking camera as he expansively marvelled at the Somerset girl's feat and counted out the yardage. At about 19ft 11in, Kent and our tracking cameraman simultaneously hit the wall. Clang.

\*   \*   \*

Peter Morley had brilliantly planned it, Graham's expertise backed it up, the company obviously threw money at it, so we did resplendently at covering the funeral of Winston

Churchill. Certainly we matched the BBC for once, in verve as well as solemnity. They had their Richard Dimbleby still – but Peter called up the likes of Laurence Olivier and Richard Burton to read the speeches and Graham organized the OB shots of London's dockland lowering its cranes, and the funeral train wending its way over the points and intersections out of Waterloo to the burial-home in Oxfordshire. Both were utterly stupendous shots and Graham was very rightly proud of the statuette he was awarded for them. As we all were for the many awards the superlatively good and 'soberly imaginative' Morley won. I would have loved to have worked for him more.

Meanwhile, there was the lovely grot of which I had to take full-ish charge. Surely memories are made of more than this? Idling away a full 20 minutes at Moor Park golf-course, looking at nothing but monochrome landscapes because no golfer was in view of our little three-camera scanner . . . or, at our first-ever evening soccer recording, dropping Austria's final, winning goal at Wembley on the cutting-room floor and gormlessly sellotaping on two interminable National Anthems instead. Most of the nation probably felt they had snoozed off. There was also the time the network pulled the plug on the crucial last over of the Gillette Cup final at Lord's (ITV cricket still has to get over the shame of that) . . . and the occasion when we unconcernedly held a full frontal close-up of a young gymnast changing vests at the Albert Hall; only when we panned down did we realise 'he' was a she. (If the non-existent Austrian goal was the nadir, you might call that the 'Nadia'.)

We were responsible for ITV's only go at covering Wimbledon. It had been a BBC preserve since its first ever Head of Sport, Gerald Cook, had written to SW19 in 1936: 'Could we try television next year? We would be tackling unknown quantities – we are not sure whether we can achieve yet a satisfactory picture link between Wimbledon and the Alexandra Palace, as the new apparatus has not been used over such distance before. . . .'

With a day to go to the 1937 Wimbledon, the picture was not working – till it was found that (as a BBC memo said) the 'cause of interference with the link from Wimbledon has been traced to Hornsey Central Hospital. They have now agreed so far as possible to suspend Diathermy activities during the times we are transmitting tennis pictures'. So history was made. The first match seen was between Bunny Austin and George Rogers. Freddie Grisewood was commentator, and the *Daily Telegraph* reporter said '. . . televiewers could observe every movement of the players; even the passage of the marks of the lawnmower over the grass was distinctly visible'.

ITV was just as green when we pitched our tents on that hill above the Centre Court in 1965. We looked like the bedraggled English before Agincourt compared with the BBC's 'village' next door. In the quarter finals that year, the defending champion Roy Emerson crashed into a netpost while trying to retrieve a dinky little dropshot from his opponent. He twisted a knee and we lathered ourselves up into speculation about who might now win the tournament. I decided to set up a debate on the matter there and then. I raced to the Press tent to grab a few sages. In my rush, I neglected to notice they were sozzled. For the few statutory guineas they agreed to stagger up to our makeshift, marqueed studio. Okay, cue, and I asked Sage No 1 if, in view of Emerson's accident, he now thought the tournament was wide open? 'Old boy', he slurred intimately, first to me, then the camera, 'I think you can safely say that the Wimbledon Championships of 1965 are as wide open as [Miss So-and-So's] delicious long legs!' (He named a very famous Italian film star of the time). Fade out.

I remained to do one very good turn in my decade as Editor of Outside Balls-Ups. Not sporting this one. Every year, the day after the BBC had their annual whopping audience for the Miss World contest, the envious ITV bosses

would tell me to invent our own beauty contest to try and
match the appeal of the sequin-and-swimsuit job at the
Lyceum.

For years, such things as Miss Million Dollar Legs, or
Miss International Cover Girl, were down to me. They were
never much cop. We got most of the girls from London
modelling agencies. It helped if they originated from
somewhere abroad, so as to spice up our show with an
international flavour. At lunch-time on the day of one such
contest, the agency rang with a message to say that 'Miss
Israel' had fallen sick and would not be competing. I asked
if they had a spare. The girl on the switchboard said they
were all out at lunch. 'What's that accent of yours?' I asked
her, sensing a trace of New Zealand or Australia. 'You'll
do', I said, 'get a taxi round here immediately'. She did. She
had a lovely figure, to be sure. But also a very, very
noticeable hare-lip. But this was no time for being fanciful
about facial fissures. We entered her as 'Miss Antipodean'.
She won Third Prize – which was a top modelling course in
Paris!

Another time – was it perhaps Miss Mini-skirt of 1966? –
I spent the rehearsals making friends with a cracking little
Cockney competitor in the finals at the Royal Lancaster
Hotel. We wuz robbed. She was eliminated in the first
batch. We danced the night away, and then hand in hand
we lolled down the Bayswater Road to my flat. At last it
was to be all right on the night. That afternoon I'd bought a
bottle of brandy and a smoochy record. And sprinkled All
Spice all over to freshen my musty pit in Holland Park. We
canoodled up the stairs. Cuddles over coffee. She kicked off
her shoes. Bra off with the brandies. Home and not at all
dry. I flicked off the light switch.

'Ere!' she exclaimed, seeing the grey light of dawn
fingering the window pane, 'what's the bleedin' time?' She
was up and away – 'I've gotta get the first bleedin' train
from Victoria. I'm in the 'eats of Miss Brighton Belle first
thing this mornin'!'

\* \* \*

Like her, we all had days which we just couldn't wait to start. Life was full of such days for me. Let's just take one at random to give you the picture. Say, May 29, 1968, perhaps. Random? May 29, 1968. It was a day of days. I was 30. Youth still so clear-eyed, fizzing, full to the brim and fancy-free that we took it all in our stride at the time. Yet, inside a handful of hours, it was the time of our lives – the day of Sir Matt and Sir Ivor, of Best and Guest and Lester. It was a sweltering belter of a heatwave Derby Day up on the Downs, with the classic of Classics won by, till then, the horse and jockey of the century. And in the sultry, thunderous Wembley evening, Man United won the European Cup for their manager to dedicate to his heavenly Busby Babes.

First, early to the Downs alongside peak-capped chauffeur, washed and brushed-up and very much Mossed and Brossed, for one of my jobs was to liaise with the steward of the Royal Box, just above the winner's enclosure. His name was Bernard Marmaduke Fitzalan Howard (plus a few others besides) and he was premier duke of all England and lord high marshal of ceremonial; and he had very little sniffing time, I'm telling you, for a Moss Bros oik with cumbersome TV cameras keen for prying shots of Royalty at gambling. He had a rubicund, pug-doggy face, and he had crossed garters with me at other events through the year. 'Get lor-st, sonny, and take those wires with you', was the tenor of his growl as he essayed a scuff at our precious cables with his bespoke little patent-leather feet.

Even Marmaduke left us alone to cover the race itself. It was like an oven as the sun hammered down, and the knife-sharp anticipation rose up to meet it. Sir Ivor was surely going to slay the bookies. We had crossed the water a few weeks earlier to film the favourite at work on Vincent O'Brien's blissful gallops at Ballydoyle, and not one of our crew had returned home without putting his house on the dramatic, wild-eyed bay with the spectacular turn of foot. We were surer for Vincent telling us he was hoping Piggott had bagged the bridle for the up-coming biggie and more so when Sir Ivor's owner, Raymond Guest, who was US Ambassador to Dublin, told us that over a year before he had plonked down £550 at 100–1 with William Hill. The engaging Guest was furious that he would miss Epsom on the 29th because he had to attend the Wexford unveiling of Ireland's Kennedy Memorial, but when the race got under way I thought it was as well he was absent because his horse was not showing at all.

The field careered like a huge colourful float down the hill to Tattenham Corner with never a mention of Sir Ivor. Round the bend and the long climb for home and still nowhere to be seen. Piggott was boxed in with the rear bunch that were already up in their stirrups peering into the distance to see who would win it, when, all of a sudden, whoosh! I've never seen such acceleration before or since. In chocolate-and-powder-blue colours resembling an old-style rugby strip, Piggott launched himself out of the scrum as the horse went for the line in a way that still defies description. It was truly stunning – Piggott still reckons Sir Ivor his most wondrous beast – and for the first and only time I threw my top hat in the air.

I had to retrieve it soon enough, for the day was only half over. Hotfoot to Wembley. No way, though, that United could eclipse Sir Ivor. Wanna bet?

United's progress to the final – an English club's first – had captivated all football, for it was surely Busby's last throw, exactly a decade since his finest side was wiped out in the slush of the Munich runway. But, like earlier in the afternoon, the early signals were unpromising. It was bitty, neurotic stuff, with United petrified of the onus on them and Benfica narrow-eyed and oblivious to romance.

The fouls went tit for tat. Eusebio did slap Stepney's crossbar with a screamer, but Best was being chopped off at the shins. Stiles was replying in kind, and Charlton was frowning and fretting, despite scoring the opening goal. The attrition wore on, the vast throng almost accepting the inevitability of Benfica's equalizer and, as soon as it came, only Stepney's galumphing last-ditch flop when Eusebio was clear put the thing into extra-time. That was my cue. And the game's for immortality. And the moon's, which now was suddenly raging down above the floodlit beacons. And now United began to play.

I was still in my Epsom topper and tails; I had conned my way round the touchline – no cop man enough to challenge my nobby outfit – so I was crouched immediately behind Stepney's net at the tunnel end. Extra time meant we could steal a march on the BBC and, at the final whistle, grab anyone to interview on the pitch and go live into News at Ten. So the climactic faraway flurry of goals by the mesmeric Best, bounding Kidd and bald, brave, blubbing Bobby were only 'sensed' from my end. But I saw in close-up how the prowling Stepney, edgy till the very end, was crying too, and then, with the tumult quite overpowering, we got our handheld shots and interviews at the final whistle as Bobby fell weeping onto old Matt's chest, the two survivors of Munich. (You can see me in some of the press pictures, on the pitch in full finery.)

Afterwards we searched and searched for Bobby. The celebrations were in full swing and he was nowhere to be found. We discovered him at last, being consoled by Pat Crerand, sitting in the litter and jetsam under the grandstand itself, still in tears. We crept away, for there was another party that my gear might gatecrash to top and tail this day of days. It was already in full swing at the great room in the Savoy. Raymond Guest had already flown in, bringing with him Teddy Kennedy and the Irish President, Eamon de Valera, no less.

What a hooley. Sir Ivor wasn't there, mind, nor was William Hill – but everyone else was. And as the early hours got later, the double celebration got wilder. Racing and football came together – and there drinking alone at a table was one Irishman I recognized. It was George Best, waiflike, winding down, and sadly sullen amid the crazy carnival. He shrugged off congratulations with a forced, dismissive smile. But he accepted a drink, and we left him to his moping. It was some 10 years later that he explained to me how that night had demonstrated to him that he was no longer part of his team's laughter or tears. 'I was there', he said, 'but I knew I didn't belong'. All around George that night had been men and women celebrating the achievement of their lifetime's work and determination. 'It should have been that for me, too. Instead, although I couldn't quite phrase it at the time, it was the beginning of the end for me'.

May 29, 1968 was in a way, I suppose, the beginning of the end for a whole generation – and come to think of it, I bet old Bernard Marmaduke went to bed that night at Arundel quite pleased about that at least.

\* \* \*

The end of this chapter had begun for me as well. It was a good way to go. Mainly thanks to Grahame's verve, we won awards for programmes we did on Somerset Maugham (*The Writer Lately Dead*), and the terrible floods in Florence (*Italy My Italy*). When Sir Laurence read my script, full of corny 'testaments to human grandeur', which he made seem tremendous, at the run-through he said to me, 'Which way d'you want me to piddle off, old boy, camera-left or camera-right?' Not that it mattered, but 'Camera-right, please, Sir Laurence', I said, decisively. Hey Mum, I've directed Sir Larry!

Often, Grahame and I just went to 'observe', to assess the (often remote) possibility of covering an event in the future. Thus, with equal facility, we might on a whim have ordered a chauffeured limousine to drive us to Stratford to take in lunch and the matinée, or nip over the pond, first class, to see Muhammad Ali fight when he was in his stupendous prime before they banned him as a draft-dodger.

It was too good to last. Nor did it. First Grahame and I

fell out. Towards the end of the 1960s, we were filming athletes training at altitude in the Pyrenees. One evening after the shoot and before supper, Grahame burst matily into my room. I was supine on my bed with no trousers on. Grahame's luscious-legged PA, Suzanne, was next to me in all her glory. Nothing was actually happening. But, in TV especially, bosses take a totally irrational and proprietorial interest in their (always female, and usually beautiful) PA's welfare: that is, if the boss himself can't have her, nobody else can. We wrapped up pronto, and travelled home in a seething silence. It was the end of a beautiful friendship in more ways than one.

We got back to find that Rediffusion had lost its contract. The London midweek company would now be Thames, full of keen-eyed accountants and new-broom budget officers. Grahame was made Head of OBs. I was first officially called Head of Special Projects and then – as there did not seem to be any, not special ones, at least – I was shunted to Current Affairs, in effect the early evening show called *Today*. The old, laughing OB team did come together just one more time – in Mexico for Pelé's beguiling World Cup in 1970. Which was where, almost by a fluke, I began writing on sport.

# 9

Not that I had completely lost the habit of writing during my years in television. For many of these, the loafer in me wangled nine-month contracts. This allowed me summer days a-cricketing, as well as hunks of time in France. In the early and middle 1960s, two General Elections hurried upon each other. In both I enjoyed doing what I could to help our old Stroud MP, Ben Parkin, who was now defending a precious majority in North Paddington. (Dad came up for a couple of weekends, tweed jacket and mud on his boots, and at the Cross in Harrow Road gave me just a glimpse, but a warm one, of his old trenchancy on top of a stepladder which he had learned all those years ago a mile or two away at Speakers' Corner). Ben safely kept the seat, both times with increased majorities. One night, licking envelopes at Ben's HQ in Chippenham Road, I met one of Ben's workers, Stella, a rotund, elderly barrel of mirth with a broad French accent who was married to Teddy, an incorrigible Polish chef not as dedicated as his wife to the Labour Party. 'Hey, Frankie,' he would say, 'c'mon, we go drink Bayswater [which he pronounced Byze-watt-tor]; bew-tee-foo girls Bayswater, no?'

Stella worked winters on the clock counter at Selfridges,

and Ted, on and off, for all the top restaurants in town. Summers they would spend in the tumbledown old French château Stella was left by her father. Not the deep south, quite, but certainly the warm – perched high on a plump wooded tump in the sublime Lot valley, well off the tourist beat of the Dordogne. Ben had holidayed there a couple of times. He suggested I come too.

It became an annual trip. More like a ritual. As soon as the midnight boat-train eased away from Victoria, I would begin growing my beard. Duty-free would stock me with untipped Gitanes. A first-light taxi across Paris for a greedy breakfast at Gare Austerlitz and the purchase of a few foolscap exercise-books. After the Biarritz flier passed Brive, give it quarter-of-an-hour till you passed a string of waterfalls, which meant it was time to begin getting your gear together. Out at the 10-second stop at Gourdon, where Michel from the Beauregard bar would be waiting with his rickety Maigret Citroën – and after a relaxing, Pastis-swallowing first day, I would be up with the cockerels and at the end of the garden, deliberately writing 'Chapter One' or 'Act 1, Scene 1' on the first page of my first exercise book. Six weeks or so later, a heavily bearded pard would be jauntily striding across the concourse at Victoria Station – pack of 200 Gitane under one arm, completed longhand manuscripts under the other. The Novelist's Return. Every time I was convinced this was It and A Major Talent would be hailed by the TLS in no time at all. The following week at TV House, Kingsway, secretaries would fretfully be typing up the masterpieces – pointedly and wearily sighing as they did so in the places where they were definitely meant either to laugh or to cry, but not to sigh, dammit. Ah, well: they are all still in a drawer somewhere.

But the fun, and the sun – and Stella's cooking. (Teddy never went near the stove on his holidays: he was permanently i/c the booze cupboard, and was sometimes to be found contentedly asleep inside it). I wrote like an idiot by day. Girlfriends from London would visit; or, mostly, girls I wanted to know better; 'my French summer pad' was a good chat-up ploy in a Kensington bistro in winter. Some even turned up, intrigued – 'just passing through' – with their wretchedly protective boyfriends, who were invariably assholes. Many were called and a few even succumbed for a brief interlude – till our evening drinking and the stench of the 'chemical' loo drove them away. Anyway, at times, Château Veyrières seemed like an annexe of TV House.

Outside TV, my best friend of those happily hectic times was Tony Lias, with the gaunt good looks of a rangy, unkempt Dirk Bogarde, and a devotion to and appetite for drink and redheaded voluptuaries ('haven't you noticed, their very smell is enticingly different down there, old chap?'). I met Tony on my very first evening as a timorous sub on the *Guardian* in 1963. He took one distasteful look at me, in my Burton's suit and my hair plastered down and parting-straight. Within five minutes he had scribbled on a piece of paper and passed to me this – asking, deadpan, if I could come up with a 30-point Bodoni Bold headline for it across four columns:


'You sit upon the Foreign Deske
In a suit – My God, how peske!
Drip, I bet you smoke De Reske?'


(De Reske was a slim, cheap, unfashionable cigarette which they sold in those days in 'fives'.)

By midnight we had agreed to meet in the Anglesea – and from then on we were inseparable comrades for years. He was Oxford, had been commissioned in both the Army and RAF, was a published poet, a cricket nut (and an accurate out-swing bowler with a tutored, flowing action), and already a couple of times married. Most things that 'happened' to him were drink related, as they say. But everyone has to have a Lias at some stage in his development, and certainly Tony was mine. He taught me a lot – especially how to laugh at the nincompoop time-servers of 'authority'.

Like most poets who like to unwind with a drink after (or during; and then unwind again) composition, Lias regularly burned his literary efforts in exasperated disgust. But I have kept one which I liked, about cricket, and another, apt for those times of ours together, about women in the morning rush-hour:

Girls decant from buses bright with rain,
Sleep on their faces like the sheen of apples
In a glass orchard, wink of a new coin.
No night-anxieties tug now at their nipples
Or trouble thighs forgetful of all sex.

For one brief hour they are not dangerous.

It is 10 years since I heard from Lias. On England's cricket tour to India in 1982, the office cabled me an urgent message at Bangalore to ring such-and-such a pile of numbers back in England and with the utmost urgency. I could only presume it was a sister with bad family news. As always from India it took an age to get through. Tony had obviously been having a-few-to-catch-up since he had read the *Guardian* that morning. I gathered through the incoherence that some metaphor I had used in my match report – say, 'the gnomic Fletcher, with the impudence of a front-garden friend of Snow White, danced out to drive', or some such drivel – had been first coined by Tony and he wanted payment for the line else he would sue.

From India, later, I dropped him a line – doubtless, pompous – with a few ideas for writing jobs, or whatever, which might possibly be up his street. On my return home, this 'Dear Frank' letter was waiting:

'Which direction is my signpost pointing in? I'm always

annoyed (though not unamused) when you keep asking what I'm "doing" about anything. Well, what do you *expect* me to be doing, old cock? And if I was perhaps doing it, are you sure you'd recognize it? So leaving my future choices and activities to me, what are YOU doing, old boy, old cock? Perhaps you could *send* me some notes on the self-abnegating, socially useful life? With some addenda on how to become a good Socialist? Or even a good Catholic?

'Meanwhile (while I wait for your guidance, I mean) I shall continue to dig up weeds and think what it is *best* for me to do. The trouble nowadays is that if one wished, say, to help other alcoholics in a more constructive way than spouting at AA meetings or handing out tea and biscuits, one would need a Ph.D. in Social Dynamics, or some such crap.

'One last question. If you were not paid a *salary* for what you are doing, would you consider yourself productive in, say, a Marxist sense? – Love, T'.

My early evening television show was presented by Eamonn Andrews, the one-time 'voice' of Sports Report that had so beguiled my Saturday tea-times when I was a boy. Dear Eamonn, the last time I saw him, just before his sudden death a few years ago, he was insisting that, no, he would wait his turn in the queue at Dublin Airport like everybody else (a back-log had set in due to fog) and he would not dream of preferential treatment from the Aer Lingus staff. No matter that he probably owned the airline. Nevertheless, it gave us our last few hours – nipping contentedly into our clink of duty-free – talking about his beloved boxing. The first world heavyweight fight he had seen was Marciano v Cockell, and invariably his tales just took it from there . . . dada, dada, dada, dedum, dee-diddly-dum, de-*dah*!

Sometimes after our early evening show, Eamonn would take one or two of us – his favourites like Andy Allan or David Boardman – for a meal (perhaps at Wheeler's in Ken High Street, or the 'big' Ark just nearby), and then back to his house south of the river for long late nights if Graine was in Dublin. Always boxing – and yarns about those taut romantic days of 'live wireless', when lines would go down from Highbury or wherever, leaving him to pad desperately. Eamonn would delight in his own mimicry of the Finnan-haddie cackle down his earphones of Angus McKay, his ferocious and famous producer, or the smoked-salmon smoothness of John Webster's reading of the results. Those evenings with Eamonn made us all little boys again.

One thing, mind you, I could not do – ever – was write a link for Eamonn in the show, which had a pot-pourri, magaziny format. Andy and David could knock them off in seconds; the pretentious poove of a pen-man in me had Eamonn trying to unscramble high-flown sub-Joycean Celtic cadences when all that was required was a link from, say, pollution problems in the Thames to an interview with the new Mayor of Lambeth.

Boardman was a pal in the cricket freemasonry. So was Robert Fleming, with whom I shared the high, wide and rickety flat in Holland Park for a dozen grand years of diverting bachelordom. Robert had been born in Australia, but of very English parents (thespians who had met on a colonial tour in the Casson-Thorndike caravan). They settled in the sun to bring up their baby to be as English as Eton: they sent him 'home' in his 20s, kitted out with everything necessary from a W1 tailor, an ice-pick sharp pukka accent (which reverted to raucous Oz only when he was appealing for lbw off his own bowling) and even membership of MCC. Robert was a Light-Ent director aspiring to less frivolous things when I overheard him in the club at TV House moaning about Graveney's recall at 40 to the England team. Narrow-eyed tenners were duly slapped down on the table – and we cabbed up to St John's Wood there and then, with Ray Dicks holding the stakes. I duly collected, of course, when Tom made his memorable, tear-stained 96 against Hall and Griffith, and Robert and I became friends for life.

He was a tall blond, his Trumper-trimmed and pomaded hair crinkled by the Sydney sun. He looked rather like a heavyweight Nicol Williamson on form in a cameo 'English' part. Robert introduced me to his 'Jolly Rogers' cricket team which toured every weekend all the most blissful village grounds of Sussex, Surrey and Kent – and also, in his Light-Ent capacity, to a string of long-leged, long-larynxed light-vocalist hopefuls looking for a chance on Opportunity Knocks. First thing most mornings, even if 'auditions' for length of leg and larynx had taken up much of the night, Robert and I would inevitably be 'on guard' for our ruthlessly contested squash match. At the top of the road, then seemingly unknown to anyone else, the GLC parks department rented a court for next to nuppence. For years the ferocity of our morning championship scarred the walls black and the air red with oaths. Our last match, for Holland Park's all-time title-of-titles in the early 1970s, ended bitterly, both of us realizing we had finally kicked the habit.

It was a dramatic withdrawal: 7–7 in the fifth and retching for breath. I went for the ultimate, unforgivable ploy – allowable only on this parquet-floored snakepit. Robert was in the very wind-up of his crucial service, when I croaked the command, 'Hold it!' He allowed the wretched rubber onion to bobble, unbouncing, to the floor and he turned his blood-shot eyes to mine, aggressively. 'I am not', I said as firmly as I could while attempting to focus my glare on his brow, 'I am not going to continue this match with you looking like that. You win, Bob ol' friend, I concede the game and set. Let's go and have a drink on it'.

'What do you mean, you swine?' he said through heaving gulps of breath.

'The last time', I lied, 'I beat someone with that blotchy, purply-mauve forehead I see on you, he died in the showers even before he had squeezed out his Vosene'.

'I don't believe you, you bastard!' he said. But the poor fellow's defiance lacked conviction.

'Be it on your own head and sickly brow', I told him, as

An obviously overtired Bollinger Bolshevik failing to get the joke of the best Prime Minister we never had. (*Colin Elsey, Colorsport*)

Guyana 1981: Just days before he died, English cricket's esteemed 'Colonel' Barrington explains the art of Mrs Malaprop to FK and Mike Gatting. (*Patrick Eagar*)

1984, with Bobby Charlton who could, as Geoffrey Green put it, 'billow an opponent's net as if a gale had struck it'. (*Jeff Goddard*)

Certainly England's most resplendent all-rounder. Ian Botham sets off from John O'Groats on the first of his stupendous charity walks in 1985. The joker on the right failed to make Wick, let alone Land's End. (*Adrian Murrell, Allsport*)

he turned to serve for the match. He ran not a step for either of my returns. I won 9–7. Game, set and match. And *finis*.

If Stephen Potter, onliest 'inventor' of gamesmanship, would have beamed approval at my ploy, it was only because I had been brought up in a hard school. David Miller, new chief sports correspondent of *The Times*, played a few squash games with me. He was just as much an unfit tub as I was – if anything, the beginnings of his beer-pot were more advanced than mine, and his general co-ordination, in modesty, less sharp. He would always wear, even in the hottest and most torrid of lost-set battles, a shrunken, creamy old Cambridge University sweater, to which he was entitled having won a Blue at soccer. David always beat me. Only after reading Potter did I discover why: 'At Oxford, though never a Blue, I used to wear a Blue's tie, particularly when playing games against nice men who knew I had no right to wear the honour. This simple trick, which is said by psychologists to induce the "pseudo-schizophrenic syndrome", or doubt, is most effective in moving ball-games'.

* * *

It was David Miller who encouraged me to have a real go at sportswriting. He was *The Sunday Telegraph*'s truculent soccer correspondent when I got to know him in the mid-60s. We had called him in once or twice when OBs needed some advice on tight-scripted footer matters. When the new OB team asked me to help out for a sabbatical month in Mexico for what turned out to be the last of the romantics' World Cups in 1970, David urged his friend, John Hennessy, sports editor of *The Times*, to use the odd bits from me. And so, I suppose, I caught the bug. I will be ever grateful to DM, not only for the introduction but for his guidance since. When I can get near his slipstream, that is.

Miller still lives life at his old-fashioned winger's lick. As John Moynihan once described playing with him: 'He collects the ball, sprints the length of the right-wing touchline, centres perfectly . . . and runs on past the corner-flag, full pelt, to make a phone call'. David used to keep a sailing cruiser at Burnham-on-Crouch. After some long, late nights at a faraway foreign athletics tournament or somesuch, he suggested on our arrival home that a few days unwinding at sea might be just the ticket. Blow winds and crack your cheeks! wasn't in it as, from Heathrow, David headed his horsepower at the east coast of England. In an Essex village, a bobby flagged him to stop: 'Not that you're doing anything actually unlawful, sir – but just tone it down a bit'. Such has been my regular admonition to DM down the years. Later on that storm-tossed car journey, David spied a phonebox and leaped out for a check-call. He came back, waterlogged but delighted: 'Goodie! A gale warning. Force 10. Fantastic'. Once he sailed me round the Isle of Wight in another raging storm. He did not, I swear, narrowly go past the Needles – but threaded right through them. I have never got drunker faster.

DM is still at it, girdling the globe at top speed, usually driving himself. A couple of years ago we were in Rome. He came into the hotel white with fury. 'I've just heard some absolutely disastrous news', he said, grinding his teeth and calling for a Campari. It was surely either that *The Times* had sacked him or Marita had left him. 'What is it, old friend?' 'The bastards are closing the Brenner Pass for repairs next winter'.

In complete contrast was the boss to whom David introduced me when I arrived in Mexico for my débutant's bow for *The Times* in the summer of 1970. Geoffrey Green never once in his life disobeyed the exhortation, 'Don't Drink and Drive'. Simply, he never drove. How lucky I was with this first of my sports-writing mentors.

I nervously shook hands with my chef-de-mission, Mr Green. He said we would discuss my role that night over a few drinks at the British Embassy. A few! I woke up at dawn in the flowerbeds, was marched inside by a security man at gunpoint – to find Geoffrey, well primed whisky glass still in his hand, amiably getting a chap to rustle up some breakfast. Twenty years older, he had drunk me not only under the table but under the azaleas.

Another time, in a dim and dangerous São Paulo nighterie, a sinister Black Power chappie swung Geoffrey around and menacingly demanded which side 'whitey' was on? A beatific smile, and 'I'm with the Rainbow People, baby' – and in a trice the world was a different, laughing place and they whisked him away to their faraway mountain hideout so he could hear their music and join in with his mouth-organ.

Green was, in his time, an elegantly gifted correspondent for *The Times* at cricket and tennis. He was also the paper's Sports Editor. But he will be remembered as the most bewitching of all writers on soccer. When he joined the paper in 1938, soccer reporting was bound in a grey tradition of archness.

Suddenly Green was stirring in metaphors of freshness and gaiety. Grey became purple. A great game was suddenly adorned by a great artist. The Hungarians of 1953 just didn't beat England, they 'lit winking, flashing lights all over Wembley, every move a flare going through a prism'. Bobby Charlton was more than a fluent forward, he was 'the dashing leader of the line on a white charger, releasing rockets that, with a clap of thunder, lift the opposing net as if a gale had struck it'. Greaves wasn't just a sharp goalscorer, he was 'the floppy-trousered pickpocket of the penalty area'. Finney never just ran up the wing, but 'glided like a yacht on a lovely day'. Quality teams wouldn't coast to victory, they would resemble 'an errand boy free-wheeling downhill with his feet on the handlebars, whistling the while'.

Geoffrey's first 'trial' match report for *The Times* was 1,000 words on a school game between Bradford and Shrewsbury in November 1938. There was no question of his ever leaving. He became an irresistible morning read. Yet it might all have been over just 20 years later – lopped off at the peak of his glory; like his truly beloved Busby Babes. He was all set to fly with Manchester United to a European Cup match in 1958, the same trip on which half the team, the glorious budding flower of British football, and a famous slice of the press corps were rubbed out in an instant on the icy slush of a Munich runway. But at the last minute the manager of *The Times* cancelled Geoffrey's tickets and spared his beauty, kindness, and skill for us for just over 30 more years, and sent him to Wales v Israel instead. And when he returned from Cardiff the curtains were drawn in all the little parlours and front-rooms of the land. A whole country hunched about in black armbands. Football itself was numbed. And in a way it has never recovered its joy. As Geoffrey said towards the end: 'The game's not much fun any more. It's all penguin football now, bingo between goalposts; 4–3–3 was bad enough, now it's something like 4-and-an-eighth – 6-and-seven-eighths isn't it? Anyway, when you'd seen the Hungarians in 1953, that was probably it'.

When they threw a banquet in a posh London hotel to give thanks, on his retirement, to the former England soccer manager, Sir Alf Ramsey, they chose Geoffrey Green to make the main speech. It was an earnest, worthy sort of do, as you might expect, boring speeches by solid citizens in dinner-suits. Geoffrey topped up his beaker of scotch, took a large slug and began: 'Alf baby, so they've sacked you. Come out to grass with me and a few fellow old grey buzzards who are forming a group, The Squandering Stars, and we've bagged the pitch in the Marble Arch underpass. So start practising, Alf baby, 'cos it's a-goin' to go something like this'. At which he whips the mouth-organ out of his pocket and liltingly serenades poor bewildered, unsmiling Sir Alf with the whole of 'Moon River'. End of speech. Laughter, love, and the largest of drinks all round.

My last foreign job with this tall, irreligious saint was in the early 1980s, I suppose, on one of Ipswich Town's expeditions into Europe, to a tinpot little Netherlands town called Enschede. The night was so long and liquidly meandering that by dawn neither of us could remotely remember the hotel we were meant to be staying in. We had to book into another, put our heads down for a couple of hours, then get off to the match. *The Times* hadn't booked him a phone for some reason, so I lent him mine. At the final whistle, I was still frantically and blearily scribbling some sense into my scrambled brain, by which time Geoffrey, without taking a note, had picked up the phone and dictated without a pause some 2,000 words of brilliantly cogent, dramatic and stirring words full of stars and moons and rainbows. When we got home he wrote me a note of thanks for the phone. I still have it, naturally: 'My dear F, Thanks for the help, the fun, the fiver, the laughter, and the gurgle of the gold-stuff into the dark hours – Geoff'.

He always said he would happily settle in the next life for being the Moon River boatman. And when Jenny and his beloved daughter, Ti, rang to tell me in 1990 that he had gone and they were at last taking down the Christmas tree in the little cottage in Twickenham – it was a permanent fixture: well, wasn't every day Christmas Day? – I put the phone down with a dull heart. But at once, yes, I cupped my hand to an ear, and could hear that haunting old lilt of the Moon River boatman wafting down from the fresh green banks of Elysium on his tinny old mouth-organ.

\*   \*   \*

Johnny Haynes was England's captain and unquestionably Fulham's finest-ever footballer. But he was never what we reckoned to be your actual Fulham-type player. For one thing he was far, far too good. For another, he wasn't half eccentric enough.

Haynes suffered 18 glorious, exasperated years for Fulham, carpeting out the world's most sumptuous passes to a motley crew of single-jointed unappreciative nuts; a Brylcreemed Schweitzer among the pygmies.

Going down to Fulham on Saturdays when Chelsea were playing away was part of the corduroy scene in the 1950s and early 1960s. They were, as John Moynihan said in his joyous chronicle of the times, 'a Saturday afternoon team, offering a feeling of animated recreation rather than solid professionalism . . . a side of happy, sometimes comic triers watched by garrulous actors, serious actors, pantomime players, band-leaders, stuntmen, starlets; tweed, black leather, green leather, pink ankle-length knickers, baggy overcoats over armour-plated suede, cheroots between thumb and first finger'. They were days when a joint was a jazz cellar, LSD was a couple of Friday fivers, a trip was a moonlight bedsit flit – and dope, more often than not, was Bedford Jezzard's latest signing from the Hellenic League.

Liquid lunch, then long walk alongside the cemetery past tiny, prim houses called 'Hazeldene', to marvel at Haynes – and to groan and wring our hands with him when the little men forgot to run on to – or even ran away from – those lancing, expansive long passes. He was too good for us, too; and, really, we turned up to love the fellows who forgot.

What a litany: that loping trier, Maurice Cook, who could never quite fathom what Johnny was at; it was like Laurel and Hardy. Every resigned dismissive shrug by Haynes made Maurice simper with inferiority. And could it have been Maurice who ran out one afternoon with that high-stepping dressage I'll-show-'em swank – and promptly doubled-up with a torn hamstring and was stretchered off even before the kick-off?

Over the years they came and went. But mostly came and stayed: Arthur Stevens, grizzle-haired wigman, who'd be wound up at the start to run the full 90 minutes – but only in straight lines. 'They Also Swerve' we used to plainchant at him. Arthur was the original subject of the legendary theatre-bill phrase 'This will run and run' – F. Cashin, *D. Sketch*. Then there was Jimmy ('Give it to the Rabbi') Hill – who, of course, we still know and love. Jim, to be sure, scored many thousands of outstanding goals – but on double-checked reckoning he also muffed about 971 sitters (plus two half chances). One now famous actor once said on the terraces that Jim only patented that piratical growth on his chin because he thought it might make him play like Charlie Buchan (don't strain yourself working it out, corny humour's changed too).

And what about Killer Keetch? Blonde and butch, fancy in his pointed Eyetie patents, but a devil in boots – no shinpad had an earthly. Horrors, we even loved him that afternoon he got stuck into Bobby Charlton. He'd be jeaned and conspicuously casual down the Portobello on a Saturday morning – after a casual canter down Rotten Row – sniffing out bargains for his junkshop (sorry, high-class antiques emporium), outstanding headscarfed brunette snuggling into his armpit; at 2.30 (unless stated) he'd wickedly set about some unsuspecting and innocent No. 9 shirt; by 6.30 he'd be downing a few swifties at the Queen's Elm, settling himself up for 10-ish and eyeball-to-eyeball confrontation with outstanding blonde over the candles and white tablecloths of L'Écu de France or some such gracious nosherie. (Why didn't Parky write a book on Keetch, for heaven's sake?)

Earlier, there was Eddie Lowe, the statutory baldy at wing-half alleged to have lost all his hair overnight through the shock of reading one of Walter Winterbottom's coaching pamphlets on peripheral vision. Or Jim Langley, bow-legged back with convict's crew-cut who, astonishingly, played for England and didn't let us down (though we were terribly worried for him). He taught that tubby antelope George Cohen all he knew about overlapping, and George became the best in the biz, one of England's 1966 heroes.

Our last great joy at Craven Cottage was the young Rodney. In a way Marsh was more of a genius then, simply because he hadn't yet realized it; only we nobodies were telling him and he, sheepish then, thought we were taking the mickey. For one season, just about the final one of those lovely winters, we'd go and watch Marsh in the reserves. Once, the goalkeeper was injured and Rodney excitedly bagged the polo-neck and gloves for himself, but when the first corner came over the dear nut tried to tip it over the top with a flying bicycle kick. Own goal!

Rodney, as a teenager, rated self-education. His bible was *Pear's Cyclopaedia*. He carried it with him everywhere and learned pages by heart. On away train trips George Cohen would solemnly have to hear him – 'Right, ready: World's Longest Rivers. Ready?' – and he'd close his eyes and recite 'Amazon twenty-eight billion yards', or whatever, 'Limpopo nineteen billion . . .', right down to the blooming Arno. When Rodney went deaf and almost had to pack up completely after he had nutted the crossbar with an almighty clang, it was sad, era's end – but it was also pure, undiluted Fulham.

But of all of them, most pure and undiluted Fulham was Tosh Chamberlain, winger supreme. It was Tosh who refused to get up after a hard tackle, saying he'd sit the game out 'until that bleeding ref apologizes'. It was Tosh who once snapped the flag clean in two when he mistimed a corner kick (if the stick had carried we all bet that Maurice would have nodded it home). It was Tosh who once broke the ribs of his own goalkeeper, Tony Macedo, with a ferocious back-pass. Tosh was the only one who'd audibly swear back at Haynes – indeed once the referee Mervyn Griffiths, Bethesda Chapel and all that, almost booked him for it.

The team's much slicker now. And there's an impressive grandstand covering the bank from where we used to watch the Boat Race – and so miss Fulham's only goal of the month. The thing to remember about all the foregoing list of loves is that, for all the memory of endearing incompetence, those sides were, more often than not, in the First Division – or rather, they were quite often there, and once in, it must be said, they spent all their time frenziedly trying to stay there. (Someone once tried to get a new nickname going for them, the Fokker Wolves – 'bloody miraculous how they stay up'.) But they finished tenth in the First Division once, in 1960. And they're no newts to FA Cup semifinals. They lost in a replay in 1962, and in 1958 Manchester United, rebuilt by Jimmy Murphy after the Munich crash, beat them by 5–3 with all the world praying for a Fulham defeat. The atmosphere was too much for Macedo, whose fine talent in goal had been instrumental (with Haynes's) in getting them that far, but on the day he flapped and fumbled like a school-girl.

In the mid-60s, I admit it, I had a brief fling with the hoops of Queen's Park Rangers, when Fulham sold Rodney Marsh to them. He took the Rs up to the First Division, and won the League Cup for them at Wembley against West Brom; and a congregation of some 4,500 of us with banners and bugles, crocodiled a few miles up the Harrow Road to the dilapidated old concrete shrine. The quavering chant of Rod-nee! Rod-nee! had the traffic stopping on the North Circular when taxi-drivers got out of their cabs to clap the parade and offer us a thumbs-up. (The musicians John Tilbury and Gavin Bryars were Rangers fans, and they incorporated the few bars of the chant in a piece they arranged for a concert in the Purcell Rooms. The reviewer wrote in the *Musical Times*, 'Did Marsh really score in Cardew's treatise or was it an hallucination?') Rodney remains my favourite footballer. Sometimes he would take the breath away with his daring – tilting at massed defences with that sort-of Max Wall run and dribble, like a forward-tripping waiter with a full tray. Time and again the ball finished up behind the mesmerized goalkeeper. Ah, Rod-nee!

\*     \*     \*

It would have been the same for me, I suppose, and George Best had I lived in Manchester in the 1960s. Later, I was to spend a day with George when he was living in California, and another when he was back at the home of his mother-in-law in Southend. Not a bottle to be seen on either occasion, so I know him as a lovely boy, companionable and matey, and fascinating on soccer. After Pelé, has there been a better? I had astonishing good luck in my early days as a sportswriter to be hired by the BBC (possibly because of my TV 'experience') to present a half-hour retrospective on some of the sporting legends of my time. It was called 'Maestro'. I was not very good at it, but just think what a crammer-course it was for a tyro in the trade – and for a romantic child who had steeped himself in sport as a hobby ever since that day in Stonehouse he had heard Raymond Glendenning shouting out of his wireless, 'Stamps has scored!'

My first 'Maestro', would you believe, was Tommy Farr, the Welsh heavyweight boxer, whose name was made just five weeks before I was born: 15 rounds with the Brown Bomber, Joe Louis, in New York in 1937. It was relevant to start with him in a way, for that fight's commentary on August 30, so long ago, was the first live sporting event to be relayed across the Atlantic by the ocean-bed landline. They rigged up an amplifier in the Tonypandy Assembly Hall and 4,000 miners sat up to listen and, like seashells on the ear, marvelled that they could hear the sound of the waves shushing through the static. Farr lost, but only by a whisker; they sang 'Land of my Fathers' and then clocked on for the dawn shift.

As it was my first effort in front of the cameras, (however persistently Grahame Turner might suggest I spruce myself up and have a go), I was very nervous about the Farr interview. I met him the night before in a hotel near his south-coast bungalow home. He was uptight too, I think; certainly he was as crotchety as Eddie Grundy. It was going to be a disaster. Next morning, we started edgily. (I am the only man I know who combs his hair before a radio interview). It wasn't going well. Then Tommy's wife, Monty, started surreptitiously putting regular little medicine-glass measures of cough mixture ('for his throat') on the table in front of him. After three or four measures himself, he offered me a slug. I hadn't got a sore throat. 'Get it down you, boy!' he insisted. I took a large slug. It was Monty's home-made cowslip wine. A few more each and we sailed through the interview, Farr being quite brilliant. 'Would Ali have beaten Louis?' was my last question. 'Ali?' said Tom scornfully, 'Ali wouldn't have hit Louis on the bum with a handful of rice!'

I did about 15 'Maestros' with its meticulous, worrypot producer, Jeff Goddard, my boyhood heroes coming to life in the chair in front of me. We even did Stroud's own Pat Smythe, subject of my first-ever 'proper' profile on the *Stroud News*. Dear Pat, once she had stopped being moonily misty about her beloved nags Flanagan, Tosca and Prince Hal, she just wanted to introduce all the dogs on her lap to the camera – just as Fred Winter, bless him, was keen to break off horsy-talk and get his cherished rose-garden into shot. He would have much preferred us to be 'Gardeners' Question Time'. One solitary tear dribbled down Bobby Charlton's face when I asked him how often he thought of his United team-mates killed on that icy Munich runway. You could hear only the camera motor. 'They were lovely lads, all of them,' he muttered softly at last.

Barry John, as carefree and mischievous a sprite as he ever was in the face of All Black terrorists, got me totally blotto the night before in a Tiger Bay Chinese restaurant. Next morning, he carried me through the interview with such deft and smiling charm that nobody suspected our combined hangover weighed as much as Colin Meads. The Maestro.

Denis Compton was next. Still full of the joys then – and, still is. (Whenever I see him now, I remain as mesmerized as that first day I saw him at Old Trafford in 1949). Denis's yarns flowed like Tommy Farr's cough mixture. Once, the crowd had barracked the Aussie demon, Miller, who had made what seemed from the ropes to be a threatening gesture as Denis walked in to bat. 'Actually, he was asking me what had won the 2.30 at Newmarket'. Another time, in India, Denis was bribed one lunch interval by a wealthy businessman who desperately wanted Compton's side to win. He said he would give Denis so many rupees a run. By the close of play, he came in with 258 not out, did a quick multiplication and knew he was suddenly worth a fortune. He was met at the pavilion door by a servant of the businessman with a sealed note on a silver tray. It read: 'Gone to Calcutta on very urgent business'!

Fred Davis astonished me by saying he never for one moment thought of practising between tournaments. He hadn't even got a snooker table at his Worcestershire farm. From a cloud of smoke in his lovely house in the Dales, Fred Trueman emerged, took his gigantic pipe from his mouth and jabbed it fiercely in my chest, 'Ye call me "Fiery Fred"? Don't be absolutely ridiculous! Y'only call me that because Fred rhymes with Fiery!' Somehow, we got on to the subject of women's lib. Said Fred, 'You should treat women the same way as any good Yorkshire batsman used to treat a cricket ball. Don't stroke 'em. Don't tickle 'em. Just give 'em a ruddy good belt!'

In the film on Lester Piggott, his good friend, Teasy-Weazy Raymond, the hairdresser and racehorse-owner, recalled the evening Lester won his first Derby on Never Say Die in 1954 when he was 17. The BBC wireless rang up to ask for an interview. In those days the Corporation expected nation to speak unto nation for free. There was a long pause on the phone, then the teenager told them his thoughts on the day would cost them £50 – a huge whack at that time. They coughed up. Lester has never lost the knack.

We spent a couple of days with another fast operator who lived dangerously. In his opulent home above Lake Geneva, Jackie Stewart said he had known what I would ask, so he and Helen had lain in bed that morning and counted all their true motor-racing friends – not just acquaintances – who were now late motor-racing friends. 'We gave up counting when we reached 63'. Most touching moment with

Stewart was when talk got around to childhood heroes. He raced upstairs to rummage in the attic – and came down with his boyhood autograph book, started when he was a garage mechanic in Dumbartonshire. There they all were, his sacred squiggles . . . Hawthorn, Ascari, Farina, Brooks, and, most coveted of all, Stirling Moss.

Geoff Duke drove me sedately around his Isle of Man hairpins on the pillion of a little 2-stroke machine – as Stirling Moss did around Mayfair on the back of his Lambretta. Which was inadequate preparation when, years later, one of his successors decided on a very hairy revenge.

Some weeks you forget what opinion you expressed on a certain matter the week before. This can make life difficult for a columnist (it is a phenomenon perfectly sent-up in *Private Eye* by Glenda Slag, who cannot remember what she thinks from one paragraph to the next). I was caught out spectacularly by Nigel Mansell. *Punch* asked me to do a piece on 'the three most boring men in British sport'. I knocked off a thousand of the best – Nick Faldo, Steve Davis, and Nigel Mansell were my choices – posted it and thought no more about it. Not even when the phone rang and the men from Mr Mansell's garage said he had a good idea. I accepted the invitation listlessly. Just another job. Bit of a doddle, actually. Be driven round Silverstone as Nigel talks you through the curves and the course for the upcoming big race at the weekend. Oh, and by the way, it would be in a Ferrari F40, so it would be the nearest any non-racer could get to simulating the experience of an F1 whizzer at full throttle. Okay, sure, a goodish wheeze, I supposed, and not a bad gimmick either, seeing as I'm a famous sluggard in my little staff-car Escort in which even venerable tractors have been known to leave me standing when lights turn to amber on market day.

So I tootled down unconcernedly for my pootle with good ol' Nige. I even got down early to give myself a half hour in the delicious library-hush of that browsers' bookshop in

Brackley main street. It was a benign midsummer morning.
Heavyish rain squalls had scooted off eastwards after
freshening up the day, and now a heat haze chummily
settled over the heart of England. There was no better place
to be in all the world than in the mellow greenery of the
rolling shires. Silverstone looked absolutely glorious. So did
the Silverstone girls: there is no more obliging, civilized
bunch of administrators in all British sport.

The message was that Nigel would meet me at the Ferrari
pits in 20 minutes. Meanwhile, have a coffee, look at a few
press handouts and, oh yes, good luck.

Good luck? Ominous, that. Even so, the penny was taking
a long time to drop. I flipped through the bumph. I must
have read that the F40 could reach 202.87 mph flat out –
but seeing as I, to my certain knowledge, had never reached
102.87 mph on four wheels in my life, it did not register. I
do recall, however, that my subconscious did order another
coffee – black, this time – and a large slug of Perrier, after
I'd glanced through the presskit crits.

'The F40 reminds me of a German shepherd dog from
which you risk getting a nasty bite' (Michele Alboreto, *Auto
In*); 'I had the feeling that I was in the car I had dreamed so
much of driving when I was still racing' (Giancarlo Baghetti,
*Auto Oggi*); 'It was not we who were testing the car, but the
F40 that was putting us to the test' (Giancarlo Perini, *Gente
Motori*); 'Keep an eye, above all, on the cleanliness of the
road surface; a stream of diesel left by a tanker could be
lethal' (Duilio Trufo, *Auto-capital*).

And a motoring lady for *Auto Week* called Denise
McCluggage (who should have been travel correspondent
for the *Glasgow Herald*, I thought) had written that
'nothing in my entire life was as red, as swift, as
aerodynamic, as powerful, and as far-out as my test drive
with Eddie Cheever'. She summarized the whole experience
simply as – 'Gulp!' These were now, suddenly, my thoughts
exactly. Gulp! What the hell had I let myself in for?

They brought me crash-helmets to try for size. Already I

felt like using one as a sickbag. There was something of the dread and doom of an execution squad as they led me to the pits. I'd left home, dammit, with no more than a cheery cheerio. No final cuddle for the kids. Your past life swims before you. Wasn't I the guy, aged 12, who'd fainted cold when he got off the Big Dipper at Battersea Funfair in 1951 when Mum and Dad took us up to the Festival of Britain? Sheer, unadulterated terror.

For Christ's sakes, I may be a cricket writer, but I've never been strapped into a net with a crash-hat on and been expected to take my chances with Malcolm Marshall. This is what they were asking me to do now with this Nigel bloody Mansell.

Could I make a bolt for it? Yellow-bellied blue funk isn't against the law, is it? Say you must go to the loo – and vamoose to the dear old beguiling blue Escort, and I could be back, cowering, behind the shelves of that Brackley bookshop in no time. They'd never think to look for me there.

I even flunked that. There was a throng around the car: cameramen and cognoscenti. Lots of 'good lucks', lots of envy, too. Lord, if they only knew. The red, sleek, low-slung, dangerous tube seemed to be glinting in the sun with a sadist's smile. So did Mansell's grin of greeting, I thought, betray a similar curl of cruelty. He was slighter, less well-built than I expected. His handshake was firm, and I noticed (when your life's on the line, you obviously log these minute details with perfect clarity) that as soon as he released the wet flannel which was my palm, he wiped it dry on his overall. How could I have ever publicly called this sadist 'boring'?

They helped cram me, quivering now, into the cockpit. I couldn't fasten my belt. I was in a real state. Mansell leaned across, still grinning, and did it up for me. That was decent of him. So look here, pull yourself together, man. He's not only a good bloke, good ol' Nige, but he's so obviously one of the very best drivers of a motor car in the whole world.

Well, it's his job, isn't it? Stands to reason. He'll only potter around. Would he do anything really scary? Of course not. You'll be as safe as houses with the best driver on the planet. Sit back, old son, and enjoy it. Didn't you hear how those mechanics and people out there envied you this experience? Yes, it's going to be okey-doke. Just enjoy it.

I was calm now. Could I, I asked, clip this little microphone to your overalls, Nigel, so you could talk me round the course? Sure, said Nige, but although my brain now seemed serene and settled, my hands were still twitching, so the nice chap clipped it on himself, and also plugged the cable into the tape-recorder which I was holding in my lap. He chuckled in, I hoped, a matey, reassuring fashion, and asked: 'Do you like doughnuts?'

What a funny question! I just smiled a gormless, sheep's smile – strangled almost at birth as, all of a sudden, a ridiculous retch of revs and high-pitched screams erupted in an explosion like the world had gone off its rocker. We were on our back wheels, spinning like a crazed top. Outside, smoke was all around our pirouetting red pot. Every brain cell was in a stampede of palpitating panic, and every emotion and sense cascaded with rivers and floods of fear. The prancing, rearing horse of Maranello gone dreadfully, dangerously mad.

With diabolic footwork, Mansell's prologue to this torture-chamber turn was to taunt me with a devilishly meticulous balance of clutch, power and steering that had us wrenched terrifyingly and dizzily through half a dozen 360-degree turns – before we leapt careeringly, and still crazily, in an alarming, convulsive forwards-spiral up the pit lane like we were snaking uncontrollably down a twisting hallway to, if not hell, then at least to oblivion.

I have never been so petrified in all my existence. Please, good God willing, I will never be so wretchedly so again. Now this cocky, cruel little man beside me was actually talking. In my utter petrifaction, I heard not a word. Another stunned, cold sweat broke out on my brow when, days later, I had to force myself to play back the tape. This, verbatim, is what he said – all above the wailing wall of noise: 'Enjoy that start, did you, eh? [chortle, chortle]. . . . A hell of a lot of power, eh? Nought to 112 in 12 seconds. . . . That was Copse. Hang on, the track's still very slippery at the moment. . . . Wa-hey! . . . from second down to Maggotts in top; I'd be slowing from about 160 down to under 100 for Becketts in the race . . . lots of brake, down to second . . . and now flat out to Chapel – wa-hey! still very slippery, and now absolutely let it rip down Hangar . . . wa-heeee! Close your eyes, a bit bumpy here. . . . Stowe's an even quicker corner today after the rain. . . . Enjoy that, eh? [diabolic chuckle]. . . . Up to fifth, 150-plus . . . Abbey . . . now, foot down, push for 200 to Woodcote. . . .'

And then the tape went dead. It had slipped from my sopping fingers to the floor. My other hand, knuckles pure white with tension, was pressed to the dashboard.

Woodcote? Woodcote? Wasn't that where Scheckter caused that almighty pile-up a few years back? Hell, what is this raving Brummie doing to me? Slow down, can't you? Surely we're coming to the pits now?

No, not again, not another lap! Please! It seems such a perilously tiny corridor. The barriers blur past like mur-derously intent tracer bullets, just lining up my eggshell skull in their sights. I've heard it said you don't feel a thing. But, oh, my dear wife, my children!

This deranged nut alongside me is still rabbiting on, matter-of-fact. Still chortling. Still saying the track is slippery, but not slowing down an iota . . . except, what's this? He's braking. Merciful heavens! Hail Mary, full of grace, the Lord is with me. . . .

'A couple more doughnuts for your photographer,' says Mansell, and there on Chapel Curve itself, he prances us through the terrifying twirls again, and I'm now almost dead with fear because I know, just know, those bastards back in the pits didn't close the door on my side properly. . . .

With an excruciating, gulping surge, we're careering ahead again in an unbearable tumult of acceleration down Hangar . . . and engraved on what's left of the tatters of my mind is that overhead camera shot of this same blithering bastard at my side when, at Adelaide, his tyre burst at full pelt in a crazy catherine wheel of sparks and flames and fury. What if that happened to us now? Didn't Jackie Stewart once say that 90 per cent of grand prix accidents were caused by mechanical failure? My God, come to think of it, it'd serve this Mansell creep right if a wheel blew now. That'd wipe the stupid grin off his face, and stop this insane commentary dead.

Jackie Stewart also said that driving a grand prix car at full lick was so coaxingly rhythmic and sensitive it was akin to making gently passionate and voluptuous love. Well, you can tell him from me, that it's more like a harmless civilized gentleman being attacked by a horde of Amazon cannibals and then left for brain-dead in the jungle.

My mouth was too dry to utter even a scream. How can 20 or 30 racers, jockeys strapped alongside each other into these snarling beasts (like I was now), have time to think, let alone adjust – let alone dice with each other for sport – when the curves and corners come at you in such a crazed and quickfire kaleidoscope? Their eyesight, distance and depth-perception must be phenomenal.

We had stopped, I could re-focus. I was safe. Alive! It was heady. Glorious. Alive-alive-o! Still quivering uncontrollably, though. That was to last for a good two or three hours.

Well done, said everyone. Golly, you lucky blighter. Was it a fantastic experience? 'Absolutely fan-bloody-tastic!' I said, trying to revert from lockjaw to a smile. 'Nothing to it', I told the clamour of congrats-chaps clustering around us, 'a great thrill, a truly memorable experience. Good ol' Nige'.

I sauntered, gingerly but trying to be serene, to my little blue Escort. For my next trick – well, how about blindfold and naked in a barrel over Niagara? A cinch in comparison. Moral: Careful whom you call 'boring'.

# 10

In the early 1970s Brian Jones, who had been chief sub during my first spell on the *Guardian*, was now deputy editor and hinted it might be worth my while applying to join the sports desk permanently. I was delighted when John Samuel took me aboard. He had become sports editor in 1968 and at once the pages began to attend to the real world. For example, pre-Samuel, the only horse-race meetings covered were the Derby and Grand National, and then by a 'colour' writer who only incidentally bothered to mention the winner. Samuel's zestful, hoppity mind and relishing rubbing of hands reminded me of the old actor-manager of legend. The same sort of qualities I found in Alan Coren when he edited *Punch*, for which I was later to work, in tandem with the *G*, for 10 happy years. (If ever I became wealthy, I thought, I would buy them each an astrakhan-collared coat). Samuel's organization was such that, for all his mod innovations, the sports pages' trad idiosyncrasies and surprises were retained. It was a tremendous piece of luck to be allowed to join. David Gray daily handed down his tablets to a respectful tennis world; lovely, gentle Bert Barham was soccer correspondent, spanning until his untimely death the two splendiferous generations of Donny Davies and David

Lacey; so, from the first, I had opportunities to get in the drinks, having carried to all points of the compass the typewriters of the rugby correspondent, David Frost, and the athletics and boxing sage, John Rodda. They were, to a man, very good to me. At the 1980 Olympic Games, Christopher Booker wrote his one-off classic *The Games War* and observed John and me at work (and play). Forget the Booker flannel, but it is not often the 'watchers' are watched:

> [I saw] a lot of Frank Keating – a sensitive soul of great charm, brought up as a 'Catholic Socialist' in Gloucestershire and given to bestowing 'love' and 'bless you' in all directions (much to the puzzlement of the Russian waitresses) with a slightly harassed eccentricity. Frank forms a kind of double act with his *Guardian* colleague, John Rodda, a mine of statistical information who wrote a history of the Olympics with Lord Killanin. In action in the pressbox at the Lenin Stadium – Keating all wild 'artist's impressions', which he jotted down in a surprisingly tiny pencil handwriting, Rodda all stop-watches, charts and cool efficiency – I came to think of them as a kind of latter-day Quixote and Sancho Panza.

Soon after I had arrived back, Peter Preston took over as editor of the paper and not only reaffirmed at once both its strong 'family' bonds and its basic belief in intellectual freedom for the writers. (These two characteristics encouraged me to turn down tempting job offers from Harry Evans, of *The Times*, and a couple of other big guns). Peter, happily a sports nut himself (if supporting Millwall FC qualifies one), also encouraged John to streamline matters so that sub-editors subbed and writers wrote, and no more a bit of both. Much as I had enjoyed my subbing shifts, a regular column, a wandering brief, and a company car was much more of a dare. Especially when a cricket season was about to start.

Because of its direct line of correspondents – from Sir Neville Cardus, through Denys Rowbotham, to John Arlott – the long-celebrated glory of *Guardian* sport was its cricket coverage. It was my astonishing good fortune to rejoin the paper when I did. One of the sports pages' later luminaries, Matthew Engel, was to write in the *Guardian Book of Cricket* of '. . . a second golden age. There was some vintage stuff in the paper in the early 70s: Arlott in his pomp, Cardus firmly back in the fold for his last years, wit and craftsmanship from Eric Todd and Brian Chapman, the young Blofeld . . . and, after Cardus died, Ian Peebles contributed a series of quite scintillating essays'.

The phone. The unmistakable, fondly loved and carefully enunciated post-*Punch*-lunch purr of my confrère and TV colleague, Bill Grundy (who deputized on our evening show on the day Eamonn was jumping out on the unsuspecting with his glossy red album). 'Listen, chook, if you've begun trying to write on cricket for the *Guardian*, you'd better come to supper tonight with Sir Neville himself. Baker Street Steakhouse, sharp at 7'. Could I bring Pam? 'Sure, the old boy will doubtless prefer her to you, now you come to mention it'.

He did too. Well, nobody could fail to prefer Pamela. She had a shapely tall splendour about her, and rich brown hair cut short in a pageboy bob. I regularly lunched in the 'little' Ark, a cheery bistro just off Notting Hill Gate. Pam ran the next-door bookshop with her friend, Shelagh. If there were no tables free, I would pop in and browse a while. Or pretend to – peeping over the top of a book at Pamela as she sat reading or marking up the stock; saucery-hazel eyes; black tights, the longest you could buy; and black everything (except nature and shining spirit), she looked like a bookish Françoise Sagan heroine on the Left Bank, in the good days. Au revoir, tristesse: for after weeks of this bashful browsing, I gathered the courage – and we 'walked out' together contentedly for two years or more. As well as an innate sex-appeal, Pamela had the most appealing and generous serenity I had come across till then, except in my mother.

So no wonder it was a happy and illuminating night with Bill and the grand old man. Cardus was already well into his eighties, but as chirpy and animated as a bird at a bird-table, his memory sharp and keen on Beecham and Mahler, on anything and everything – from Hammond's cover-drive in 1928 to Duckworth's reading-matter (*The Count of Monte Cristo*) on board the *Orion* with Allen's team in 1936. Just like 'Piggy' Rice, my first headmaster at Douai – and almost word for word – he said the secret of life (in this case my ambition to write on cricket) was 'to get on the front-foot at every opportunity'. The kind old knight was 'glinting' in more ways than one. As we were going home, Pam told me Neville had spent the duration of the meal – except when cutting his steak or supping his water and wine – with one, still, hand content and snug, but not at all active or mischievous, resting up her skirt at the top of her thighs. She did not mind at all; and there were more of those rewarding steak-bar outings before the good and resplendent emperor of cricket writing died in his 88th year in 1975. His encouragement, sure, but even more the sheer pleasure of those few times in his twinkling company make me a very lucky man.

Likewise meals with John Arlott. Just to be in his presence was a singular pleasure. In the six or seven years before he retired from the microphone, and as the *Guardian*'s cricket correspondent, it was my fortune (and joy) to travel often with John; to the Test matches, when I would knock off for the *Guardian* a little sidebar piece of waffle alongside his report; but best when we zig-zagged round the shires, him in his element planning the alfresco lunch we would have – and with whom – me carrying his battered old typewriter case, and keeping the scorecard up to date when not being gently ordered to nip out of the ground and across to the county stores for another couple of slices of rough terrine or an extra hunk of Cheshire. He would always keep a safe hold on his briefcase, which held four bottles nicely, and the corkscrew. He would also be maître of the onion-slicing, paring with the meticulous relish of a needy peasant the pungent, tear-jerking bulb — just so — with his penknife.

Once I got out of bed on the wrong side and wrote a crosspatch piece in the paper about the ultimate pointlessness of writing on sport. By return of post came a kindly admonishment from John, handwritten in his famous purply-black Quink:

> It is clear that sports writing is not — or should not be — important in the pattern of literary life; just as sport is not — or should not be — important in the shape of world history. The fact remains that many unimportant — and important — people retain a deeply romantic and nostalgic feeling for sports, for the great sportsmen of their childhood, and abiding interest and loyalties in the sporting events of today.

Such concern for a tyro, such generous, uncomplicated concern, made you want to pinch yourself. Was this same man — 40 years on — this same little boy's wireless idol? The same spinner of tales and wonder? The voice, all down a lifetime, had kept the boy in touch with his roots, with his Goddards and Graveneys, his Miltons and his Wilsons and his Barnetts. ... And now here was that same voice, actually asking an opinion of the child, or topping his glass for him in affectionate, paternal comradeship. Mind you, I was not the only one hook-line-and-sinkered all that long lifetime ago.

On June 11, 1947, from the terrace of a small villa in the sweltering Apennines, Dylan Thomas put down his bottle and picked up his pen to reply to a letter from his erstwhile BBC wireless producer in the talks department:

> My dear John, Thank you for writing. It was very good to

hear from you. Though I hear your voice every day: from Trent Bridge at the moment. You're not only the best cricket commentator – far and away that; but the best sports commentator I've heard ever: exact, enthusiastic, prejudiced, amazingly visual, authoritative, and friendly. A great pleasure to listen to you. . . .

Later that month Dylan wrote to another English friend, Margaret Taylor: 'I hear John Arlott's voice every weekend, describing the cricket matches. He sounds like Uncle Tom Cobleigh reading Neville Cardus to the Indians. . . .'

He was to continue to do so for another 33 years. On the last day of the centenary Test at Lord's in 1980, Arlott signed off, handed over to the next commentator without frills, stood up, and with scarcely a glance at the field below him, turned, took a large slug of the red wine in his glass, mopped his brow with a red-spotted hankie, and walked away, embarrassed by the three cheers of farewell which sounded for him round the famous stadium. And I was there. And he said to me, 'C'mon, m'boy, let's get a drink downstairs'.

It was, to start with, a sad meal that night. But John was ebullient. Freedom. Who knows of cricket, who only cricket knows? For there was still the voice, the humanity, the books, the pictures; the tearfulness when he talked of his beloved Thomas Hardy heroes (which he so associated with, not forgetting the heroines); the desperate love of his family and close friends; the always insisted 'accident' of his good fortune in life ('relished and relishable' as he would say). But I will remember most, I think, a day I spent in Alderney when he was still, just, in his great bullocky, bright-eyed power, only two or three years after he had clocked up his three-score-and-ten, and just before the sicknesses set in.

The isle was full of silence and the house full of treasures. In the hall, a grand and ancient old wireless set – it had belonged to Haley when he was BBC's Director-General.

Watercolours of Winchester and needlework of Worcester. In the kitchen, Toynbee's lively and glorious oil of *The Nets*, drawings of Hardy and Dylan Thomas and a striking portrait of Elizabeth David. In the Long Room, the first editions (Hardy, Hazlitt, Betjeman and all) and on the walls Lowry and Rowlandson, Lancaster and Beerbohm.

John's beloved father, Jack, ended up keeping the graveyard neat at Basingstoke. He wanted the boy simply to get a job with a pension. John began in local government and then in the police force. When he started making his name with the BBC, father and son embraced 'and cried together at the wonder of it all'. His third cricket book, on the Australians of 1948, was dedicated 'To my father who knows nothing about cricket and cares less but who wos werry good to me'. The last sentence in that book reads: 'Is there, I wonder, anywhere in the world such a human, generous, unenvious, shop-talking, enthusiastic, mellow, craft-versed sporting community as English cricket professionals?'

We walked down from the solid and singular house on the hill to collect the mail at the post office: 'I do love my post'. Then we strolled on down towards the sea-wall, via the Albert and the morning's first bracer, a Fino sherry in tomato juice. Then another when we had settled ourselves in the hotel bar's conservatory, which gave us a spectacular view of the relentlessly angry waves snapping and fretting and fizzing and dying against the harbour wall.

Pat, good Pat, herself doting and doted on, was waiting with lunch back up the hill. But he called for one more mammoth pre-lunch bracer, watched some more gloriously savage white horses tilt again at the Becher's of the sea-wall, and reflected softly in probably the most celebrated British voice after Churchill's: 'I'm not talking remotely about cricket, m'boy, when I tell you it ain't half a bloody old game, ain't it? It ain't half a bloody old game'. He pondered on his words, shrugged, chuckled, and ordered two more of the same.

To John I will be forever in debt. In late night bars around the world I noticed I was increasingly spending my time heatedly defending both the bonny goodness and cricketing chivalries (let alone the remarkable talent) of Ian Botham, and the wisdom of keeping up the sports boycott against the racists of white South Africa. On both subjects I would take heart: for my champion was John. Well, not only had he been instrumental in bringing Basil D'Oliveira out of his bondage, but after Basil had played for England – and when the South African government in its embarrassed pique refused him entry with his new England colleagues – Arlott spoke at the Cambridge Union against the motion, 'That politics should not intrude on sporting contacts'. Seconding the minister of sport, Denis Howell, Arlott's was a mesmerizing denunciation of the motion (overturned dramatically by 334 votes to 160) proposed by Ted Dexter and Wilf Wooller. 'It is political commitment and political belief that can make a man think that his opponent's views are so obnoxious that he will abstain from playing any game with him as a protest against what the other man believes . . .' John said. 'Any man's political commitment, if it is deep enough, is his personal philosophy and it governs his way of life, it governs his belief, and it governs the people with whom he is prepared to mix'.

The last piece of journalism John ever wrote was a tribute to 'the immense humanity' of Botham, 'the most agreeable of my sometime neighbours in Alderney' (the Bothams have a holiday cottage on the island). It appeared in the January 1992 issue of his beloved *Wisden Cricket Monthly*. Turn back three pages, and there is the announcement of John's death. He wos werry good to me.

So in a different way (less mellowed by time; just a short passage of friendship but sun-streaked with warmth for all that) was another celebrated *Guardian* cricket writer who helped drag me aboard, shake me down, and dry the dampness behind my ears. He had been a Test player. That first day, June 22, 1946, that Dad had taken me to the

Gloucester Wagon Works, he was in the Middlesex team. He batted both times immediately preceding the roller, made 0 not out and 2 (c Emmett b Scott) and took nought for 10 in four overs.)

I had heard of Ian Peebles, of course. Even to a short-trousered sports-nut in the wartime West of England, the name made for a good quiz question: Name Scotland's English leg-spinner who had diddled out the Don a decade before? I suppose I must have read him too, in the *Sunday Graphic* or *Everybody's*, though the erudite sparkle was lost on an oik who, at that age, was voracious only for the facts and figures of the Gloucestershire scorecard in our local *Citizen*. I must have been in the same room as Ian for the first time that midsummer Saturday in the early 1960s when, as sporting dogsbody on the *Slough Observer*, I conned a pass for a day to the sanctum of the Lord's press box. Here were the giants of this tyro's trade. I quaked as they eyed me with haughty disdain: golly, they all used fountain pens, and flashy cigarette holders, and drank wine. And never seemed to be watching the cricket! I was convinced I would never make the grade. Ian was then on the *Sunday Times* – and was to relate years later:

'There were rivalries, feuds, enmities, and prejudices . . . the few notorious dislikes belonging among people in the same newspaper group. For my part, I look back on much help and co-operation, and a great deal of good company and interesting talk. Fun and jest from the astringent wit of Jim Kilburn to Clive Taylor's amusing drolleries. *The Times* crossword was a great solace, and Kilburn, Bill Bowes and John Solon were each and collectively shrewd performers. The nice acid tang in Alex Bannister's quips were accentuated by a gravelly drawl. Asked about the health of a colleague, whom the enquirer knew he cordially disliked, he replied, "All right, I believe – between fits" '.

I never knew that generation. By the time I was revelling in a brief run on the cricket writers' circuit, towards the end of the 1970s, those urbane and leisurely reporters had long clipped-in their fountain pens for the last time, and the game (with a few outstanding exceptions) was being covered by real Fleet Street pros, with biros and a relish for gossip columning, if not downright crime-writing. They still didn't watch the cricket, but now they weren't even bothering with the *Sun* crossword.

It was in that company, however, that I met Ian for the first time – as colleagues and soul-mates, too, for in his late 60s he began to contribute an occasional series of quite scintillating essays for my paper, the *Guardian*. We would meet at Lord's and he would hand in his copy to be passed on to the sports editor – and then take me to lunch, me purring with delight at his soft-told tales of wine, wickets, and song (he was pretty good on women, too!). He taught me, without the slightest pretension, a little more each time about wine, and in return, at every lunch, I would insist he told me how he got Bradman at Old Trafford: '. . . when he had made 14, he again came down the wicket and played the same off-drive, only to snick the ball to second-slip, where Duleep made no mistake. A roar went up from the crowd that must have lasted a full minute and, for the moment, I had fulfilled my purpose. A well-known artist named Nevinson wrote later, in a book entitled *These Savage Islands*, that he had returned to these shores in the midst of a bank crisis, and various other disasters, to find, much to his disgust, that all the evening newspaper headlines said simply "PEEBLES DOES IT".'

Ian being a son of the manse, and me a Catholic, each time over our final one-for-the-stroll back to the office, I demanded to hear the classic faux pas of Lord Lionel Tennyson, with whom Ian had toured India in 1937. On board ship, his Lordship had made great friends of the then Prime Minister of Australia, Joe Lyons, a devout Catholic and proud father of a large family. 'They got along splendidly', recalled Ian, 'and whenever there was a pause in the conversation, Lionel was ready to fill it.

' "You've a lot of Catholics in Australia", he said.

' "Yes, indeed", replied Mr Lyons, with pardonable pride, "about a third of the population".

' "You want to watch 'em", cautioned Lionel. "You can't trust 'em – and what's more, the buggers breed like rabbits!" '

Happy days. In the winter of 1979–80, I was sent with Brearley's men to cover my first Australian tour. It was a thrilling experience – richly enhanced by a series of letters received, almost weekly it seemed, from Ian. I knew he was ill but had no inkling of it from the fizz and chuckle and exhortation contained in those regular signals on air-mail flimsy. I stayed at Melbourne's Windsor Hotel, mellow, brown-stained old relic then from Ian's own touring days, years before. This delighted him. 'Make sure you walk to the ground every morning', he insisted, 'through the park with its trees and grasses, and exquisite masses of flowers and colour'. Or, 'Get yourself a haircut, and go to Mr Brown's establishment and see if, behind the barber's chair, he still has the framed picture of Sammy Carter catching Jack Hobbs behind the wicket in 1921, a very notable catch'. Or, 'Remember in Australia that all cricket grounds are Ovals, and are tended not by groundsmen but by curators. Wonderful cricket grounds they are too'. The same warm flavours that permeate the beguiling *Bowler's Turn* that's open before me as I write.

When young Graham Gooch was run out for 99 in the Melbourne Test, almost by return came a four-page letter-essay on 'Great Knocks of 99', which was worthy of any all-time anthology (as long as the cavalier spelling was checked: as his friend, Mr Swanton, said in his introduction to the reissue of *Batter's Castle*, Ian had 'a positively mediaeval indifference to spelling'); and then, by next post, another engaging reflection on running between the wickets at Melbourne in the 1937 Test, when Ian's fondly remembered and scatty Middlesex comrade, Walter Robins – the same bald 'snobby Robbie' with whom my dear Bomber Wells had crossed swords – had come in to bat on the fifth evening, with 534 runs still needed and four wickets down. Maurice Leyland was still there, having battled his way through an intensely hot day against a spirited attack:

'It was with great relief (having scored nought in the first innings) that Walter steered O'Reilly's first ball through the gully and was off like a whippet from the trap. He was back for the second in a flash and, seeing no fielder in the vicinity of the ball, set off for a third. Halfway there he was aware of a figure by his side. It was Maurice, whom he had lapped. At once Walter turned back; Maurice plodded on to safety where, in a cloud of steam and sweat, he literally "sat on the splice", blowing like anything. As Walter advanced to make his apologies, Maurice tottered out to meet him. "Take it easy, lad", he gasped, "we can't get all these roody roons tonight".

'PS: Keep up good work: I have a very drinkable Côtes du Roussillon for you when you return'.

Brearley's cricketers and their caravan of hangers-on returned from that tour to Heathrow airport on 21 February. I went home to the West Country for a few days' R & R before looking forward, amongst other things, to returning to London and splicing the bottle with Ian. Such tales to tell him. Within a week, on February 29, the newspapers said he was dead. He was 72.

\* \* \*

I came late to golf. Dad and Uncle John made us all laugh with their occasional pretensions with their half-set of jumble-sale hickories on Minchinhampton Common or the Lilleybrook course in Cheltenham. Slices, hooks, divots, air-shots, and curses in equal measure. The first time I found myself riveted in front of the television was the first time the BBC covered the Open in colour and chubby little Tony Jacklin, in his Lincolnshire poacher's lilac cardie won at Lytham. A dear friend from my brief passage on the *Slough Observer*, Doug Kelly, was now a bigwig in the Aer Lingus publicity office and he organized more than a couple of sponsored freebies for me – to have a swipe or two around the golf courses of my forefathers' kingdom and to report back (a) for their brochure and (b) for the *Guardian* holiday page.

I spent a sublime few days playing a spanking new course in the west. Chairman, champion, captain, and initial course-record holder was the area's delightful parish priest, Father Brendan. He had spent the previous five years holidaying in the United States and raising money for his course. He lived the life of Reilly. Mass each morning, Benediction on Sundays, and Confessions on Saturday evenings when a queue of old biddies would be waiting expectantly to tell him of their venial sins of the flesh – for Fr Brendan was dashingly handsome, so he was, so he was.

The remainder of the week could be spent lolling in his swank new clubhouse, when not endeavouring to beat his own course record on the heavenly green undulations of his very own 18-holer above the frothing Atlantic Ocean. Might I write 'a week in the life of' Fr Brendan for the *Guardian*? 'Surely to goodness, m'boy, I'd be delighted'. The piece duly appeared, a loving evocation of how the other half live. It was headlined 'Pastor With Putter'. I sent him a couple of copies. He was delighted, and asked for more, plus some to be sent to his friends in America. A month or two later, the *Catholic Herald* asked if they could use the piece in their 'Holidays in Ireland' supplement. Sure, I said.

Within a week, Fr Brendan rang – from Dublin. 'Jesus Mary and Joseph, you blackguard, you've ruined my life! May ye rot in hell, sor! The Archbishop read your confounded package of lies and slander in the *Catholic Herald* – and has posted me permanently, to care for the souls of the capital's drug addicts and prostitutes. You rogue, you're the Devil's own apprentice, sor!'

Forgive me, Father, for I had truly sinned. (I wonder if he's still there. I have never enquired. I wonder, too, what his handicap might be now).

So golf was not my game – until Pat Ward-Thomas, doyen of the writers post-Longhurst, suggested I come up to

my first Open at Royal Birkdale in 1976. Pat was an
enchantment always and an enigma most of the time. A
blue-flamed Tory and a genially soft and patient putter-up
with the untutored likes of me. He adored his wife, Jean,
and golf's daily match-up and fight-to-the-death between
character and talent. He smoked like a liner's funnel, was
resigned to his malignant cancer, cursed officialdom and 'the
shits of the world' with rapacious rancour, and could charm
vultures out of gum trees. In profile, as he tap-tappingly
woodpeckered away on his 'writer in the press tent, he
looked a replica of Goya's Duke of Wellington (except I
don't think His Grace smoked Senior Service). I had arrived
at his side, nervously, on the first day of the 1976 Open. I
felt shy and flustered, and knew I looked scruffy and
unshaven. 'C'mon, old boy', sighed Pat, appalled, 'try and
smarten up a bit, we're dining with Jack tonight'.

Talk about starting at the top. At Southport's Prince of
Wales Hotel that evening, Pat pleaded fraternally with
Nicklaus to please keep going for a few more years. 'Just see
me out, Jack. I just can't be churning out reams on all these
college boys who seem happy to pick up $100,000 a year
with a stream of straight but anonymous rounds'.

With his endearing grin, Nicklaus put a huge arm round
the spindly old writer's shoulders and assured his friend,
'Okay, Pat, I'll keep trying to win till you go, I'll see you out
and happy'. Then he momentarily frowned, and said:
'Okay, you know when you want to get out – but I wonder
if I will know for sure the exact time that I'll need to leave
the stage for good?' Said Pat: 'You, Jack, will go the very
moment you admit to yourself you can never ever win
another Major'. Said Jack: 'You're wrong, I think. Even in
my dotage, when they push me in a wheelchair on a fishing
trip, I guess I'll be dreaming what I've always dreamed
about – making three pars and a birdie on the last four
holes, to win a Major by a stroke'. And the two pairs of
dazzling blue eyes stared fiercely, and very affectionately, at
each other.

Gloves off for the final time; last village innings, at 50, Ibberton, Dorset, 1988 (caught deep long-off, 22). (*Bob Franklin*)

Probably the world's most resplendent all-rounder: with Daley Thompson, on the day he retired at Trondheim, Norway, 1992. (*Tom Jenkins, Guardian*)

Happy ever laughter . . . though Tess sleeps this one out. (*Rob Judges, Country Living*)

Immediately came the two epic, Kiplingesque summer weeks of the 1977 and 1978 Open Championships. Disaster and triumph. Nicklaus treated them just the same. At Turnberry in 1977, he was involved in that unforgettable stroke-for-stroke, 36-hole finale to the Open when Nicklaus shot 65 and 66 – yet lost by a stroke to the two 65s of the new pretender, Tom Watson (third-placed Hubert Green was 11 shots behind them). At the very height of their struggle, before teeing off on one of the closing holes, Watson turned to Nicklaus and said, 'I guess this is what it's all about'. Nicklaus, the old champion, knew exactly what he meant. 'You bet it is!'

Just 12 months on, to the day, it was Nicklaus alone who was walking in solo state up the 18th at St Andrews, garlanded with affection like an emperor home from the crusades, and the cheers rose as if to make an almost tangible proscenium over the vast lawn of the 18th fairway. And later, when he was presented with the battered old claret jug, as he stood on the last green at the prizewinner's table, I looked at Ward-Thomas as we sat on the sun-parched turf in the front row of the huge throng. Rivers of tears were running down the clefts of each of his lined and teaky-brown cheeks. Tears of pleasure. Jack had seen him out: it was Pat's last Open.

Glory be, I was as lucky with PWT's successor on the *Guardian*. In press tents hither and yon, the long, lanky, peripatetic Peter Dobereiner would fold legs under a rickety trestle table, light a cigarette, plonk it – spiralling smoke – in an ashtray, let a smile twitch about his lips and attempt to continue my education: 'My boy, take the sentence, "This is a magnificent test of golf", and translate it as, "I hold the course record". Likewise, when Dave Hill is quoted as saying, "This course is nothing but a cow pasture", he is really saying, "I missed the cut". Beware, too, of Gary Player's favourite quote: "This is the finest golf course I have ever seen of its kind". That is the verbal shorthand for, "The commissioner has warned me that the next time I criticize a host club in public he will have my guts for garters".'

When he left the *Guardian*, to return to his first and last love, the *Observer*, Peter sent me a precious farewell present (so typical, when it should have been the other way round). It was an Oxford University Athletics Club programme for an evening match on Thursday May 6, 1954. 'Event 9, One Mile, 6 o'clock'. It was the day young Doctor Bannister beat the clock. There were only 100 programmes printed. It has been carefully framed. I daresay it is priceless.

As was my tutelage as a sportswriter.

# 11

Which moment, or event, riddles the spine still, continues to detonate a little puff of pleasure in the cockles – a palpitation, a catch of breath – when I recall the witnessing of it? Ali against Cleveland Williams? Laver v Rosewall in Dallas? Coe and Ovett in Moscow? Daley Thompson in Athens, or anywhere; Nicklaus (and PWT) at St Andrews, or Europe's first Ryder Cup at the Belfry? The youngsters Gooch and Gower at Kingston? Viv in Antigua, Holding in Bridgetown, or my old Tom Graveney at Lord's? Botham most places? 'Lillian Thomson' at Melbourne? And Rodney, sure? Ditto Best, Law, Charlton? Hurst, Moore, Peters at Wembley? Pelé in the Aztec that day? Sugar Ray in the early hours in Las Vegas? An evening with Carwyn James? The Baa-baas' try? And Blanco's; and Slemen's? Red Rum and Dawn Run; Sir Ivor and Nijinsky? All of them – and much more where they came from.

Everything relies, as the dramatic unities insist, on context. Other times, of course, I wasn't there – but I remember vividly why I wasn't. I listened to Willis at Headingley while interviewing Zaheer Abbas at Bristol. I watched Foreman dismantled in the jungle at the Dominion, Tottenham Court Road.

I had a ringside ticket in my trouser-pocket, the night Muhammad's fists gored 'Enry's eyebrows at 'Ighbury. At South Ken tube station, as I was setting off for the fight, I managed one of my few public 'chat-ups' – with a Scandinavian girl, to boot. We, as they say, 'alighted', next stop, at Knightsbridge on the Piccadilly Line, and walked back to my then happily regular haunt, the '19' at Mossop Street (Jonah Barrington was a sometime washer-up there and one of Tony Lias's lovely redheaded wives was a waitress) where nice, winking Talbot gave us the 'upstairs-2' – where the table was so narrow you could eye-gaze and eat and thigh-touch (since known as 'doin' a Neville') at one and the same time.

We each, the Brit and the Swede (OK, probably a rasher of Danish, actually) attempted all three with relish, but we had not even got round to ordering Jean's apple-pie by the time Talbot came up to announce that Ali had bloodily sliced Henry's temples into red Christmas streamers. Alas, I cannot remember what happened later that night with svelte Miss Scanda – but if it was still 1964, it would not have amounted to much on my part. The night remains memorable for my optimistic and pathetic perversity in preferring the remote possibility of plundering the purlieus of pantie-hose to watching a world heavyweight champion-ship title fight. What a ridiculous young fellow I was.

Nevertheless, the point is made: you don't have to have actually been there in person for famous sporting days to remain memorable. Like, what were you doing the day Arthur Ashe beat Jimmy Connors in the final of the 'Gentlemen's' Singles at Wimbledon in 1975? Again, I had a ticket in my pocket; not to report the thing, but to act as legman for David Gray; all I was expected to do was produce a few daubs of colour for Monday morning. So when the phone rang, I was anybody's. It did. Twice. First, a friendly call from our esteemed drama critic, Michael Billington – why not pop round for drinks that very evening.

Second call, out of the blue, was from a long-ago and passing acquaintance from telly days – well, 'passing' in as much as I had often dared myself to make a pass at her. If 'fancied' was the word, then I 'fancied' her. She had been a researcher a few offices up the corridor at Rediffusion. I'd bumped into her once or twice since. Now she was something in films. Her name was Sarah-Daphne, pronounced Sara-Daff. Had I a spare ticket for the Wimbledon final, she wanted to know? Of course not, sweetheart. Well, why not let's go out for lunch and watch the final on your TV? Okay. I said, I would do a piece on old Dan Maskell's gushing vocab – and then perhaps she would like to come to Mike B's drinks party?

Such days change your life – as, on this midsummer Saturday, Jimmy Connors was to find out to his cost. The young champion could not have been a more vibrant favourite. All year he had been on song and as sharp as a lark on the wing. But Ashe simply slowballed the pace merchant. (It was rather like Ali encouraging Foreman to punch himself out: nobody had dared do that to the fearsome George before, so he didn't know what to do: just as Jimmy didn't here). Arthur just returned all the kid's whizzbangs to him in a gentle parabola then, when he served, sliced the balls wider and wider. At each rest period, Arthur towelled himself in a trance while, alongside him, Jimmy fannied and fidgeted and read and re-read a note from his beloved Grandmother, lately dead, which said, 'Don't let them get at you, boy'. Once, towards the end when all was lost, the bewildered, heroically despairing Connors answered heaven and a heckler with the plaintive shriek, 'I *am* trying, f'Chrissakes!'

That epic final, more than any other, was one of those few sporting events which might have been heightened and more sharply focused by television than by actually being there, seeing as it was all taking place on the two chairs under the umpire's stepladder: Arthur's mystic, eyes-closed yoga, Jimmy's fretful despair as his capture became more certain.

Sara-Daff was as riveted as me. I perceived my stock to be already fine fettled with her: the pre-Wimbledon tournament that year had been on the grass in Nottingham and I had spent a couple of days up there working with Ashe on a profile. Now I could boastfully add snippets to the match we were watching with some 'insider's' stories. Sara-Daff seemed reasonably impressed. A good first-base. Good enough to be sure, for we stayed together four years. She was a singular smasher – a square, open, expressive face – dimpled and moled to perfection, although she wouldn't thank you for mentioning that. For certain types of smile the tip of her tongue would fractionally peep between her teeth, which I found remarkably appealing, don't ask me why. She had a timeless, country-girl's look – golden wheatsheaf hair, box-top shoulders, and a homely, hammocky, well-filled bra. She might have been typecast to play the lead in the spate of Thomas Hardy films of that time, parts which always seemed to go to too-sophisticated actresses like Julie Christie. There was a mischievous, sparky, full-bloom-of-youth Diane Cilento about our Sara-Daff.

We laughed a great deal, and drank even more, convincing ourselves what a good gamble we had made. I liked her Cornish folks and she liked mine from Glos. Robert sportingly left the flat; we stayed on, and then bought a dinky, thatched-honeypot cottage at Lower Chute on the Wilts-Hants border. We giggled and fought, both with the manic intensity of a Keystone one-reeler. We spent our salaries like we'd left both bath-taps running. In the end we realized we had committed ourselves to something which had been founded on nothing much in the first place. Sara-Daff was the first to mention it and, bravely, the first to do something about it.

I returned from Brearley's 1979–80 Australian tour to find a note. Sara-Daff was 'staying with friends'. She returned 'for one last try'. This kind of ultimatum pressurizes everything. When has 'one last try' *ever* worked? I was soon off with Bill Beaumont's rugby Lions to benighted, soul-destroying South Africa. (As I was being grilled by the khaki-shorted cops in Cape Town about my work-permit not allowing reports from townships – 'only rr-ugg-bee, mun' – the phone rang at the police station. A personal call; I thought it would be the Editor enjoining me 'stick it out, brave soul'. But it was Sara-Daff in tears saying the cat had died. The cops thought it was a coded message).

Within a fortnight of my being (most happily) thrown out of South Africa, I was on the plane to the Moscow Olympics. Daley danced and Seb ran. Sara-Daff and Marita Miller met David and me off the plane at Heathrow. We all had a memorable, relieved slap-up in the Ark which went into the early hours. When I woke up next morning, Sara-Daff had gone and so had all her stuff.

I was half heartbroken, half relieved. I played desperate court to the former feeling, and drank more than a few solitary, celebratory draughts to the latter. It is often more comfortable to be the left than the leaver. Anyway, the US tennis championships were about to start. . . .

\*     \*     \*

As if I hadn't had enough to be going on with that year. One of the most palpitating passages had been three days and two races with Sebastian Coe at the Moscow Olympics during that dreamy, drowsy, heatwave fortnight in the late summer. The classy, spike-sparking Steve Ovett – nearly, but very much not quite, one of the all-time greats – was given the first race, the 800m final, on a plate by Coe, who ran like a nervous schoolgirl. Seb knew it, too, and when the elated Ovett, atop the podium, stuck out his mitt to shake Coe's hand, the expression on the face of the dejected silver medallist looked, in the memorable words of Clive James, 'as if someone was handing him a steamy turd'.

To say the least, Coe had to reinvigorate body and, especially, mind, for the upcoming 1,500m race. Few gave him a prayer. It was, for a start, Ovett's speciality race;

anyway, Coe's spirit would surely take more than three days to recover. Seb was brooding in the village when his father and coach, Peter, brought in a telegram from England. It was signed by an unknown Mrs Mullory, and said simply: 'Get your bloody finger out, Coe, I've got money on you'. They don't know to this day who Mrs Mullory is – 'but Seb and I looked at each other', said Peter, 'and the look said "She's damn right", so out our finger we did get'.

The gun! The first two, jockeying, laps of the four-lap final were dawdles enough to set up an explosive, extended, finish. I can remember the dryness in my mouth almost as well the steam-hammer clump of my heart as I sat high above the clustered little knot of colours circling the strawberry-red track. Which of the two, compatriots and deadly rivals both in the all-white rig, would be the one to pull out ahead and make an extended necklace of the colours behind them?

Suddenly, eruptingly, on the back straight, with about 190 metres to the tape, both Coe and Ovett put in a simultaneous kick. In a moment, only Straub, the East German in blue who had made all the early running, looked remotely capable of catching them. No realistic hopes, for now Coe put in another semi-kick, and was a stride-and-a-half up on Ovett. It was now down to this: Ovett had the most chilling, killing final sprint in history so far, but could Coe draw the string from it before they hit the last 50 metres? On the crown of the final bend, another split second semi-kick from Coe. Dammit, the little wraith was accelerating, then accelerating again, then again, going up through the gears, then up further ... Ovett and the game Straub were having all the juice sucked from them.

Another kick off the final bend by Coe did for them. The little man put in two backwards glances, left and right, as he glided into the straight – and no one was gathering himself at his shoulder. Ovett's final, famous, surge had been strangled. Another half-kick at 40 metres out, just to run the flag up the pole, and Coe was now running to the line on instinct only – arms outstretched and face contorted in an orgasmic expression of relief and exultation. He had run the last 800m of his 1,500m faster than any man before. His last 300m had been covered in 39 secs, the last 200 in 24.7, the last 100m in 12.1. Incredible. As comebacks go, it remains top-rated on my Lazarus scale alright.

There had been something else to interrupt a sulking row with Sara-Daff. This took 20 times longer than Sebastian's last dash: the Borg-McEnroe tie-break, the first ever played in a Wimbledon final. Borg was a man of the Seventies. This was to be the last of his five successive Wimbledon championships. The young pretender McEnroe was to go on and win three of the next four Wimbledons. This was the first, horn-locking encounter between the old and new champions of the herd. The tie-break – Borg up two sets to one, and 6–6 in the fourth – took an astonishing 34 points. Back and forth, each pinging the ball harder and more nervelessly than, you felt, at any time in their careers. For a fourth, then fifth time Borg reached match point. For a fourth, then fifth time the Kid, with utter daring, fought back to level . . . and then, in turn, five, six, seven times got to set-point to level the match 2–2. At the seventh time of asking, McEnroe did it. Momentarily, the old cabbage-green place turned scarlet with the emotion of it.

The same sort of spent feeling came over all who witnessed The Barbarians Try at Cardiff in 1972. One day, much later, I sat down the men who scored it and said 'what actually happened?'

. . . KIRKPATRICK . . . TO BRYAN WILLIAMS . . . THIS IS GREAT STUFF . . . PHIL BENNETT COVERING . . . CHASED BY ALISTAIR SCOWN . . . BRILLIANT . . . OH, THAT'S BRILLIANT . . . JOHN WILLIAMS . . . PULLIN . . . JOHN DAWES, GREAT DUMMY . . . DAVID, TOM DAVID, THE HALFWAY LINE . . . BRILLIANT, BY QUINNELL . . . THIS IS GARETH EDWARDS . . . A DRAMATIC START . . . WHAT A SCORE!

Cliff Morgan's commentary on The Barbarians Try is bound to spool through the minds and hearts of all us nuts.

Not Phil Bennett's try really. Nor Gareth's. But the Magnificent Seven's.

Bennett's was the coruscating opening move, as he gathered the difficult bobbler under his own posts and, as a furious wave of adrenalin-charged All Blacks bore down on him, in the very act of turning he drove his right foot into not one, nor two, but three sidesteps . . . brilliant, oh that's brilliant. . . .

'At the time I was intent only on getting out of trouble. I sensed they were right on top of me. Perhaps the whole beautiful, amazing thing wouldn't have happened if I hadn't heard Alistair Scown's menacing footsteps bearing down on me. As it was it was a bit of a hospital pass I gave to JPR, wasn't it?'

. . . JOHN WILLIAMS . . .

'Well, certainly I nearly lost my head as Bryan Williams lunged at me. But what utter brilliance by Phil. I remain convinced that the whole thing was really Carwyn James's try. Unique to the Barbarians, who disapproved of coaching, they asked him to give us a talk before the game.

'There was a lot of needle in the game; both we and the All Blacks were treating it as an unofficial fifth Test decider after we (the Lions) had beaten them, coached by Carwyn, down-under 18 months before. Now, before we went out, Carwyn soothed us, calming and relaxed, told us to enjoy it; and I'll never forget his last words, to insist to Phil, who was full of trepidation, hadn't played long for Wales and certainly not for the Lions, to go out and play just like he did for Llanelli.

'So he does, then gives it to me, and as I'm almost scalped I see John [Pullin] outside me, and pop it to him, and do you know I still think to myself sometimes "where the heck did he come from; what's John, our trusty old hooker, doing there?" '

. . . PULLIN . . .

'Tell him I was there because speedy running forwards are not a new phenomenon. I'd been doing it all my career, but nobody seemed to notice. The try still vivid in my memory? Well, has to be. They seem to replay it every week on TV. Can't escape it. Seriously, there was a real needle to the game. "Exhibition match" was our last thought. A 3–0 win would have been enough for me.

'I suppose, looking back, it would honestly have been normal for me to have kicked for touch when I got the ball, but at the time it never entered my mind – I was back in New Zealand playing for Carwyn and the Lions and he drilled us all tour that if someone else had a bit of space then you pass it on to him. And John Dawes was moving quite nicely, wasn't he?'

. . . JOHN DAWES, GREAT DUMMY . . .

'Ah me, the dummy that never was! But I'm eternally grateful to Cliff, telling the world I was a purveyor of great dummies. And I'm not going to argue with 35 million viewers, am I? In fact I was already looking to put John [Bevan] off down the wing, but the "dummy" was more my eyeing the opposition as if I intended to pass. Anyway suddenly they weren't there any more, I was through the gap and now looking for support inside.

'The fascinating things are: would Benny, who was pretty much a novice in international terms then, have dreamed of opening up if Carwyn's last words hadn't been to "sidestep this lot off the park, like you do at Stradey"; and that Gareth, if you study the TV replay, had covered right back from the halfway to our own line and when John passed to me, Gareth was actually well behind us, so he covered a heck of a lot of ground in that single minute.

'And incidentally, tell old Pullin that if the "mismove" had been invented in 1973, he wouldn't have got his pass and been world famous now'.

. . . DAVID, TOM DAVID, THE HALFWAY LINE . . .

'Is that really me, taking the ball at such a helter-skelter in every one of those million TV replays? I wish the BBC would stop them. Well, the world and his wife thinks I'm still 23 and an electric athletic of under 14 stone, and then they see my middle-aged spread coming through the door and say; "That's never him, the guy in the Baa-Baas try — can't be, impossible".

'No, actually, whenever I see it I think of two blokes from Gloucester way. Well, of course I had only been told I was replacing the injured Mervyn [Davies] on the day of the match. Hadn't played for three weeks seriously because of my knee, see. The Saturday before, I thought I needed a run-out to get a bit fit, so asked some pals up at Cilfynydd for a game.

'They were playing a little club at Gloucester called Hucclecote. No problem, they say, so off we go to Gloucester and I turn out in the centre. Foggy, I remember, which is perhaps the reason that I seem to score a try every time I get the ball. Tons of them, haring through the centre just like that. Great. Knee great too, so no worries by the end of the week when I'm called up for the Baa-Baas.

'Except little me's surrounded by all these all-time greats. The only sadness it, I'm not in the programme, being such a late call-up. It also worried two blokes in the great crowd, too. They were from Hucclecote. It said "Mervyn Davies" in the programme. They must have thought they'd either had too many beers or were in the middle of a bad dream. "Stone me, if that's not the bugger who played in the centre for Cilfynydd against us last Saturday".

'That evening they sought me out to settle their argument. "Hello, boys", I said, "Sure, I'm the local valley boy from the centre for Cilfynydd who made good in a week, and gave the pass for Derek Quinnell's magnificent catch this very afternoon".'

... BRILLIANT, BY QUINNELL ...

'Funny you describe it as a slip catch on the run. That very thing, ridiculously, was going through my mind as I held it. That there I was on the Arms Park, and I was thinking about a boyhood triumph all those years ago at Coleshill Sec Mod when my Form 2A played the big boys from 4A in the school cricket cup final and I took a truly wonderful catch at silly mid-on, just like this one I had just taken off Tom. And I'm pretty certain that childhood winning catch was off the bowling of form 2A's little Phil Bennett himself.

'When we got back with the cup that afternoon our form master, Mr Brace, said "Quinnell, a truly magnificent, magnificent catch, but remember you only field at silly mid-on because you're built for comfort, not speed". That's what I was thinking as I scooped up Tom's pass at my bootlaces – till I was soon enough exploded out of my reverie by this series of banshee shouts behind me.

'I knew Gareth was coming up like a train, screaming for the ball like a raving idiot – jeepers, what a din. So recalling Mr Brace again and my lack of speed, I just pop the ball out to the left and let John [Bevan] and Gareth sort out who takes the pass. I guessed it would be Gareth, mind you, for he wanted something to show for having run so far so fast, which was not his usual practice if he could help it, was it?'

... THIS IS GARETH EDWARDS ... A DRAMATIC START ...

When they talk about it, Derek will chaff Gareth that he was only allowed to make his name for posterity thanks to Quinnell's 'magnificent unselfishness, when I could easily have run in the ball himself'. In fact, Edwards had to pin his ears back and go like a fury to catapult in at the corner. Typically, he just says it was 'a privilege to finish such a move'.

... WHAT A SCORE! ...

In the grandstand, the game's eminence, 75-year old Lord Wakefield of Kendal, turned and shook hands with the Barbarians' celebrated president, Herbert Waddell, and whispered in his ear: 'My friend, I will now die a happy man'.

Meanwhile, not far away from the two old men, Carwyn James took a deep, satisfied pull on his Senior Service and smiled his private, contented smile. I rang him up and asked him to write, for the *Guardian*, of the moment, rare and unforgettable, when you can play at a level outside the

conscious when everything is instinctive, but as clear as a
bell because you have practised it so often and, especially,
dreamed it – that unique moment when sport, lovely sport,
not only achieves, but assumes, an art form.

There have been three great 'collective' tries logged by
history. I saw them all. I was there on 21 May 1980 in
Potchefstroom's quaint little, low-slung grandstand. This
time, the estimable Quinnell himself was producer-director.
High on the Veldt, the sun was dropping and time was fast
running out for the beleaguered British. 16–19 – it was
going to be the Lions' first defeat outside Tests in South
Africa in eight years and 26 matches. The referee, as the
football commentator once put it, 'was looking at his
whistle and preparing to blow his watch'. The frantic,
counter-attacking wave came and came again as the ball
went through 33 pairs of hands in a move lasting one
minute and 36 seconds – an unbelievable amount of time, if
you think about it.

On and on it went, from hand to hand, from left to right,
forwards and backwards, forwards and backwards and
forwards again ... Quinnell always there, rucking and
running, alongside his tiny West Walian lieutenant, Richards.
It was almost touch rugby. O'Driscoll, Williams, Rees, and
Phillips; Patterson, with the fast fingers, kept switching the
options; cool hand Renwick was always there, and the
pacing Woodward. What started as a rather forlorn gesture
of defiance – the referee could not blow the final whistle till
the ball was dead – rolled on and on to a crescendo of
heroic proportions – as the doughty Scot called Hay turned
into a tackle on the touchline only a few feet away from me,
to show the spring-heeled Slemen a gap through which he
drove the killing, thrilling thrust.

Pandemonium – and 50,000 South African hands smacked
palm-to-palm in generosity and wonder. The old Empire
came together again for just a fleeting moment or two.

The third try, in March 1991, may, in all truth, have been
the best. Well, context is all. This, by France and inspired by
Serge Blanco, was run in during the intensity of a Grand Slam

finale. Grandeur, it was. England missed a long penalty and all eyes and senses, certainly those of the England XV for a fatal moment, relaxed and prepared for a 22 drop-out.

Suddenly all hell broke loose or, rather, the incomparable Serge Blanco, dusky warrior-captain of France, did. 'Moi, moi', he shouted to Berbizier, who fielded the ball. Blanco has always put his trust in gods who favour the foolhardy. He was now across his line but still 10 yards short of his own 22. In a trice the ball was with Lafond outside him and the wing's left hip took out Andrew, first to spot the danger; an instantaneous finger-tip pass inside allowed Sella, at speed, to round his own despairing white marker.

Sella was over the 22 and momentarily clear as England regrouped and frantically funnelled back. The stalwart Probyn had tanked across to confront him on France's 10-metre line. Sella feinted to knife inside him, so stopping the prop in his tracks, and, as he did so, he turned in a dummy-scissors loop and fed on the outside again the delicate Camberabero. The pit-a-pat fly-half could now snipe across the halfway mark.

Then, with dainty exactness, he chipped the ball over the head of the retreating Hodgkinson, caught it in full-pelt stride and was now up to England's 22. Though England's bold general Carling had, remarkably, made it across the field, he could only fling himself at Camberabero a split-second after the Frenchman had dapped the most perfectly weighted cross-kick to within five metres of the posts.

This took out the corner-flagging Hill and left Saint-André to compose himself, collect and triumphantly launch himself at the line as Guscott's all-in, last-gasp dive lassoed his ankles. The palpitating thing was done. Eh, voilà. Parc des Princes erupted.

\*　　\*　　\*

I could write a book on cricket tours. But in these abroad thoughts from home it is not the actual cricket which leaps to the mind, but the dotty little snippets of life before and after close of play. Like flying into (I think) Montserrat in the seat next to Geoffrey B. and noticing, when he opened his famous tooled-leather businessman's briefcase to get out his whacking, heavyweight Robert Ludlum novel, that the rest of the case was (literally) choc-full of nothing else but neat stacks of Cadbury's fruit-and-nut bars. There must have been at least three dozen in there. 'It's for me energy', quoth Geoff.

I thought of my own childhood when I walked up the hillocky path, past Captain Cook's Cottage, through the park between the MCG and the Windsor Hotel. I was 25 yards behind Derek Randall, and kept my distance – for there, in his reverie and without a bat, the England ragamuffin man-child was miming every stroke in the manual . . . forward-defensives, opulent cover-drives, meaty square-cuts, feathery leg-glances . . . for all the world like a bouncy schoolboy in front of his mum's full-length mirror; and every shot, of course, accompanied by a click of his tongue, and every follow through held, just so, with a hum of pleasure and the momentary grin of a Bisto kid. He had just scored a famous Test century, but was still a boy. What touching and timeless flavours of relish and exuberance did Randall bestow to his Test match days.

On and on, the flickering memory spool careers back, higgledy-piggledy. . . . Gatt with his interminable tapes of his beloved *Lord of the Rings*; Willis with his pills and his potions and his humours, his grit and his courage, and the full works of Wodehouse in his bag; Bob Taylor exchanging smiles in a mutual admiration society with Mother Teresa; Botham's utter hooraymanship everywhere; ditto Gower's sheer class and charm both at the crease and away from it; 'Sir' Geoffrey's truly sublime serenity – as if he'd climbed Everest after a lifetime of trying – the evening he took his pads off at Delhi the day before Christmas, having passed Sir Garfield's all-time Test aggregate of 8032 runs. And, within a fortnight, he was gone from the Test match scene forever.

Oh, sure, real cricket, too. Cricket to savour on those three tours of mine. Like a square-drive by Clive Lloyd in Barbados, played late off the front foot, which was as withering as it was breathtaking. Or a double-century at Madras which combined utter grandeur and almost sheepish modesty – it could only be by Viswanath, that tiny one-off with the bashful, marsupial eyes. There was a penny-pinching, wizard's spell of slow bowling by Emburey at Trinidad, hour upon hour in dark glasses and on a batsman's pitch. And Viv's inevitable century in Antigua's first-ever Test – a rasping first 50 for the island, and a careful, coddled, considered second 50 as a wedding-present for Miriam.

At Sydney one night, under lights – the brightest of which was a gloriously raging moon, hung dramatically in the purply-black South Pacific skies – the carrot-topped David Bairstow bristled out to join his compatriot Graham Stevenson with three overs and two wickets left, and 35 to get against Australia. Lillee and Thompson were pawing the earth, and The Hill was hooting and happy. Said Bairstow as he greeted his mate, 'Evenin', lad. I reckon we can piss this, y'know'. They did too. Almost with the same dismissive unconcernedness as Botham had shown at Indore two winters later, when the Baron of Beefy bazooka'd 122 against Central Zone in 48 minutes and off 48 balls – having blocked 11 of the first 14 he received. When Botham posted his century, Gatting, at the other end, had generously scored but three solitary singles.

Our 1980–81 Windies tour was dominated by politics. England called up a substitute for the injured Willis. Whether by stupidity or design, Lord's sent out Robin Jackman, chirpy Oval sparrow with the little legs, long run-up, and klaxon-like appeal to the umpire and the heavens. For the previous nine winters, Robin had been coaching or playing in South Africa, a fact to which Mr Forbes Burnham, the demon-king who then ruled Guyana in his Chinese dungarees, did not take kindly.

The day after Jackman's arrival, England played a pre-Test one-dayer in a jungle-clearing down in Berbice. Having heard Mr Burnham growling about apartheid on the early morning state radio, a few of us played truant from the cricket and strolled up from the Pegasus hotel in our Bermuda shorts and Panama hats to the British High Commission. We must have looked like a bunch of Brits in one of those Pinewood films: Melford of the *Telegraph* playing the lugubrious twitcher John le Mesurier; Woodcock of *The Times* as Robert Morley, mopingly mopping his jowls with a spotted handkerchief; Fitzpatrick of the *Guardian* a Mancunian Richard Wattis; Hodgson of the *Star* a glum Peter Ustinov; and me, happily typecast as Richard Todd or a youthful Trevor Howard.

A couple of ragged sentries saluted us and we were ushered into the presence of Her Majesty's representative in Guyana and non-resident Ambassador to Surinam, P. L. V. Mallet, Esq., CMG, Winchester & Balliol: previous postings, Sweden, the Sudan; club, Brooks; hobbies, cricket. He sat at his desk under the Annigoni portrait. He was dressed in a Persil-perfect tropical suit. This was probably the biggest day of his career. There was a tiny blob of egg yolk on his chin.

Whitehall had just phoned, he said. 'Looks like bad news, I'm afraid, chaps'. The phone rang again. It was his man in Berbice. He winced, then replaced the receiver to announce, 'England 34 for 3, Boycott, Gooch and Gower all gone'.

The match didn't last long. As soon as the team returned to the Pegasus, a silent, sinister official in khaki and wire specs served Jackman, his perkiness only momentarily embarrassed, with his 'immediate revocation of entry permit'. No cricket team can ever have packed more quickly. Then the rickety airport bus wouldn't start, and the team's beloved assistant manager Ken Barrington, who had once owned a garage in Surrey, fiddled around under the bonnet and got it going.

A small, glum crowd saw us off. 'With that bastard

Burnham depriving them of their cricket, I'm surprised he's not got a full-scale evolution on his hands', muttered Barrington. We relished Ken's unending stream of malapropisms. They even came in pairs, like opening bats. Of the West Indies pace attack, he said, 'The ball comes at you non-stop like a high-philosophy bullet, and if it wasn't for batsmen's helmets we'd have quite a few fertilities around'. Or even trebles: once he told Bob Willis, 'The secret of bowling in anyone's cup of tea is to keep the batsman in two-man's land till he surrenders his wicket like one of them Japanese Kalahari pilots'.

At least Barbados let Jackman play. A week later, when the Test series resumed at Bridgetown, darling old Ken sat, fraught and chain-smoking in the pav as England, his 'boys', collapsed miserably to 122 all out. Nothing changes – except later that evening, March 14, 1981, Ken Barrington died of a heart attack.

Next innings, his eyes still moist with tears, young Gooch goes out to face Holding, Roberts, Croft, and Garner with only one determination in his soul – to dedicate his defiance to Kenny's memory. And how. Gooch's 116 of England's 224 all out (only two others made double figures) was heroism of quite memorable resplendence.

On tour, the telephone dominates the day more than bat or ball. There was dappy Don Mosey, that duke of disgruntlement, finally getting through to the BBC sportsroom from the banks of the Berbice River in downtown, downtrodden Guyana. They were all out at lunch. Only a temp was on. 'I don't know who you are, but do you want to give some news?' she asked. 'No', spat the emperor of irony, jowls a-wobble, as he slammed down the phone, 'I want to give a pint of blood!'

Another time, at Jammu, where we needed hot-water bottles and could see the Himalayas from the bedroom windows of the Hotel Asia, two nights running 'Ernie Embers' tried to ring his Suzie in Melbourne. Both times he was told 'Suzie is out at the café with Kurt'. Embers felt hurt about Kurt. Third night of calling, the same answer. 'Are you sure that's Melbourne whatever-the-number was?' asked Emburey. 'Oh no', said the voice, 'this is not Australia, this is Maubendorf, Austria'.

In those days, of course, almost every story from outside the office was telephoned through to copytakers who, muffed in headphones, would take down the reams of daily rubbish which seemed so important on the night. They had to change their paper every three or four paragraphs, and each time re-type and number the story's 'catchline' on every succeeding sheet.

One evening, David Gray, our esteemed but extremely verbose tennis writer, dictated page after page of guff from Wimbledon. The catchline was 'lawn tennis'. When the drooping copytaker finally finished David's marathon, her phone immediately rang again. This time it was a two-thousander from Terry Coleman with some wordy feature on poets laureate. Every time his name was mentioned in the piece, which was often, one of the greatest of our royal scribblers came out as 'Alfred Lawn Tennison'. It wasn't spotted by any of the subs and ran through all editions.

Off the top of my head, even from this distance, I can remember a few, and all doubtless down to me, when I was subbing – and too many sprinted evening trips across the road and back from the Blue Lion. How about 'A rash of no-balls by Willis had umpire Fagg regularly gestating throughout the day?' Or 'Banks saved a certain goal when he died despairingly at Davies's feet'. I suppose even next morning I had to be quite pleased with, 'The last batsman, Albeit Carefully, survived to lunch'. Hooray for Albeit.

And on and on. . . . 'Compared with Leeds's all-white strip, Chelsea took the eye with their irresistible passes and royal-blue skirts'. . . . 'Uttley can play anywhere in the scrum – a typically English futility player'. . . . 'A stony-faced Barrington last night accused Griffith of chuckling' . . . 'Somehow Bedi regained his crease after being strangled halfway down the wicket'. Even mixed doubles . . . 'The tall, blind, goalkeeper, Bailey, was discomfited in keeping out a rocket of a shit from Jones. . . .' 'The game featured a second period hat-trick from Tony Hand and some sound neckminding by John McCrone in the British goal'. . . . 'Ian Greig, captain of Surrey for the lost five years, is to step down at the end of the season' . . . 'Bridgend 9 Newbridge 4: The quest for two pints has become the over-riding factor in the inaugural season of the Heineken League'.

Once, in my first days as a sub on the *Guardian*'s foreign desk, not long after that ludicrous lovelorn trek up the length of Africa humming 'Maria', I almost caused a diplomatic incident by rushing up a headline on the stone but failing to check it at proof-panic. The darling of the British left at the time was President Nkrumah of the newly independent Ghana – soon to be exposed as a dictator and crook; but not quite yet. Our reporter in Accra sent over a good piece about Ghana's allegedly democratic referendum on some matter or other, describing how, nevertheless, armed members of Nkrumah's People's Party were on hand in the polling booths to 'explain' voting procedures to the populace, while others were organizing victory revels in the streets before even the X's had been crossed on the ballot papers. I put up the reasonable and ambiguously suggestive headline 'Ghana Takes Referendum in Party Spirit' and never gave it another thought. Next day, all hell . . . diplomatic bags full of apology, screaming ad-dabs from excitable blokes in the Ghanaian Embassy, me hauled over the John Coles by our then Political Editor (now dear old, tweed-coated 'Hoon-doot-edly' of BBC News). What had been printed in all editions on the front page had been the unequivocal headline 'Ghana Fakes Referendum in Party Spirit', which was a far different kettle of certitude than our reporter with his nudge-and-wink had dared to intend. Nkrumah thought of slinging him in a dungeon, apparently, and John considered throttling me. But in the end, like the 'democratic' referendum itself, it all became water under the bridge. As it usually does on daily papers. For there is nothing more *passé* and pointless as yesterday's paper to a daily journo. Or even today's. Tomorrow is all.

So the *Guardian*'s most crass misprint must remain the one enshrined in brass and on permanent display on the wall of a Fleet Street wine bar. *The* Fleet Street wine bar, El Vino's. When the management of that estimable step-in-and-buy-just-the-one decided to honour the *Guardian*'s revered and veteran critic of opera and theatre, Philip Hope-Wallace, by erecting a plaque to him in his favourite cubbyhole (back room, middle left), the paper was telephoned and asked 'Does he spell Philip with one "l" or two?'. And answer came there 'two'. So the unveiling ceremony was quite ruined for Philip – or so he sighed; deep down it suited his world-weary despair of the modern way of the world and particularly proved how tiresome to him the 'new' *Guardian* had become as opposed to its stolid and meticulous old Manchester self when he had first joined it.

'What else can you expect, my dear boy', he would elegantly seethe, while at the same time looking to catch the waitress's eye for the setting up of a freshly delectable bottle of fizz. Then another sigh, and he would launch into a blazingly observant, always hilarious tale of the latest woes that had befallen him and modern England. He was the funniest (I suppose he would prefer the more wry 'drollest') raconteur I can ever hope to meet. And by far the most generous man who ever kept his loose change in a war issue leather purse. His true tales of the excruciating or otherwise personal habits of world-renowned sopranos or tenors or conductors would have my mouth agape. He was just as riveting on famous buses of his time that failed to make St John's Wood from the Strand. Or of his days as a junior clerk in the London Gas & Coke Board. Or when he was the equivalent of Uncle Mac on Radio Normandy in the 1930s. It just depended on what came up in the cubbyhole conversation that day ... say, 'Princess Louise of Battenburg', or 'the Peru national airline', or 'Rod Laver's backhand' (tennis was the only 'untiresome' sport), or 'Hay-on-Wye', or 'Noël Coward', and it would trigger-off the entrancing flow. I went to sit at his feet, and always ended up rolling on the floor (once or thrice, literally). Philip would sit with his back to the offending plaque so he could see the end of his world go by – and also shout a sharp 'Door!' whenever some tyro barrister forgot his manners. He especially enjoyed pompous men being slung out of the place for breaking the loony stipulation of El Vino's that 'gentlemen' should wear a tie. Once that veteran bow-legged Hollywood hero, Jack Palance, as tall as he was rich (and father of Holly, a longtime darling friend and Holland Park neighbour of mine), had no sooner seated himself in the honoured chair next to Philip than he was asked if he wouldn't mind leaving and returning with a 'proper' tie. The film star was wearing a resplendent, buttoned-up silk shirt on which, from top-to-tummy-button, had been exquisitely hand-stitched a wavy 'tie' of genuine, rare boa-constrictor (or whatever) snakeskin. 'Whaddya mean, man, this shirt – and tie – cost over six-hundred dollars', said the affronted Mr P. No matter. Not in England. Not in El Vino's. It was, doubtless, the most expensive shirt-and-tie ensemble ever to grace the hostelry – but it was stitched to the shirt and so would definitely not do. We had to cadge him the management's spare and mangy, soup stained and wine reeking, old club-striped length of tat which was kept for such eventualities, and he had to put it on *over* his own opulent creation before Philip could pour the first glass of welcoming Bollinger.

Television had been fun while it lasted, but it was all swank, pink-shirted modernism going places, much less a benignly raffish meeting of minds and cronies as journalism. To me, late to Fleet Street anyway, and an unconsidered sports hack to boot, those regular sessions at Philip's knee were as richly and generally rewarding as they were stimulating. If you remembered a tie and bagged an early place – often, in my case, prearranged with my dear pal, Johnny Moynihan – the giants of the trade would pass by the Hope-Wallace den, morning and evening. A whole alphabet of inky stars: well, offhand, how about the W's alone? Colin Welch, cricket loving wit, and Michael Wharton, who lived on liquor and fish-fingers, the two successive and dazzling Peter Simples from the *Telegraph*; the two journos' journos, Keith Waterhouse, white haired and wondrous, and Dick West, another Holland Parkite; Geoffrey Wheatcroft, his satchel overflowing with review copies; Alan Watkins, politics, rugby football, and all-round gusto; and the peacock, Peregrine Worsthorne, who wrote in his obituary to Philip in the *Guardian* – 'It was almost obligatory before settling down to write a leader or feature to cross the Street to El Vino's to have a drink with Philip. As a result there was a little bit of Philip in about everything one ever wrote. His influence was pervasive, and much more than his champagne went to our heads.'

Or how about the M's? Moynihan; or the *Mirror*'s ace court man (juicy cases a speciality) Brian McConnell; the wickedly gabby gossip with the Basil Brush chuckle, Peter McKay; or, on Saturdays before the match, the onliest McIlvanney, of the *Obs*, who would breeze in for a bubble or two with his sports editor, the kindly and exuberant Clifford Makins in his opera cloak. . . .

I just sat and listened; enthralled.

As it turned out, had we but realized, those days represented the last glorious, but dying, convulsions of old Fleet Street – that same invigorating roistering, those tangential unorthodoxies of intellect in full spate that had so captivated Dad in his youthful Chesterbelloc days. Before he put up his hand at a Land Association meeting and became a farmer.

Suddenly Philip died, and almost in sympathy his ancient newspaper ways of centuries – hot metal and nicotine, black ink, and liquid gold in the glass – was detonated; so explosively, it seemed almost between editions, that Fleet Street turned into the incomprehensible world of shimmering dayglo green screens and the Anglo-Jap jargon of computer gobbledygook. Overnight, olde Fleete Streete was fragmented; those legends in my little lunchtime were dispersed hither and yon to razor-wired modern factories up and downriver, with no pubs nor other newspapers nearby; creepy-hush carpets on the floors, and no-smoking orders slapped on every wall by zoot-suited admin wankers or crèche-campaigning single-parent lesbians in blue and baggy boiler suits of corduroy who call themselves office managers. They are the masters now. The great and good Waterhouse hit the button on the dismantlement of El Vino's veritas for journalism when he lamented the lost days in an essay in the *Guardian* in 1992 – when Fleet Street was a gossip mill: 'perpetuating a line of slander and calumny unbroken since Dr Johnson's day; but there was far more to it than mere tittle-tattle . . . in the back room of El Vino's you could take a crash course on the political issues of the day, or get expert assessment of the chances of the latest libel action or, as a complete ignoramus on sport, learn all you needed to know on the subject from rubbing shoulders with ace sports writers . . . When Fleet Street roared with argument, as it did day after day and night after night, it was the sound of newspaper folk sharpening their wits . . . Wappingization doesn't only mean not smoking or drinking, it means not meeting, not exchanging ideas'.

Then, glory be, just as Fleet Street began to disperse, terminally, to its mineral-waters-all-round and pukey screen-green, out of the blue Alan Coren, bless his cherry-red waistcoats, offered me a weekly essay in *Punch*. It was a daunting 2,000-er but, for me, good loot, in which respect I felt I owed myself a bit of catching up, for now there need be no temptation any more even to consider leaving the *Guardian*. (In 1981, for instance, Harry Evans had offered me a top job, for bundles of booty, on *The Times* sports pages, and it was one sleepless night and some fond and genuine entreaties from John Samuel and Peter Preston before I came to my senses; but I very nearly succumbed to Harry's charm and Mammon; I also rang up Dad to ask his

advice in the middle of that deciding night: 'Just think of
two proper nouns before you make your decision, m'boy –
"Mr Murdoch" and "all the tea in China". Goodnight!'
(Within a year, it turned out, Harry Evans had been
Murdoched, and the senior sports column had happily gone
to my old friend and mentor, David Miller, who remains
pluperfect in the job). There was also a juicy carrot dangled
by the *Telegraph* to be a general colour magazine writer,
and 'polite enquiries' of my availability from one or two
other papers or magazines, including a bizarre dinner and
B&B at Headington Hall with the grizzly bear, Robert
Maxwell, which came (thank God) to nothing once the fat
man had been called up to London to sort out a union
dispute in mid-evening. I obviously did not impress, for all
the flattery I never heard another word. (Perhaps, as with
dear old Tom White at Guildford all those years ago, I had
asked about the Pension Fund). So Coren's invitation to be a
*Punch* regular, to fit in with all my *Guardian* assignments,
was heaven sent. It also put the tin lid on a dotty and
youthful ambition. Back on the *Hereford Times*, when I was
20, I had sent with tremulous speculation to the then *Punch*
editor, Malcolm Muggeridge, a tyro's effort at a 'humorous
essay', about a Herefordshire hedging match. It came back
pronto in my own stamped-addressed envelope, not even
with a rejection slip. Okay, Mal baby, I got the message.
(Once I joined, over 20 years later, the disappointment of
that curt fob-off of boyhood was alleviated when Miles
Kington told me that the magazine's first editor, Mark
Lemon, had spiked essays by Thomas Hardy and Charles
Dickens).

Occasionally Alan suggested I invite a guest for Punch's
famous Friday lunch. Once I took John Arlott, who was
surprisingly nervous when I met him beforehand in El
Vino's for a preliminary snort. He said he did not know
what to expect. But once the claret was tapped he held 'the
table' spellbound. Another time I took good, beady-eyed
(and exceedingly bushy-tailed when you get to know him)

Bob Willis when he was captain of England. Daft, I know, but I always felt dauntingly honoured (I suppose 'chuffed' should be the sports-hack's word) whenever I sat down to lunch at that huge table, heavily scored like an old school desktop by the initials of staffers down a century-and-a-half. (Before Prince Charles came to lunch one time, his detective had to inspect the room. 'My God, sir', he said to Alan, 'you've certainly had trouble with vandals, haven't you?').

On it had guzzled and gossiped: Garibaldi, Mark Twain, Wodehouse, Betjeman, A. A. Milne, A. P. Herbert, and even Thackeray – the last admitting that he wrote for *Punch* 'because of its good pay and great opportunity for laughing, sneering, kicking, and gambadoing'. Hooray to that. And an even more illustrious string of artists – Tenniel, du Maurier, Keene, Bateman, Heath Robinson, Emmett, Pont, and Fougasse, right up to the legends in my Friday lunchtimes, like Larry and Tidy, Handlesman, Jensen and Dickinson, the superlative Wally Fawkes (Trog), the consistently brilliant Michael Heath, and the gently zany, wholly original Michael ffoulkes, a dear man who would take me on to the Wig & Pen once Alan locked the port away at teatime. The artists would generally cluster round one end of the table, the writers at the other where Alan presided with the genial confidence and gusto of a man described on the dustcover of all his books as 'unarguably the funniest writer in England'.

I was sorry that my particular friend (who was that dustcover blurb's 'arguable' for his weekly challenge to Alan for all-England's heavyweight title), Miles Kington, did not stay long as assistant editor in my time before he was lured away to *The Times*. Miles had joined the magazine in the late 1960s, when Alan was deputy to the previous editor, Bill Davis, a former *Guardian* financial editor with an appealing European background and Fizz, who had been hired to clout some circulation strategies and commercial oomph into the old institution. 'One day, Davis came back from a long, executive, planning lunch,' Miles remembers, 'to find me, Alan and David Taylor playing a ferocious

game of indoor cricket with a tennis ball. I think it was the
occasion that Alan, with a hook shot for six, dislodged a
pile of magazines and commented, "Hello, a bit of trouble
among *The Spectators*, I see!" Anyway, Davis just looked at
us, shook his head, and went sadly into his room. We
continued our match.'

Miles said when he first arrived and was assigned a desk,
he cleared it out. He found Basil Boothroyd's slippers, a
letter from A. A. Milne to someone in 1939 saying he didn't
think the war was going to last long, and a first edition
review copy of *The Savoy Cocktail Book* with a slip inside
saying, 'Please Do Not Review Before June 4, 1926'.

It could not last. One of my neighbouring columnists in
the magazine, Melvyn Bragg, defined a *Punch* 'shock issue'
as one which investigated the decline of the English club:
'Punch is male, leisured, not intellectual; like a certain type
of Englishman, it likes tea, claret, and cricket, and that's
about it'. I remember one lunch when Alan invited as a
guest the then junior health minister in Mrs Thatcher's
government, Virginia Bottomley; she sat throughout the
meal wearing a forcedly brave but freezer-cold stare of utter
incredulity at the *Boys' Own* banter. The chair I used to try
and bag at lunch was next to the sublime film critic, Dilys
Powell, or the wine writer, the effervescent former *Manchester Guardian* man and dead ringer for Mr Punch
himself, Cyril Ray. Both Dilys and Cyril were in their 80s. It
was certainly not aiming at the young readership was
*Punch*. United Newspapers, who owned it, decided to get a
grip. The drama critic, Sheridan Morley, who liked to walk
around the office in his socks, reckoned the moment *Punch*'s
number came up was the day a United Newspapers' account
executive ordered him to put on his shoes. Increasingly, all
these men in suits with their ABC figures, point-of-sale
marketing, vendor-friendly covers, and product targeting
development pushes took over the bus. As Bill Tidy said,
'They thought they were dealing with a commodity. They
wanted 6½ ounces of whimsy and a pound of belly laughs.
Well, humour doesn't work like that.'

Coren, alas, finally had one too many tilts at the Suits and left. It was a sad day. Three stalwarts, David Taylor, Russell Davies and the splendid droll, Stanley Reynolds (whose sons, like those of Sheridan Morley's as well, were being schooled, coincidentally, at Douai) each had a spell in the editor's chair. The circulation of *Punch* in my ten years had dropped (only partly my fault, guv) by 20,000 copies to around 50,000. United tried a last revamp and appointed a talented turk from the *Mail on Sunday*, David ('I'll make *Punch* hip, trendy, and hot') Thomas. Appalled, the old guard walked out in a fearful huff. Thomas asked me to stay. I rather liked him and I did. He did not have much hope, so if encouragement was all one could offer that seemed fair enough – at least till my weekly stuff began to stick out more and more like a sore thumb in a pair of ragged mittens. It was a mercy the morning I opened a letter from that delightful enthusiast, Dominic Lawson, who had just become editor of *The Spectator*, suggesting I switch the weekly column to Doughty Street. There I remain, content, although I cannot say I was in the least bit chirpy the day that poor, put-upon Thomas's time ran out and *Punch* was laid to rest, unmourned, in its 150th year in 1992 – the very same month, as it happens, that my old Thames Television also fell, with seeming finality, off its precarious perch. How lucky I have been with editors – from dear old Geoffrey, my first in Stroud, up to two of the acknowledged finest of their times, Peter Preston and Alan Coren, who reigned in those poignant years just before bonny and *real* olde Fleet Street curled up at the toes, before Philip Hope-Wallace gathered up his bundle of newspapers, his faded white gloves and his brolly, and hurried out of El Vino's for the very last time. It was (as a *Guardian* misprint gloriously, and with even more finality than intended, had it when wanting to say 'end of an era') the End of an End.

My favourite *Gruandian*, however, is my own – some waffle about the cricketer, C. B. Fry, who was also at one time the world's long-jump record holder. 'In his Oxford rooms', I wrote, 'one of Fry's party tricks was to jump backwards from carpet to mantelpiece from a standing start'. Late into the evening, I drifted back to the sports desk from the Blue Lion, saw the first edition, which had long 'gone', and read of CB's ability to jump on to the mantelpiece 'from a standing tart'. I changed it hastily for all further editions and staggered home. Next morning I was to learn, of course, that Fry's party piece was engineered by 'a standing fart'.

Old CB himself might have been amused. In 1995, it will be a hundred years since his first Test match for England. It was at Port Elizabeth, alongside the Indian Ocean, and he scored 43. One day, 85 years later, I stood on the square there and thought of Fry. Just as, a few weeks later, I climbed high into the bleachers at Johannesburg. The stadium was eerily empty; the sun was gathering itself to set in its stone-drop, red-balled southern suddenness; I half-closed my eyes and, yes, down there in the middle I could almost 'see' the elongated, Lowry-lank shadows of the clustering fieldsmen, and hear the three distinct and successive oohs and the crescendoed applause for Tom Goddard's hat-trick for England the winter after I was born, the three wickets which saved young Jim Swanton's bacon.

In Durban, I made a pilgrimage to the quiet, winter-soft field behind the esplanade: not a soul was around; I walked from the pavilion to the square in solitary reverie, and mimed to face up, left-handed stance, to a ghostly Tufty Mann. But I didn't know which end dear old Jack, in his prime, had been at when the exultant crackle of Arlott's voice had said, that last over in 1948 . . . 'and Crapp hits mightily again . . . and England have won'.

At Bombay nowadays they play Test matches on a different field, a huge modern sponsored, steep-sided concrete saucepan. I took a taxi once to the old stadium — where Graveney, colt-slim and Pershore-cheeked, scored his maiden Test match century. In Brisbane one afternoon in the relentless sun, I thought of Charlie Barnett's blazing 69 when opening the batting in his first Australian Test over half a century before – and Sir Neville cabled back that evening to the *Guardian*: 'Barnett batted today for daring and for hauteur; he batted for love, and he batted for lust'.

\*     \*     \*

In Trinidad, I make a special pilgrimage one day down into the country of V. S. Naipaul – miles and miles of sugar cane which stops abruptly to make room for the village of Esperance. Some of the men have long caught the dawn bus to town, or are those distant specks hacking and bending at toil in the fields. Mangy terriers sleep in the shade. Serene old women squat on doorsteps watching beautiful children sleepily play.

Two plots up from the Yellow Bird Café – 'Licensed to sell spirituous liquors' and 'No obscene language here' – is a quaint and aged wooden house perched wonkily on spindly stilts. On the verandah, from a creaking rocking chair, an old lady in plum-red hand-stitched dress watches her clothes dry; they are spread around her on every available bush and rock and hedge. She is not expecting you, but when you announce yourself she beams a mouthful of gold teeth and greets you by putting both her hands on your shoulders, as is the custom.

Please to step inside, says Mrs Sumintra Rocke. At once I am transported back three-quarters of my life to that high summer morning in Gloucestershire full 30 years ago when poor old Dad had to work and couldn't come, and Uncle John and I and our Mum's sandwiches in greaseproof paper caught the first bus of the day from outside Woolworths in Stroud – and none of my heroes had the remotest clue about playing the spin bowling of a tiny man with a pencil moustache and a plum-red cap, with a pattering neat little run-up and the sleeves of his cream shirt buttoned tight at the wrists.

Sonny Ramadhin, that same mystic mesmerist who bowled off-breaks and leg-breaks and straight ones – but no

bat knew which until it bounced – arrived at this very same
house in Esperance to live with this same auntie when he
was orphaned at the age of two. The old lady's husband,
Soodhat, had a hobby. He enjoyed making picture frames in
black or silver passe-partout. This little house is a shrine to
his hobby and his nephew. A large framed picture of the
Sacred Heart had pride of place – many Trinidad Indians
are Christians – but then every available inch of wall space
in the three little rooms of the wooden house is covered with
faded sepia snapshots of one of the most legendary wizards
of tweak the noblest old game has ever known. And every
one is glazed and framed lovingly in black passe-partout or
silver-foil seconded from chocolate-bar wrappings.

There is a photograph of Sonny bowling against Yorkshire
at Bradford, the second match of that 1950 tour. That was
the day when, having taken a couple of wickets as soon as
he came on, he approached the player who had taken the
bewildered boy under his wing, Gerry Gomez, and enquired:
'Mister Gerry, will you tell me when this great batsman,
Mister L. Hutton, is coming in?' Replied Gomez: 'My dear
Ram, you've just got him out, caught in the leg trap in your
first over!'

There is a faded portrait on the wall of Frank Worrell. It
is inscribed 'Happy thoughts of years of pleasure – Frank'.
There is one, too, of Weekes – 'To Ram, my truly good
friend, from Everton'. There is a studio study of Ramadhin
himself, taken on the day he left on the boat for faraway
England and fame. He was wearing a trilby-type titfer on
the crown of his head and looked for all the world as
solemnly sinister as a Hollywood extra playing a Chinatown
hood. There is a picture of a starchy white-tie-and-tails
banquet at London's Café Royal in the summer of 1950.
Surrounded by knights with garters, peers without peer,
princes and patricians, Sonny Ramadhin is the only diner
wearing an ordinary necktie.

And there, high in the corner of this wooden-slatted little
hut, and home, on stilts is a framed newsprint photograph,

almost too sepia browned to be recognizable. You stand on tiptoe and squint. A tiny-tot of a batsman is 'shouldering arms'. The bails are in mid-air, the middle-stump askew. Sonny must have cut it out that night and sent it home to his Uncle Soodhat. It is from the *Cheltenham Echo*. The caption says, 'Another early victim for S. Ramadhin at the College Ground today was the Glo'shire wicket-keeper, A. E. Wilson'.

Our octogenarian Andy as ever was. Andy from Redmarley d'Abitot, on Gloucestershire's Hereford border under the Malverns and, now, just down the road from me.

\* \* \*

Well, didn't T. S. Eliot reckon, 'Home is where one starts from'. So Jane and I came home to Hereford in 1987 to establish the most contented of newly-married nests. Just as Mum and Dad had 60 years before. We are back in a farmhouse, too – an ancient, darling, L-shaped thing, black-and-white, and encased in greens with the blissful, daisy-chaining, sheep-speckled meadows sloping, on one side, down to the River Lugg and, on the other, the deer-running, tree-swathed steepness of Dinmore.

We are plonked slap in the middle of Marden Court farmyard, and in no time, first Patrick, then Tess, arrived – and just like me all those years ago, their first sights and sounds have been of lambs being lambed, sheep being sheared, hedges being hedged, and fatstock being fattened . . . the aahs and the baahs, the moohs and the poohs and the pongs. We are the same distance to the north of the city as Little Birch was to the south, and my good father lived long enough to come back often to his old haunts, help supervise the renovation of our great stone cider mill and press, and dandle on his knee the newest Keating with the Irish name of his forefathers.

In 1989, Dad poured his usual nightcap – one generous, treble slug of Scotch, and had a last catch-up with the *Guardian* or *Chelt. Echo*. Mum had gone to bed early. In the morning he was dead. Still in his armchair; Scotch downed; spirit departed, but a smile of serenity on his face. The Catholic papers remembered and gave him a veteran's salute: 'Stalwart Member of "Sheep-and-a-Cow Brigade" ' was the *Catholic Herald*'s headline; 'Last of the Pioneers' said *The Universe*.

His beloved Monica, our Mum, sails serenely on. To 'see out that Thatcher woman' was first base, which she made easily. In a dozen years, for sure, she will push the ball gently to deep mid-off and stroll the single to reach her hundred. She will doubtless send back the Queen's Telegram for centenarians – 'Silly old woman, why waste time sending telegrams to people she's never met'.

In 1983 I wrote a misbegotten book on rugby for the London publishers, Hodder & Stoughton. My editor, Richard Cohen, had a gimmick (probably learned from one of his more lucrative authors, Jeffrey Archer), which had all the seating in his office placed far lower than the 'boss's' high desk and table. So he could peer down at you like a headmaster and, cowering, you would agree to all his cuts in proof and pay. Jane was then Hodder's whizz in the Foreign Rights department. Richard presided over a meeting in his office. My chair was almost on the floor. Cohen's magisterial eye looming, dooming, down at me. Jane, opposite, was obliged to drape the whole length of her slender, willowy suppleness along Cohen's ridiculously low-slung sofa. So, like a Hitchcock camera's slow-pan, I had no alternative but to let my eye gently climb the inordinate length of two sublime legs, and upwards on and on till I met, with an already smitten double-take, the opal-sparks in her eyes. She blushed. And so did I.

Jane had become a director of the literary agency A. M. Heath by the time we held the launch party for my miserable book on the rugger-buggers of Britain – given some class only by Neil Kinnock's trenchant Introduction. But Jane came along. I asked her to supper; we went to the Ark. We have never been apart since. 1993 will be our tenth anniversary. From being, simply, sluggish and indolent and happy which, lucky bore that I am, I always have been, now something altogether more transforming had entered my life – a blessed and golden joy. Jane's glow and goodness, and the purity of her beauty, pervades every cranny of my spirit and every nook of our home. And another case of Irish stew: her pa's a Sinclair from the north, her bonny mother an O'Sullivan from Michelstown, not a million miles from Dad's garrison at Bandon. Everything comes back together if you wait long enough.

Although less frenetically passport-stamped, I remained a scribbler and swankpot around the babel-babbling stadiums of the world. When I put down my pen now, I start packing, full of expectation, for the dust and drama of the Olympic Games in Barcelona (with a day off, perhaps, to see if Maria might still be finger-clicking good in some foot-stamping cellar!)

\*       \*       \*

In the late summer of 1991, I left Jane and the kids, burrowingly brown-sugared in the sandcastles of Tenby, and went to watch the cricket at Swansea. Glamorgan were playing the mighty West Indians, hot from an immense drawn series with England. I sunned myself in front of St Helen's hill-top pavilion, looking out on Dylan's 'boat-bobbing bay'. Closer, what deeds had been done down there on the green all through the century and beyond. At cricket, and rugby too, for Wales played heroic matches here. Then, inside, I looked for the brown-stained old portraits of teams and talents frowning down from their old-fashioned frames – and feelingly murmured to myself the lines of another poet. In 1948, John Arlott had brought his friend Dylan for a day at the cricket, and it was John who went home, refreshed, to reflect:

> On this turf, the remembered of rugby –
> 'The Invincibles' – came by their name ...

Their might has outlived their moustaches,
For photos fade faster than fame.

On the way home to Hereford next day, I had a date on the banks of the River Wye, at the Nyth, a burbling salmon beat which marks Offa's Khyber between Builth and Hay. And there he was, my friend, the dear, raging Wye swirling about his waders in mid-stream.

On this legendary stretch, war torn long before Offa, the fletchers would fish for supper after cutting the twangy ash-bows from the steep banks, the same sharp humdingers that did the job for the captains and the kings at Crécy and Poitiers and Agincourt. The South Wales Borderers were the most celebrated of arrow-men. Now, as the waters pizzazz down in a froth from Plynlimon, it suddenly fizzes into a succession of gorges and gutters, rocks and deep pools. The very perfect lair for a serious salmon man to lie in ambush with his fly. The great prized and silvery flappers from the seas have fought their instinctive way all this distance in search of their gravelly spawning grounds. Now, at the Nyth, they might pause for breath in one of its deep, dark gutters, before fighting on, up against the rapids.

Either way, our grand all-rounder and Merrie Englander is waiting. Four-square in the raging waters he waits. Still. Dry fly. Moist eyes narrowed. Intent, determined. It is Ian Botham.

Over 60 years before, the grand literary waterman, H. A. Gilbert, wrote in *Tales of a Wye Fisherman*: 'Beware the Nyth, a succession of gutters which are narrow cracks in the solid rock mostly filled by fast streams; evil places to fish in high water, not only because the wading is generally difficult but also because a hooked fish is not easy to handle in such catches'.

This week, I learned later, the Wye was running six inches higher than it should have. Botham casts on – a curving, expert, loose-wristed swipe. Intent. Silent himself . . . the rushing water now just an insistent, but unnoticed hiss.

Of a sudden, more intent. He's got on. Can he hold it? Can he play it? This calls for the utmost delicacy now. Feather-light touch on the whipcord wrist. This way and that . . . diving, leaping, squirming. Hold on. Give and take. . . .

Finally he lands it – and the intensity of the battle was such that it is as if the very cascading waters, the birds, the buzzard and the ravens and chattering little things and sweet-singer woodlarks are all applauding too, like so many vast throngs have done for him on cricketing paddocks the wide world over.

It is Botham's first Wye salmon. Never, I warrant, has he looked more sportingly satisfied. Not at Headingley, nor Indore – nor even last week when he hit the winning blow for England to level the series. It is a 12-pounder, no great shakes, but silvern-strong and powerful alright. The great cricketer weighs it in, talking to it like a friend almost – 'You poor old bugger, all that way, all those dangers, all those battles to get up here, and you go and fall for my old homemade "Golden Shred" marmalady-yellow fly'. And in his triumph, he shrugs, as if to say, 'That's the name of the game, old chap'.

So it is. The name of a game which has evolved down aeons. Just as his 'own' game – now moneyed and manipulated, flattered and filmed and ludicrously fan-dangoed – cricket would be nothing at all, nothing, if not firmly rooted in its past. The very manner of Ian Botham's playing of his game makes it evident that his nature understands this well. He plays his cricket, as he fishes – as villagers did a roll of centuries ago. Exactly like . . . well, as Cardus once told me: 'Although I saw Dr Grace only once, the sight was enough for me to know that he played his game with the whole man of him in full action, body, soul, heart, and wits'. And us small-time loiterers who hang around the fringes of the so-called big-time, we are forever just as powerfully in debt.

I was fortunate enough to play over 30 years of unending

(as they seem to me now) summers in the direct and beguiling inheritance of the long-ago yeomen of olde Englande, those shepherds and carters and cowmen and foresters who invented the game on the rolling soft downlands of Sussex, Hampshire and Kent. The fields of those southern counties, by lucky fluke, were the ones I trod for much of my adult cricket.

First with friends from Douai, all round the Home Counties as the Old Augustinians: occasionally Aubrey would drive me in his purringly-old green Riley; mostly it was the train; we played Beaumont, up above King John's Runneymede each summer; and at Tilford, where they filmed the classic *England, Their England*; at Edenbridge and Westerham; and at Halstead, where in the evenings after the game, dear good 'Hoppy' – D. W. B. Buxton-Hopkin, who had been Douai's head Smoothie the day at the Douai Dance when I had dispatched Miss Delia Fortescue with that delicious pearler – would play his honky-tonk piano for the singsong.

Then when I met Robert Fleming (the day of Graveney's triumphant, tear-stained return to a Test at Lord's) and we set up our flat together he soon introduced me to a wandering band of blokes who had to work the week in London. We called ourselves (old hat, but endearing) the Jolly Rogers. Every weekend we went off by car or train to sport in civilized serenity with the villagers of such as Coldharbour, with its postage-stamp pitch; or Stonewall Park, with the cattle softly grazing at deep extra-cover, and the grand house lording it behind the bowler's arm; a Fleming from Stonewall Park now plays for Kent; his first two Championship scoring shots were sixes; his great-grandfather played for the Gentlemen of England at Lord's and hit an all-run *seven*. That's what I mean about the beauty – and necessity – of the game's antecedents. Then there was Fordcombe, with its always scrumptious teas in the village hall; or Staplefield, with the pub at third man to the left-hander, if I remember correctly. And Chiddingstone, where we would meet at the Castle for a pint of cider, then hump the gear through the waist-high cornfield to the flat, green pitch on top.

Brockham Green, a favourite of the Tourist Board calendar photographs, has its church on the green and the pub where deep fine-leg should stand. We played at Leigh (cider in the Seven Stars); at Dormansland; at dinky, verdant Forest Green. At Shoreham, Tony Lias and I put on 70 together in the sun. At Staplefield, for summer after summer, they had Charlie, a veteran, wiry-strong, horny-handed old demon bowler — a Tom Cartwright type, a 'Shack' — who would relentlessly skittle us with his unwavering persistence. Once, in the late 60s, we turned up, to hear the old man had collapsed and died the week before, actually in the middle of his bowling spell. Lias went home and wrote a lovely poem for his widow, who was the scorer and tea-brewer:

When skipper handed Charlie the new ball,
That end was taken care of for the day;
Charlie'd grin boyishly, then wheel away
Until he'd snapped up six, or eight, or all.
This once, however, Charlie couldn't scoff
So lightly at his sixty years and odd;
For halfway through his umpteenth over, God
Overruled skipper, and took Charlie off.

At Moorhouse, near Westerham, Robert and I put on 30, our highest ever partnership (I never could run between the wickets with Aussies). H. G. Wells used to watch cricket at Moorhouse. The other day I came across his diary. Did you know that his father was an early pro cricketer for Kent, hired by local squires to strengthen their teams? The old boy used to exasperate the young writer, but when he died, in 1898, Wells wrote enchantingly of his dad: 'His yarns of gallant stands and unexpected turns of fortune, of memorable hits and eccentric umpiring, albeit sometimes incredibly to his own glory, are full of the flavour of days well spent, of bright mornings of play, sunlit sprawling behind the score tent; warmth, the flavour of bitten grass stems, and the odour of crushed turf. . . . One thinks of stone jars with cool drink swishing therein, of shouting victories and memorable defeats, of eleven grown men in a drag, and tuneful, and altogether glorious homecomings by the light of the moon'.

Exactly. Substitute an Austin A30 (or Aubrey's green Riley) or BR Southern Region for 'drag', and those, a century later, were our days, too.

For a few successive years I 'got up' my own team each year to 'take on' that of another old, grand writer like Wells. The fixture started because a TV friend lived briefly at Little Chart – sublime, enclosed, village green ringed by a speckle of ancient houses. H. E. Bates lived in the loveliest, and he'd sit at his gate in his deckchair, rheumy-eyed and purply-cheeked mellow, working out his batting-order while Mrs Bates, alongside him, served lemonade or the tea from a succession of great, plump, expensive, teapots. Every one of those games was blessed by high, hot, summer suns of olde Englande, and a novelist's sussurrus of tinkling breezes in the beech leaves. The Darling Buds of August.

*     *     *

Of course, not far from the old iron bench which looked from its high Doverow perch across to the Severn, I had served a good and earnest apprenticeship as a boy. If I have any, without a doubt the team which taught me that generosity of spirit was the nub of village cricket – my beloved Stroud Stragglers of Gloucestershire. They were a bunch of gentle, craft-versed, working countrymen.

In the early to middle 1950s, even before I joined the *Stroud News*, we'd tramp up and down the tight-packed golden valleys in our whites – or white shirts, at least. Very few cars, then. Laurie Lee's men would give us two games a summer on the molehills of Sheepscombe; so would the villagers of sun-strewn Selsey; and Eastcombe; and Minch and Amberley up on the top. So would the host of little factory teams with their own lovingly rolled fields which dotted the once-busy canal tow-path from Chalford to Stonehouse.

> Patient, dramatic, serious, genial,
> From over to over the game goes on,
> Weaving its pattern of hardy perennial
> Civilization under the sun.

Now here's a thing. I've just looked it up: Gerald Bullett's lovely poem was first published in October, 1937. The month that I was born.